A Gazetteer of Archaeological Sites in Lesbos

Nigel Spencer

BAR International Series 623

1995

Published in 2019 by
BAR Publishing, Oxford

BAR International Series 623

A Gazetteer of Archaeological Sites in Lesbos

© Nigel Spencer and the Publisher 1995

ISBN 9780860548041 paperback
ISBN 9781407349299 e-book

DOI https://doi.org/10.30861/9780860548041

A catalogue record for this book is available from the British Library

This book is available at www.barpublishing.com

BAR Publishing is the trading name of British Archaeological Reports (Oxford) Ltd.
British Archaeological Reports was first incorporated in 1974 to publish the BAR
Series, International and British. In 1992 Hadrian Books Ltd became part of the BAR
group. This volume was originally published by Tempvs Reparatvm in conjunction
with British Archaeological Reports (Oxford) Ltd / Hadrian Books Ltd, the Series
principal publisher, in 1995. This present volume is published by BAR Publishing,
2019.

BAR
PUBLISHING

BAR titles are available from:

       BAR Publishing
       122 Banbury Rd, Oxford, OX2 7BP, UK
EMAIL   info@barpublishing.com
PHONE +44 (0)1865 310431
FAX   +44 (0)1865 316916
       www.barpublishing.com

To my parents

TABLE OF CONTENTS

ACKNOWLEDGEMENTS

The initial research for this volume was carried out during a three-year British Academy Major State Studentship in the Department of Classics at King's College London (1988-1991) where my doctoral thesis (*Asty and chora in Early Lesbos*) was completed in 1993. For help and guidance with the thesis thanks are due to my supervisor Prof. John Barron and to Prof. Susan Alcock. Subsequent work was continued first during my year as Research Officer for the Pylos Regional Archaeological Project at Reading University (1991-1992), and then (from 1993) as a British Academy Postdoctoral Research Fellow (generously funded by Swan Hellenic/P&O) at the Institute of Archaeology, Oxford. Additional funding was offered by the Dover Fund of the Hellenic Society (in 1993) in order to study aspects of the island's epigraphy (presented here in Appendix 1). I am grateful to both King's College and the British Academy for allowing me study leave to continue my research in Athens from March 1989-April 1991. This allowed me to use the excellent facilities at the British School in Athens and to have access to the collections in the other foreign schools in Athens as well.

For illustrative material in this volume grateful thanks are due to the following bodies and individuals. Fig. 1 was drawn by Pam Schaus. Figs. 16 and 28 were reproduced by permission of Dr. Makis Axiotis, fig. 17 courtesy of Prof. Dr. Hans-Günter Buchholz, figs. 18 and 31 are from the Winifred Lamb archive of the British School at Athens, and fig. 30 reproduced by permission from Verlag Philipp von Zabern (Mainz). The photographic work for figs. 16-32 was carried out by Bob Wilkins and Jennie Lowe at the Institute of Archaeology in Oxford.

In Lesbos a permit to visit known archaeological sites and study topographical problems was granted in 1990 by Mrs. A. Archontidou-Argyri, Ephor of the 10th Ephoreia of Prehistoric and Classical Antiquities. I would like to acknowledge the cooperation of Mrs. Archontidou-Argyri and Mrs. Lilian Acheilara, both for allowing me to carry out my work and also for many stimulating conversations concerning the archaeology of the island. Of the archaeological service team based in the island, thanks are also due to the following for all their information and advice: Eleni Bomboulaki in Methymna, Basileios Kalaitzis at Messa, Kostas Sapkas at Klopedi and Sophoklis Roumeliotis at Skala Eresou. To Mr. Kalaitzis I must give special thanks for readily putting at my disposal his considerable knowledge of many sites in the island.

In addition to these people, others in the island have given great assistance to the completion of the work. Foremost among these is Dr. Makis Axiotis who discussed details of his extensive and thorough survey work in the island and generously allowed me to reproduce illustrations from his own study of the island's history and archaeology (Περπατώντας τη Λέσβο). During my research I have also benefitted from useful discussions with Mr. Miltis Paraskeuaidis, a distinguished scholar of the island's archaeology. Deborah Ruscillo helped in the completion of the work by checking specific points in local newspapers and other works in Mytilene library during 1994-1995. Michailis Bathrokoulis, the former mayor of Skalochori, furnished me with much local source material for the area of Skalochori, and Mr. Stamos Stephanou in Mytilene kindly showed to me his extensive collection of casts of Archaic and Classical Mytilenean coins. I would also like to put on record the extreme kindness shown to me by many villagers during my numerous visits to Lesbos which meant that visits to sites otherwise difficult to reach with public transport (such as ancient Antissa) were made both easier and much more enjoyable.

Sincere thanks are due to the whole Canadian team involved in the excavations in Mytilene town from 1989 onwards under the directorship of Prof. Hector Williams (University of British Columbia). Both he and Prof. Caroline Williams always made available to me their finds within the island, putting their great knowledge of the archaeology of Lesbos at my disposal. I thank them especially for the freedom to look at unpublished finds from their excavations and read reports of their work in advance of publication. Prof. Hector Williams also offered translations for Turkish words. Prof. Gerry Schaus (Wilfrid Laurier University) generously shared his detailed knowledge of the west part of the island. I am also grateful to Dr. Grant Head (Wilfrid Laurier University) for many useful discussions on the geology and topography of the valley of Eresos. Dr. Machiel Kiel (Utrecht University) kindly discussed details of his research into Lesbos during the Tourkokratia and communicated to me the views of Dr. Dimitris N. Karidis (Athens Polytechnic University) and Dr. Dr. Hedda Reindl-Kiel on the same period of history.

Prof. Dr. Wolfgang Schiering and Mr. Federico Utili (University of Mannheim) provided information regarding the excavations of Johannes Boehlau at Pyrrha. I am also very grateful to Prof. Dr. Schiering, Mr. Utili and Christof Boehringer (Göttingen Archaeological Institute) for providing me with slides of unpublished material from Boehlau's excavations, now stored in Göttingen, and for examining the Göttingen archives on my behalf. Prof. Dr. K. Fittschen at the German Archaeological Institute (DAI) kindly granted me permission to examine the sherd collection of material from the island and Dr. Martin Kreeb supervised my visit in March-April 1995, patiently answering any questions which arose.

I must also thank the British School at Athens for allowing access to the archive of unpublished material from Winifred Lamb's excavations at Thermi, Antissa and Methymna. Of the staff and former students at the British School with whom I discussed particular points, I thank Dr. Jan Sanders (Director, Beaver College), Dr. Guy Sanders (former Assistant

Director), Dr. Lin Foxhall (Leicester University), Dr. Graham Shipley (Leicester University), Mr. Richard Catling (Oxford University), Dr. Eric Ivison (Dumbarton Oaks), Mr. Graham Joyner (McQuarie University), Dr. Jane Francis (Concordia University), Dr. Philip Baker (Brighton University), Miss. Catherine Dyer (London University) and Dr. Yaprak Eran (British Institute of Archaeology at Ankara). Dr. Susan Sherratt (Ashmolean Museum, Oxford) and Mr. Mervyn Popham (Oxford University) helped clarify the precise nature of the Middle Bronze Age pottery from Perama (site 54). Both Mr. Charles Watkinson (Oxbow Books) and also my mother kindly read through the manuscript at short notice and made numerous perceptive comments which improved the text immeasurably.

Thanks are due to Dr. Richard Jones (former Director of the Fitch Laboratory) for an introduction to the pottery stored in the sherd archive of the laboratory and also to Dr. Ian Whitbread (Director of the Fitch Laboratory) and Dr. Sarah Vaughan for information on the geology and petrology of Lesbos.

Finally, I would have gained hardly any of the information which I did in Lesbos without a basic understanding of the modern Greek language. For the latter I have to thank the eternal patience of my teachers Miss. Lilian Phanara and her mother Mrs. Panagiota Phanara.

Institute of Archaeology, Oxford.

June 1995.

ABBREVIATIONS AND SELECT BIBLIOGRAPHY

The abbreviations used throughout the text (including the appendices) for journals and series are given here together with those employed for specific books and articles to which reference is made on more than one occasion. This second part of the abbreviations list also serves as a select bibliography for the volume. Abbreviations of the names and works of ancient authors correspond to those listed in the introduction to *LSJ*.

Journals/Series

AA	Archäologische Anzeiger
AAA	Athens Annals of Archaeology (Ἀρχαιολογικὰ ἀνάλεκτα ἐξ Ἀθηνῶν)
ArchDelt	Ἀρχαιολογικὸν Δελτίον
AE	Ἀρχαιολογικὴ Ἐφημερίς
AJA	American Journal of Archaeology
AK	Antike Kunst
AM	Mitteilungen des Deutschen Archäologischen Instituts, Athenische Abteilung
Annuario	Annuario della Scuola archeologica di Atene e delle Missioni italiane in Oriente
AR	Archaeological Reports (supplement to *JHS*)
BCH	Bulletin de Correspondance Hellénique
BSA	Annual of the British School at Athens
BZ	Byzantinische Zeitung
CIG	Boeckh, A. (ed.), *Corpus Inscriptionum Graecarum* (Berlin: Officina Academica, 1828-77)
EMC	Echos du monde classique. Classical Views
Ergon	Ἔργον τῆς Ἀρχαιολογικῆς Ἑταιρείας
IG	Inscriptiones Graecae (Berlin 1873-)
Ist.Mitt.	Istanbuler Mitteilungen
JHS	Journal of Hellenic Studies
Klio	Klio. Beiträge zur alten Geschichte
Lesbiaka	Δελτίον τῆς Ἑταιρείας Λεσβιακῶν Μελετῶν
LSJ	Liddell, H. G., Scott, R. (eds.), *A Greek-English Lexicon* (rev. ed. Jones, H. S.; supp., Oxford, 1968).
PAA	Πρακτικὰ τῆς Ἀκαδημίας Ἀθηνῶν
PAE	Πρακτικὰ τῆς ἐν Ἀθήναις Ἀρχαιολογικῆς Ἑταιρείας
RE	Pauly-Wissowa, Real-Encyclopädie der klassischen Altertumswissenschaft (Stuttgart, 1894-)
TAPA	Transactions of the American Philological Association

Special abbreviations and Select Bibliography

Acheilara and Archontidou-Argyri, 1986	L. Acheilara and A. Archontidou-Argyri, 'Χρονικά κ' εφορείας προϊστορικών και κλασικών αρχαιοτήτων', *ArchDelt* 41 (1986), Chronika 196-212
Acheilara and Archontidou-Argyri, 1987	L. Acheilara and A. Archontidou-Argyri, 'Χρονικά κ' εφορείας προϊστορικών και κλασικών αρχαιοτήτων', *ArchDelt* 42 (1987), Chronika 474-89
Adam	J.-P. Adam, *l'Architecture militaire grecque* (Paris, 1982)
Åkerström I/II	Å. Åkerström, *Die architektonischen Terrakotten Kleinasiens* (Lund, 1966) 2 vols.
Akurgal	E. Akurgal, *Alt-Smyrna, 1: Wohnschichten und Athenatempel* (Ankara, 1983)
Aliprantis, 1972	Th. Ch. Aliprantis, 'Βυζαντινά, μεσαιωνικά καὶ νεώτερα μνημεῖα νήσων Αἰγαίου', *ArchDelt* 27 (1972), Chronika 616-17
Aliprantis, 1973	Th. Ch. Aliprantis, 'Βυζαντινά, μεσαιωνικά καὶ νεώτερα μνημεῖα νήσων Αἰγαίου', *ArchDelt* 28 (1973), Chronika 556-57
Archontidou-Argyri, 1986-87	A. Archontidou-Argyri, 'Χρονικά κ' εφορείας αρχαιοτήτων έτους 1986-1987', *Lesbiaka* 12 (1989), 56-76
Archontidou-Argyri, 1988	A. Archontidou-Argyri, 'Χρονικά κ' εφορείας προϊστορικών και κλασικών αρχαιοτήτων', *ArchDelt* 43 (1988), 451-69
Aupert	P. Aupert, 'Chronique des fouilles et découvertes archéologiques en Grèce en 1975', *BCH* 100 (1976), 591-745
Axiotis, 1991a	M. Axiotis, "Ενα άγνωστο οχυρό της αρχαίας Μήθυμνας', *Archaiologia* 38 (1991), 75-77

Axiotis, 1991b   M. Axiotis, 'Μια νέα προϊστορική θέση στη Λέσβο', *Archaiologia* 40 (1991), 79-80

Axiotis, 1992 I/II   M. Axiotis, Περπατώντας τη Λέσβο (Mytilene, 1992) 2 vols.

Axiotis, 1994   M. Axiotis, 'Πέτρινα απομεινάρια από την κατεργασία της ελιάς στη Λέσβο', *Archaiologia* 51 (1994), 31-34

Basiakos   G. Basiakos, ''Ερευνα για εργαστήρια αμφορέων', *ArchDelt* 41 (1986), Chronika 207-10

Bayne   N. P. Bayne, *The grey wares of north-west Anatolia in the middle and late Bronze Age and the early Iron Age and their relation to the early Greek settlements* (Diss. University of Oxford, 1963)

Betancourt   P. P. Betancourt, *The Aeolic style in architecture* (Princeton, 1977)

BSA   British School at Athens

Buchholz   H.-G. Buchholz, *Methymna* (Mainz, 1975)

Catling   H. W. Catling, 'Archaeology in Greece, 1976-77', *AR* 24 (1978), 3-69

Charitonidis, 1960   S. Charitonidis, ''Αρχαιότητες καὶ μνημεῖα νήσων Αἰγαίου· Μυτιλήνη', *ArchDelt* 16 (1960), Chronika 235-43

Charitonidis, 1961a   S. Charitonidis, ''Ανασκαφαὶ Μυτιλήνης', *PAE* (1961), 207-14

Charitonidis, 1961b   S. Charitonidis, 'Μυτιλήνη', *Ergon* (1961), 211-15

Charitonidis, 1961-62   S. Charitonidis, ''Αρχαιότητες καὶ μνημεῖα νήσων Αἰγαίου· Α' Λέσβος', *ArchDelt* 17 (1961-62), Chronika 261-65

Charitonidis, 1962a   S. Charitonidis, ''Ανασκαφὴ Μυτιλήνης', *PAE* (1962), 134-41

Charitonidis, 1962b   S. Charitonidis, 'Μυτιλήνη', *Ergon* (1962), 155-59

Charitonidis, 1963a   S. Charitonidis, ''Ανασκαφὴ Μυτιλήνης', *PAE* (1963), 158-59

Charitonidis, 1963b   S. Charitonidis, 'Μυτιλήνη', *Ergon* (1963), 157-59

Charitonidis, 1963c   S. Charitonidis, ''Αρχαιότητες καὶ μνημεῖα νήσων Αἰγαίου· Μυτιλήνη', *ArchDelt* 18 (1963), Chronika 266-72

Charitonidis, 1964   S. Charitonidis, ''Αρχαιότητες καὶ μνημεῖα νήσων Αἰγαίου· Λέσβος', *ArchDelt* 19 (1964), Chronika 396-400

Charitonidis, 1965   S. Charitonidis, ''Αρχαιότητες καὶ μνημεῖα νήσων Αἰγαίου· Μυτιλήνη', *ArchDelt* 20 (1965), Chronika 488-95

Charitonidis, 1966   S. Charitonidis, 'Βυζαντιναὶ ἐκκλησίαι τῆς Λέσβου' in Χαριστήριον εἰς 'Αναστάσιον Κ. 'Ορλάνδον (Athens, 1966), vol. B, 72-77

Charitonidis, 1968a   S. Charitonidis, 'Παλιοχριστιανικὴ τοπογραφία τῆς Λέσβου', *ArchDelt* 23 (1968), Meletimata 10-69

Charitonidis, 1968b   S. Charitonidis, Αἱ ἐπιγραφαὶ τῆς Λέσβου - Συμπλήρωμα (Athens, 1968)

Chatzi, 1971   D. Chatzi, ''Αρχαιότητες καὶ μνημεῖα νήσων Αἰγαίου', *ArchDelt* 26 (1971), Chronika 448-58

Chatzi, 1972   D. Chatzi, ''Αρχαιότητες καὶ μνημεῖα νήσων Αἰγαίου', *ArchDelt* 27 (1972), Chronika 579-99

Chatzi, 1973   D. Chatzi, ''Αρχαιότητες καὶ μνημεῖα νήσων Αἰγαίου', *ArchDelt* 28 (1973), Chronika 507-20

Chatziioannou   I. S. Chatziioannou, 'Τὸ 'Ρωμαϊκὸ ὑδραγωγεῖο Μυτιλήνης', *Lesbiaka* 9 (1985), 153-62

Cherry et al.   J. F. Cherry et al., *Landscape archaeology as long-term history: northern Keos in the Cycladic islands from earliest settlement until modern times* (Los Angeles, 1991)

Conze   A. Conze, *Reise auf der Insel Lesbos* (Hanover, 1865)

DAI   Deutsches Archäologisches Institut

Daux, 1960   G. Daux, 'Chronique des fouilles et découvertes archéologiques en Grèce en 1959', *BCH* 84 (1960), 617-868

Daux, 1962   G Daux, 'Chronique des fouilles et découvertes archéologiques en Grèce en 1961', *BCH* 86 (1962), 629-974

Déléage   A. Déléage, *La Capitation du Bas-Empire* (Paris, 1945)

Euangelidis, 1924-25   D. Euangelidis, ''Ανασκαφαὶ καὶ ἔρευναι ἐν Λέσβῳ', *ArchDelt* 9 (1924-25) supp., 41-54

Euangelidis, 1925-26   D. Euangelidis ''Ανασκαφικαὶ ἔρευναι ἐν Λέσβῳ', *PAE* (1925-26), 147-56

Euangelidis, 1927   D. Euangelidis, ''Ανασκαφαὶ ἐν Λέσβῳ', *PAE* (1927), 57-59

Euangelidis, 1927-28   D. Euangelidis, "Ανασκαφαὶ καὶ ἀρχαῖα ἐκ Μυτιλήνης', *ArchDelt* 11 (1927-28) supp., 14-22

Euangelidis, 1928   D. Euangelidis, "Ανασκαφὴ Κλοπεδῆς Λέσβου', *PAE* (1928), 126-37

Fagerström   K. Fagerström, *Greek iron age architecture: developments through changing times* (SIMA 81; Göteborg, 1988)

French, 1993   E. B. French, 'Archaeology in Greece, 1992-93', *AR* 39 (1993), 3-81

French, 1994   E. B. French, 'Archaeology in Greece, 1993-94', *AR* 40 (1994), 3-84

French I/II   D. H. French, *Anatolia and the Aegean in the third millenium BC* (Diss. Univ. of Cambridge, 1968) 2 vols.

Green   P. Green, 'Longus, Antiphon and the topography of Lesbos', *JHS* 102 (1982), 210-14

Hood   M. S. F. Hood, 'Archaeology in Greece, 1960-61', *AR* 7 (1961), 3-35

Iakobos — Iakobos, 'Τὰ πρῶτα μνημεῖα τῆς χριστιανικῆς λατρείας εἰς τὴν Λέσβον', *Lesbiaka* 3 (1959), 31-40

Koldewey — R. Koldewey, *Die antiken Baureste der Insel Lesbos* (Berlin, 1890)

Kontellis — P. I. Kontellis, *Ο κόσμος ο μικρός ... Μεσότοπος Λέσβου· ιστορικά, λαογραφικά* (Athens, 1985)

Kontis, 1973 — G. D. Kontis, *Λεσβιακὸ Πολύπτυχο* (Athens, 1973)

Kontis, 1978 — G. D. Kontis, *Λέσβος καὶ ἡ μικρασιατικὴ τῆς περιοχὴ* (Athens, 1978)

Koumarelas, 1989a — B. Koumarelas, 'Ξεχασμένα αρχαία οχυρά', *Aigaion* (24/4/89), 4

Koumarelas, 1989b — B. Koumarelas, 'Το οχυρό του Φονιά', *Ta Nea ton Skalochoriton* (January-June 1989), 3

Koumarelas, 1989c — B. Koumarelas, 'Αρχαία οχυρά στον Προφήτη Ηλία Σκαλοχωρίου', *Ta Nea ton Skalochoriton* (January-June 1989), 3

Koumarelas, 1995 — B. Koumarelas, ' 'Αγνωστοι πύργοι και περιβόλοι της αρχαίας Ερεσού', *Archaiologia* 54 (1995), 41-46

Lamb, 1930-31 — W. Lamb, 'Antissa', *BSA* 31 (1930-31), 166-78

Lamb, 1931-32 — W. Lamb, 'Antissa', *BSA* 32 (1931-32), 41-67

Lamb, 1932 — W. Lamb, 'Grey wares from Lesbos', *JHS* 52 (1932), 1-12

Lamb, 1936 — W. Lamb, *Excavations at Thermi in Lesbos* (Cambridge, 1936)

Laskaris — G. Th. Laskaris, 'Τὰ λείψανα τῆς ἀρχαίας 'Ερεσοῦ', *Lesbiaka* 3 (1960), 67-74

Lawrence — A. W. Lawrence, *Greek aims in fortification* (Oxford, 1979).

Lobel-Page — E. Lobel and D. Page (eds.), *Poetarum Lesbiorum Fragmenta* (Oxford, 1955).

Mantzuranes — D. P. Mantzuranes, 'Σωσομένα τοπονύμια ἐκ τοῦ ἀρχαίου κτηματολογίου τῆς Λέσβου', *BZ* 44 (1951), 410-12.

Mason, 1979 — H. J. Mason, 'Longus and the topography of Lesbos', *TAPA* 109 (1979), 149-63

Mason, 1993 — H. J. Mason, 'Mytilene and Methymna: quarrels, borders and topography', *EMC* 37 (1993), 225-50

Millar — R. J. O. Millar, *Mytilene 1990 Excavation Report - Epano Skala Site* (MS, 1990)

Millar and Williams, 1993 — R. Millar and H. Williams, 'The Roman quarry at Moria, Mytilene', *EMC* 37 (1993), 211-23

Millar and Williams, 1994 — R. Millar and H. Williams, 'Moria quarry survey, Lesbos, 1993', *EMC* 38 (1994), 235-43

Moutzouris, 1962 — I. Moutzouris, 'Μεσαιωνικὰ κάστρα τῆς Λέσβου', *Lesbiaka* 4 (1962), 50-68

Moutzouris, 1973 — I. Moutzouris, 'Οἱ 'Αγαλλιανοὶ καὶ αἱ μοναὶ Λειμῶνος καὶ Μυρσινιώτισσης Καλλονῆς', *Lesbiaka* 6 (1973), 92-104

Moutzouris, 1983 — I. Moutzouris, 'Η Καλλονή καί τα χωριά της', *Mytilini* 2 (1983), 17-31

Newton I/II — C. T. Newton, *Travels and discoveries in the Levant* (London, 1865), 2 vols.

Orlandos, 1928 — A. K. Orlandos, 'Βυζαντινὴ τέχνη· Παλιοχριστιανικαὶ βασιλικαὶ τῆς Λέσβου', *PAA* 3 (1928), 322-30

Orlandos, 1929 — A. K. Orlandos, 'Αἱ παλιοχριστιανικαὶ βασιλικαὶ τῆς Λέσβου', *ArchDelt* 12 (1929), 1-72

Orlandos, 1937 — A. K. Orlandos, *Αρχεῖον τῶν Βυζαντινῶν Μνημείων τῆς 'Ελλάδος* (Athens, 1937) vol. 3

Orlandos, 1952-54 — A. K. Orlandos, *Ἡ ξυλόστεγος παλαιοχριστιανικὴ βασιλικὴ τῆς Μεσογειακῆς λεκάνης* (Athens, 1952-54)

Page — D. L. Page, *Sappho and Alcaeus: an introduction to the study of ancient Lesbian poetry* (Oxford, 1955)

Papazoglou — I. P. Papazoglou, *Ιστορία τῆς 'Ερέσου* (Athens, 1981)

Paraskeuaidis, 26/9/29 — S. Paraskeuaidis, ' 'Οδοιπορικὲς Σημειώσεις', *Tachydromos* 26/9/29

Paraskeuaidis, 29/9/29 — S. Paraskeuaidis, ' 'Οδοιπορικὲς Σημειώσεις', *Tachydromos* 29/9/29

Paraskeuaidis, 1963 — M. Paraskeuaidis, 'Pyrrha auf Lesbos', *RE* 24 (Stuttgart, 1963), 1403-20

Paraskeuaidis, 1966 — M. Paraskeuaidis, 'Νέες ἀρχαιολογικὲς ἐνδείξεις γιὰ τὴ Λέσβο', *Lesbiaka* 5 (1966), 198-219

Paraskeuaidis, 1970 — M. Paraskeuaidis, ' 'Επίμετρον· βιβλιογραφικὰ ἀρχαιογνωσίας τῆς περιοχῆς 'Αγίας Παρασκευῆς Λέσβου' in K. Makistos, *'Η Σελλάδα τῆς 'Αγίας Παρασκευῆς Λέσβου* (Athens, 1970), 241-76

Paraskeuaidis, 1976 — M. Paraskeuaidis, 'Lesbos' in R. Stillwell (ed.), *The Princeton encyclopedia of Classical sites* (Princeton, 1976), 502-03

Paraskeuaidis, 1978 — M. Paraskeuaidis, ' 'Ο προϊστορικός οἰκισμός τοῦ λόφου Προφήτη 'Ηλία 'Αγίας Παρασκευῆς Λέσβου', *Lesbiaka* 7 (1978), 161-81

Paraskeuaidis, 1987 — G. L. Paraskeuaidis, *Μανδαμάδος Λέσβου* (Thessaloniki, 1987)

Pariente — A. Pariente, 'Chronique des fouilles et découvertes archéologiques en Grèce en 1992', *BCH* 117 (1993), 757-913

Payne, 1931 — H. G. G. Payne, 'Archaeology in Greece, 1930-1931', *JHS* 51 (1931), 184-210

Payne, 1932 — H. G. G. Payne, 'Archaeology in Greece, 1931-2', *JHS* 52 (1932), 236-55

Payne, 1933 — H. G. G. Payne, 'Archaeology in Greece, 1932-1933', *JHS* 53 (1933), 266-99

Petrakos, 1967a — B. Ch. Petrakos, ' 'Ανασκαφὴ τοῦ ναοῦ τῶν Μέσων Λέσβου', *PAE* (1967), 96-102

Petrakos, 1967b	B. Ch. Petrakos, 'Μέσα Λέσβου', *Ergon* (1967), 72-75
Petrakos, 1967c	B. Ch. Petrakos, ''Αρχαιότητες καὶ μνημεῖα νήσων Αἰγαίου· Μυτιλήνη', *ArchDelt* 22 (1967), Chronika 445-62
Petrakos, 1968a	B. Ch. Petrakos, ''Ανασκαφὴ τοῦ ναοῦ τῶν Μέσων Λέσβου', *PAE* (1968), 84-86
Petrakos, 1968b	B. Ch. Petrakos, 'Μέσα Λέσβου', *Ergon* (1968), 80-82
Pococke	R. Pococke, *A description of the East, and some other countries* (London, 1745), vol. II.2
Rouse	W. H. D. Rouse, 'Lesbos', *BSA* 2 (1895-96), 145-54
Schaus and Spencer	G. P. Schaus and N. Spencer, 'Notes on the topography of Eresos', *AJA* 98 (1994), 411-30
Spencer, 1994	N. Spencer, 'Towers and enclosures of Lesbian masonry in Lesbos: rural investment in the *chora* of Archaic *poleis*' in P. N. Doukellis and L. G. Mendoni (eds.), *Structures rurales and sociétés antiques: Actes du Colloque de Corfou (14-16 mai 1992)*, (Annales Littéraires de l'Université de Besancon, 508; Paris, 1994), 207-13
Spencer, 1995	N. Spencer, 'Multi-dimensional group definition in the landscape of rural Greece' in N. Spencer (ed.), *Time, tradition and society in Greek archaeology: bridging the 'Great Divide'* (London, 1995), 28-42
Schiering	W. Schiering, 'Pyrrha auf Lesbos', *AA* (1989), 339-77
Scranton	R. L. Scranton, *Greek Walls* (Cambridge [Mass.], 1941)
Sotiriou	G. A. Sotiriou, 'Αἱ παλαιοχριστιανικαὶ βασιλικαὶ τῆς 'Ελλάδος', *AE* (1929), 161-248
Taxis	S. G. Taxis, *Συνοπτικὴ ἱστορία καὶ τοπογραφία τῆς Λέσβου* (Cairo, 1909 [reprinted Mytilene, 1994])
Touchais, 1977	G. Touchais, 'Chronique des fouilles et découvertes archéologiques en Grèce en 1976', *BCH* 101 (1977), 513-706
Touchais, 1985	G. Touchais, 'Chronique des fouilles et découvertes archéologiques en Grèce en 1984', *BCH* 109 (1985), 759-862
Williams and Parker	H. Williams and R. J. Parker, 'A fragment of a Diocletianic tax assessment from Mytilene', (forthcoming in *EMC* 1995).
Williams and Williams, 1985	H. and C. Williams, 'Excavations on the acropolis of Mytilene, 1984', *EMC* 29 N.S. 4 (1985), 225-33
Williams and Williams, 1986	H. and C. Williams, 'Excavations on the acropolis of Mytilene, 1985', *EMC* 30 N.S. 5 (1986), 141-54
Williams and Williams, 1987	H. and C. Williams, 'Excavations at Mytilene (Lesbos), 1986', *EMC* 31 N.S. 6 (1987), 247-62
Williams and Williams, 1988	H. and C. Williams, 'Excavations at Mytilene (Lesbos), 1987', *EMC* 32 N.S. 7 (1988), 135-49
Williams and Williams, 1989	H. and C. Williams, 'Excavations at Mytilene, 1988', *EMC* 33 N.S. 8 (1989), 167-81
Williams and Williams, 1990	H. and C. Williams, 'Excavations at Mytilene, 1989', *EMC* 34 N.S. 9 (1990), 181-93
Williams and Williams, 1991	H. and C. Williams, 'Excavations at Mytilene, 1990', *EMC* 35 N.S. 10 (1991), 175-91
Winter	F. E. Winter, *Greek Fortifications* (London, 1971)
Wrede	W. Wrede, *Attische Mauern* (Athens, 1933).

LIST OF ILLUSTRATIONS

INTRODUCTION

1.1 Previous archaeological research in Lesbos

Lesbos, the third largest island in the Aegean Sea after Crete and Euboia, lies in a particularly significant location, at its nearest point only 12 kms across a narrow strait from the coastline of Anatolia and on the route northwards towards the Hellespont and the Black Sea (fig. 1, inset). In such a position, the island has served as a bridge between the Aegean and Anatolia from Neolithic times until the twentieth century, in different periods of its history forming either the easternmost limit of an Aegean political unit or alternatively the western outpost of an Asian empire.

Given this significance, it is unfortunate that discussions of the island's archaeology have not been numerous, and that there are still no accessible and up-to-date studies which can guide anyone wishing to pursue research into the island. Indeed, although it has long been recognised from literary sources that in certain periods of antiquity Lesbos was one of the leading East Greek states, the wealth of literary information about the island (especially in the Archaic period) has continually drawn attention away from the its archaeology.[1] Archaeologically the island has become a 'grey area' of the Aegean, and since the initial surveys of the archaeological remains in the nineteenth century (by Conze,[2] Kiepert and Koldewey[3]), the small number of fieldwork reports which have appeared have been brief and preliminary.

In the 1920s excavations were conducted at the Archaic temple of Klopedi by Euangelidis, and despite the great significance of the finds (comprising two temples side-by-side, probably both of Archaic date, together with traces of early Bronze Age remains between them) only three short articles were ever produced which included no detailed comment on stratigraphy or the ceramic material recovered.[4]

Later in the same decade Winifred Lamb began her work in the island which, from 1928-1933, focused upon three sites, Antissa, Thermi and (briefly) Methymna. Since Lamb's main objective in coming to work in Lesbos had been to find and examine in detail a site 'which would throw light on its [Lesbos'] early culture and provide a link between Greece and Anatolia',[5] Lamb soon abandoned Methymna after a brief trial excavation,[6] and after three seasons at Antissa[7] more time was devoted to the study and publication of Thermi[8] which clearly was of an earlier date than nearly all the material at either of the other two sites.[9] Lamb's excavations at Thermi established it as one of the most important early Bronze Age settlements in the northeast Aegean, but the outbreak of the Second World War meant that this interest in the island (and its clear significance) could not be followed up immediately.

Indeed, it was not until thirty-six years after the publication of Lamb's book on Thermi that another major study of the island was produced; Levang's 1972 work on Roman Lesbos.[10] The only other notices of new archaeological finds to appear had been the useful (but extremely brief) reports of Charitonidis, recording the antiquities which he discovered (or which had been pointed out to him by

---

[1] The prominence of Lesbos (especially Mytilene) in the Archaic period was recognised even in early accounts of Greek history. K. J. Beloch, *Griechische Geschichte* (Strasbourg, 1912) I, 218-19 (the Penthilidai), 256 (the literary sources for the Lesbian founding of Ainos), 351 (Pittakos' constitutional reforms), 374-75 and 388 (the tyrannies in Lesbos and the war for Sigeion). Unfortunately nearly all subsequent works have limited their discussions to almost exactly the same few historical events and given minimal consideration to archaeology.

[2] Conze.

[3] Koldewey (which includes the contribution from Kiepert).

[4] Euangelidis, 1924-25, 41-44; id., 1927; id., 1928. The nature of the excavation reports has meant that the dating of the two temples found by Euangelidis has relied largely on Åkerström's study of the architectural terracottas (see the entry for Klopedi in the gazetteer at #111).

[5] Lamb, 1936, 1.

[6] Only four summary reports (repeating the same few lines) were published; W. Lamb, 'Δοκιμαστικὴ σκαφὴ εἰς Μόλυβον τῆς Λέσβου', *ArchDelt* 11 (1927-28) supp., 41-42; A. M. Woodward, 'Archaeology in Greece 1928-1929', *JHS* 49 (1929), 223; Y. Béquignon, 'Chronique des fouilles et découvertes archéologiques dans l'Orient Hellénique 1929', *BCH* 53 (1929), 530; G. Karo, 'Archäologische Funde aus dem Jahre 1929 und der ersten Hälfte von 1930: Griechenland und Dodekanes', *AA* (1930), 144.

[7] Lamb, 1930-31; Lamb, 1931-32. 1931-33 are the probable dates for the work carried out by Lamb at Antissa, but it is difficult to be sure because of the ambiguous dating of the reports. The yearly summaries of fieldwork in *JHS* indicate that three seasons of work were conducted between 1930-1933, but since the publication (in both *JHS* and *BSA*) are dated '1930-31', '1931-32' or '1932-33' which three seasons within this span of four years the work was carried out in is unclear; in addition to the two articles in *BSA* cited here see Payne, 1931, 202-03; id., 1932, 251; id., 1933, 284-86 and figs. 10-11.

[8] Lamb, 1936.

[9] The material at Methymna was solely of Iron Age (specifically Geometric-Roman) date, see the reports cited in n. 6. At Antissa, a few sherds from Lamb's excavations were said to have been identified subsequently by Mellaart as being of Troy II type, but nearly all the material is otherwise of late Bronze Age date, see Buchholz, 123 (and fig. 34 on p. 122). These early Bronze Age sherds are said to be stored in the Institute of Archaeology in London but they could not be located in 1990 and Mellaart (pers. comm., 1995) has stated that he does not remember them.

[10] R. Levang, *Studies in the history of Lesbos* (Diss. University of Minnesota, 1972).

villagers) from 1960-65;[11] five short articles by Petrakos on his excavations at Mytilene and Messa in 1967-68;[12] and those of Chatzi concerning her brief excavations at Mytilene, Methymna, Antissa, Arisbe and Agios Phokas from 1971-73.[13]

Three more substantial works followed. In 1973 Kontis published his first, popular-style book on the island's history and archaeology.[14] However, the archaeological section of the book offered little new material (except for a few photographs), simply comprising a compilation of data from Lamb's excavations at Thermi and Antissa, together with descriptions of other finds made by Koldewey and the island's archaeological ephoreia. Two years later, in 1975, Buchholz published a detailed study of the *polis* of Methymna.[15] The main body of this work consisted of catalogues of finds which had been made either by Buchholz or previously reported, useful especially for the detailed lists of Methymna's ceramics, prosopographical and numismatic data, and the collected bibliographies for the island's prehistoric sites. And in 1978 Kontis published his second volume which attempted a complete survey of the island's ancient sites.[16] As with Kontis' first volume, however, the archaeological studies were of little value. Much of the work was highly derivative from Koldewey and Lamb, the details given for each site were extremely inconsistent, and (most significantly) no material justification was provided in the text for marking some sites on settlement maps of different archaeological periods (see the gazetteer entries for sites #46, #80).

Since this last book of Kontis, the only new archaeological data to be published have been the yearly reports of the Canadian School's excavations at Mytilene (from 1984-90),[17] a brief catalogue of finds made in 1986-87 by the island's archaeological service (published originally in the local *Lesbiaka* periodical and repeated, with a few additions, in the *Archaiologikon Deltion*),[18] and a large two-volume work by Axiotis (in 1992).[19] The latter work is particularly impressive in respect of the number of new sites discovered (especially in the mountainous west part of the island), the thoroughness of the fieldwork, and also for the immense detail on village histories which is presented.

This limited record of publication, even in terms of basic yearly reports in the *Archaiologikon Deltion*, *Praktika* and *Ergon* periodicals,[20] has led to serious problems in any attempt to study the island's archaeology. Many sites of great significance (such as the late Neolithic and early Bronze Age site at Kourtir, approximately five times larger than Thermi) still have no widespread recognition,[21] and the only published reports for the vast majority of sites are those by local authors which have appeared either in the island's newspapers,[22] popular journals,[23] or as part of more general village histories.[24] Many of these articles and books (and even one of the works cited above as a 'major' publication[25]) are almost impossible to find in libraries outside Lesbos, and understandably therefore the archaeology of the island has been passed over when 'pan-Aegean' phenomena in different periods have been discussed by scholars.[26]

1.2 The aim and contents of the volume

The main aim of this volume, therefore, is to utilise the complete corpus of published data (including the local, largely unused, sources) in order to present finally to a wider audience the current evidence for all the known archaeological sites in the island.[27] For other regions of Greece such works of reference have long been available and have greatly aided (and stimulated) work in those areas by offering secure bases for subsequent research.[28]

---

[11] Charitonidis, 1960; id., 1961a; id., 1961b; id., 1961-62; id., 1962a; id., 1962b; id., 1963a; id., 1963b; id., 1963c; id., 1964; id., 1965.

[12] Petrakos, 1967a, 96-102 and pls. 74-84; id., 1967b, 72-75 and figs. 73-76; id., 1967c, 445-58, 460-62, figs. 1-11, 13 and pls. 331-37α, 337γ-338; id., 1968a, 84-86 and pl. 63; id., 1968b, 80-82 and figs. 84-87.

[13] Chatzi, 1971; ead., 1972; ead., 1973.

[14] Kontis, 1973.

[15] Buchholz.

[16] Kontis, 1978.

[17] Williams and Williams, 1985; id., 1986; id., 1987; id., 1988; id., 1989; id., 1990; id., 1991.

[18] Acheilara and Archontidou-Argyri, 1986; Archontidou-Argyri, 1986-87; Acheilara and Archontidou-Argyri, 1987. A report on the ephoreia's 1988 work has appeared recently also, Archontidou-Argyri, 1988.

[19] Axiotis, 1992 I-II.

---

[20] From 1976 until 1986 not a single report on the island appeared in any of the three periodicals.

[21] A surface survey was conducted by Chatzi at Kourtir in September 1970, but only the briefest details of her finds have been published and access to all her material stored in Mytilene is denied. (See the gazetteer entry for the site at #91.)

[22] Paraskeuaidis, 26/9/29; id., 29/9/29; Koumarelas, 1989a; id., 1989b; id., 1989c.

[23] Laskaris; Moutzouris 1962; Paraskeuaidis, 1966; Moutzouris, 1973; Paraskeuaidis, 1978; Moutzouris, 1983; Axiotis, 1991a; id., 1991b; Koumarelas, 1995.

[24] Kontellis; Paraskeuaidis, 1987.

[25] Kontis, 1973.

[26] When a gazetteer of Bronze Age sites in the Aegean was produced (as late as 1979), Lesbos was conspicuous by its complete absence, despite the attention paid to the nearby islands of Samos, Chios and Psara: R. Hope-Simpson and O. T. P. K. Dickinson, *A gazetteer of Aegean civilisation in the Bronze Age, Vol. I: the mainland and islands* (SIMA 52; Göteborg, 1979). The only detailed treatment of the whole of the island's prehistory (rather than a focus solely upon the well-known site of Thermi) has been by Buchholz, 121-37; see also the recent survey by J. L. Davis, 'Review of Aegean Prehistory I: the Islands of the Aegean', *AJA* 96 (1992), 724. The similar lack of comment on the *archaeology* of the island in the early Iron Age and Archaic periods (in contrast to the numerous discussions of the island's *history* in the same eras), is commented upon in N. Spencer, 'Early Lesbos between East and West: a "grey area" of Aegean archaeology', *BSA* 90 (1995).

[27] One of the few works by a non-Greek scholar which utilised some of the local source material was that of Mason, 1993.

[28] Regions where topographical studies and gazetteers of ancient sites have had long histories include **Melos**: D. MacKenzie, 'Ancient sites in Melos', *BSA* 3 (1896-97), 71-88, later built upon in C. Renfrew and M. Wagstaff (eds.), *An island polity: the archaeology of exploitation in Melos* (Cambridge, 1982), Part I (Chapters 2-6), 9-71; **Messenia**: W. A. McDonald and R. Hope-Simpson, 'Prehistoric

The core of the book is a gazetteer of all known sites, each with its own bibliography. This gazetteer is supplemented by two appendices, the first listing a number of additional sites attested epigraphically in a corpus of Hellenistic and late Roman inscriptions, and the second discussing in more detail the Lesbian style of polygonal masonry which is a feature of a number of the sites presented in the gazetteer. At the end of the volume are two indices for ease of reference providing, respectively, a list of the sites in alphabetical order, and a summary of the chronological periods represented at each site. A series of figures then illustrates the distribution of sites from the Neolithic to the Tourkokratia (figs. 2-14), the epigraphically-attested sites (fig. 15) and some of the walls discussed in Appendix 2 (figs. 16-32).

Future research in the island will undoubtedly lead to revisions in the information presented here since it has proved difficult to clarify the precise nature of remains reported at some sites which could not be visited. Furthermore, as in many other regions of Greece, the study of (especially ceramic) material dating to the Byzantine and Turkish periods is still at an early stage, and it is to be hoped that the reports given in this gazetteer, which sometimes have been able to label sites simply as possessing material from the 'Middle Ages' or 'Medieval' periods, will receive further definition in subsequent years. Nevertheless, the importance of establishing for the first time an accessible database of sites for the island which can act as a guide to future research and fieldwork is hard to underestimate, and it was with this main purpose that the present work was undertaken.

habitation in southwestern Peloponnese', *AJA* 65 (1961), 221-60; id., 'Further explorations in southwestern Peloponnese', *AJA* 68 (1964), 229-45; id., 'Further explorations in southwestern Peloponnese', *AJA* 73 (1969), 123-77; W. A. McDonald and G. R. Rapp (Jr.), *The Minnesota Messenia Expedition: reconstructing a Bronze Age environment* (Minneapolis, 1972), 263-322 and figs. 8.11-8.18; the **Dodecanese**: R. Hope-Simpson and J. F. Lazenby, 'Notes from the Dodecanese', *BSA* 57 (1962), 154-75; id., 'Notes from the Dodecanese II', *BSA* 65 (1970), 47-77; **Lakonia**: H. Waterhouse and R. Hope-Simpson, 'Prehistoric Lakonia: Part I', *BSA* 55 (1960), 67-107; id., 'Prehistoric Lakonia: Part II', *BSA* 56 (1961), 114-75. Among the more recent examples (with special reference to the eastern Aegean), there are works for both Chios and Samos. **Chios**: E. Yalouris, 'Notes on the topography of Chios' in J. Boardman and C. E. Vaphopoulou-Richardson (eds.), *Chios: a conference at the Homerion in Chios, 1984* (Oxford, 1986), 141-68; **Samos**: D. G. J. Shipley, *A history of Samos, 800-188 BC* (Oxford, 1987), 249-66 (and for the island's *peraea*, 266-68).

Chapter 2

GAZETTEER OF ARCHAEOLOGICAL SITES IN LESBOS

2.1 Key

The entries for each site are organised as follows:

(a) Site number: The catalogued sites are numbered in one continuous sequence as they appear on all the distribution maps (figs. 2-14). The sequence begins on the east coast of the island near modern Komi, continuing south to the Gulf of Gera and the Malea promontory (#1-45), west over the uplands near Agiasos and around the Gulf of Kalloni (#46-131), west to Eresos and Sigri (#132-148), east along the north coast of the island to Antissa (#149-164), south across the highlands of the Kourouklos mountain range (#165-189), northeast to Methymna (#190-217) and across the Lepetymnos range to the east coast (#218-244). An asterisk (*) before the site number represents a site where excavations have been carried out.

(b) The site name is given in the form of its toponym, followed by the name of the nearest modern village in parentheses. In the spelling of toponyms, the form used is that which is employed most commonly in the published reports of the site, and (where applicable) a note has been added giving any dialectal variations also found in the publications. These differences are apparent most often in toponyms which are diminutives since the local version of the Attic diminutive forms '-άκι'/'-άκια' is '-έλλħ'/'-έλλħα' (eg. see #57, #212). Where the location of the ancient site is within the area of a modern settlement only the latter is given without an additional toponym (eg. for Pamphila [#17], Mytilene [#27], Methymna [#217] etc.).

(c) The grid references provided are taken from the British 'Aegean Islands' 1: 50 000 maps and are given to six figures where it is possible to locate the site precisely upon the maps, otherwise to four figures where either the site is very large or its exact location is unclear.

(d) If the exact location of the site is known an approximate height above sea level is given. (Where the height above sea-level is not known, this space has been left blank ['--']).

(e) The abbreviations for the dating of sites are as follows:
E = Early.
M = Middle.
L = Late.
N = Neolithic.
BA. = Bronze Age (Myc. = Mycenaean, H = Helladic, M = Minoan).
PG. = Protogeometric.
G. = Geometric.
A. = Archaic.
C. = Classical.
HL. = Hellenistic.
R. = Roman.
Byz. = Byzantine.
Ven. = Venetian.

'MAge' = site dated by sources to the 'Medieval' period or to the 'Middle Ages'.
Tur. = Turkish.[1]
BC = Before Christ.
AC = After Christ.
C = Century.
(Where the period to which the site dates is unclear, this space has been left blank ['--']).

(f) The probable function of each site has been classified as follows: HAB(itation), CEM(etery) or SP(ecial purpose). The latter has been applied to those sites which served a number of other disparate functions including centres of cult practice, fortifications, quarries etc..

(g) The descriptions of each site given include directions for finding the site and a description of the preserved remains. Directions are given in abbreviated form: n. = north, e. = east, s. = south, w. = west, ne. = northeast, ene. = east-northeast etc.. Unless stated otherwise, distances given are measured as the crow flies rather than along existing roads.

(h) Bibliography. Full references are provided for books and articles cited only once. Where a work has been cited on more than one occasion, an abbreviated form has been employed which can be found in the select bibliography at the beginning of the volume.

2.2 Site Gazetteer

1. *Paliochori* (Komi); 758692; 220m; LR.-Byz., 'MAge'; HAB, SP(?). At the spot known as Paliochori 1.3 kms nnw. from Komi on the slopes below the road to the e., the remains of an old settlement are apparent near a chapel of the Panagiouda. The chapel itself stands below a large oak tree on the w. bank of the Tenegias River with the foundations of an older chapel (and some broken architectural Byz. *membra*) beside it. To the n. and e. of the chapel the slopes w. of the river are covered with tiles and sherds including LR.-Byz. 'combed' wares and other glazed sherds of 'MAge' date. The river and nearby springs provide a strong water supply, and the remains of old terraces supported by 'herring-bone' stone walls cover the slopes indicating that the area was once under cultivation.
Bibliography: Axiotis, 1992 I, 155-56.

2. *Plati* (Nees Kydonies); 806728; 60m; EBA., Byz., 'MAge', Tur.; HAB, SP. The remains of habitation activity and a ruined 'MAge' kastro are preserved on the flat-topped ridge named Plati, the n. end of which stands above the e. coast of the island 1.5 kms e. from Nees Kydonies. The sheer n. slope of the ridge drops sharply to the fertile Kydona plain, and it is on this n. end that the

---

Sites defined as 'Tur.' indicate that the particular site dates to the period of Turkish occupation in the island (1462-1912) rather than signifying any particular ethnic affiliation.

ruins are most clearly visible. The earliest material, concentrated outside the kastro walls to the se., comprises EBA. sherds and lithics including dark-grey Troy I sherds, and also brown and red EBA. pieces (including sherds from pithoi and horizontally-pierced lug handles). Axiotis suggested that some of the foundations visible amongst the 'MAge' ruins were to be associated with this EBA. material and that a significant EBA. settlement had existed on the hill.

The enclosure wall of the kastro (1.5 m thick) is preserved up to 1 m high in places, exhibiting three external towers on the s. side. Inside the wall is a chapel of Agios Spyridon, a number of building foundations and a dense scatter of sherds (including 'MAge' glazed sherds) and tiles. This sherd scatter, together with further structural remains outside the wall to the s. near another chapel (of Agios Dimitrios), were taken by Axiotis to indicate that a settlement had been associated with the kastro at the n. end of the plateau.

The remains on the Plati hill have been equated with the 'Kastro Kydonion' referred to by travellers to the island during the Ven. and Tur. periods[2] and also listed as a village ('Kydona') of the 16C AC in a Mitropolitan codex. Local tradition suggests that the settlement of Kydona was abandoned at the end of the 16C AC or at the beginning of the 17C AC after an earthquake and that its inhabitants fled abroad, establishing the settlement of similar name ('Kydoniai', modern Ayvalik) opposite in Asia Minor (which is said to date from approximately the same period).

Bibliography: Koldewey, 34-35; Taxis, 93-94; Moutzouris, 1962, 54, 57-58; Axiotis, 1992 I, 149-53 and II, pl. 31; Mason, 1993, 244-45 and n. 89.

3. *Kalamos* (Nees Kydonies); 7972; --; Byz., Tur.; HAB, CEM, SP. To the w. of the kastro on the Plati hill (#2) the remains of an extensive Byz. and Tur. settlement are spread through the narrow valley of the Kydona River, and it may be these remains which are to be equated with the Tur. village mentioned in the 16C AC codex (and also in early 17C Ottoman sources[3]) rather than the remains on the Plati hill itself (see #2). Beside the modern bridge over the river which carries the main Mytilene-Mandamados road stands a two-storey Tur. hani, and a kalderimi leads inland (w.) along the valley bottom from the hani towards Nees Kydonies. An extensive area of the valley base ca. 0.6 km se. from the modern village is covered with Byz. tiles and sherds together with building foundations. A number of old wells are apparent also. The church of the Byz. settlement (dedicated to Agios Nikolaos) is preserved on the n. side of the river beside the kalderimi, cross-shaped in plan (suggesting a LByz. date, see #9, #176, #241), with its walls of mortared tile and unworked stones preserved up to 3 m in height. A Tur. graveyard was found beyond the church as the road climbs up to the plateau on which the modern village of Nees Kydonies stands.

---

[2] Buondelmonti (in ca. 1420) and Porcacchi (in 1576) both refer to a site in this area as 'Cidonea'.

[3] In addition to the early references to the site by travellers and in the 16C codex noted above (#2 and note 2), Ottoman sources record a village of 'Kydonia' in 1602, M. Kiel, pers. comm. (1995). For the problems of equating the historical references to the site (or possibly sites) of Kydonia with the archaeological remains in this area of the island (here, sites #2-3) see Mason, 1993, 244-45.

Bibliography: Taxis, 94; Charitonidis, 1966, 72-73, fig. 1 and pl. VIa; Axiotis, 1992 I, 151-52 and II, pl. 31; Mason, 1993, 244-45 and n. 86.

4. *Ormos Mystegnon* (Mystegna); 8270-8271; 10m; R.(?), EByz., 'MAge'; HAB, CEM(?), SP. To the e. of the main road which leads from Mytilene n. to Mystegna, significant ancient remains are scattered over a large area on the shore of the bay of Mystegna ca. 1.5 kms se. from the modern village. Some of the remains on the sw. lip of the low rocky plateau known as Plati which limits the bay of Mystegna to the n. (the s. end of the Plati ridge referred to in #2 above) were dated to the 'MAge' period by Koldewey. At the s. foot of this hill, and stretching along the shore of the bay, are extensive traces of ancient settlement. Koldewey counted some 20-30 marble blocks in this area which appeared to come from different buildings (and which he suggested had probably had been gathered from different locations). The chapel of Agios Giannis near the shore preserves the apse of an EByz. basilica, architectural fragments of which were found built into the later chapel constructed on top and also scattered nearby. Undated sherd and tile debris cover ca. 1.5 ha., including a scatter of sherds on the n.-facing slopes along the s. edge of the bay (suggested by Koldewey to represent the settlement's cemetery).

Bibliography: Koldewey, 33-34; Taxis, 94; Charitonidis, 1963c, 272; id., 1968a, 11 and pl. 3; Kontis, 1978, 233-34; Axiotis, 1992 I, 147-48 and II, pl. 30.

5. *Agia Marina* (Mystegna); 823704; 15m; EByz.; SP. In olive groves 2 kms to the se. of the village of Mystegna, two old chapels (one in ruins) stand close together low down on the n. slopes of the Kranies hill. At the chapel of Agia Marina (the northernmost chapel) EByz. architectural *membra*, together with the substantial walls of an older building visible under the s. and w. walls, indicate the location of an EByz. basilica. A large number of other architectural pieces from the basilica were found at the ruined Christos chapel nearby (built in 1921) together with a large sherd and tile scatter, worked blocks of dark trachyte, and a funerary stele of grey marble.

Bibliography: Charitonidis, 1968a, 11; Axiotis, 1992 I, 143-44 and II, pl. 29.

6. *Agios Thymianos* (Thermi); 807692; 200m; C.(?); HAB. Ca. 2.5 kms nw. from modern Thermi the Dendrosimon hill rises above the Tenegias River on the n. side of the road which leads nw. to Pigi. On the s. lip of the hilltop is the chapel of Agios Thymianos, and in the olive groves around the chapel a scatter of tile and pottery sherds are associated with crudely-constructed foundations of buildings. The pottery sherds are mostly grey wares. Kontis dated the site to the C. period on the basis of the pottery finds.

Bibliography: Kontis, 1978, 234-35; Axiotis, 1992 I, 161.

7. *Karyes* (Thermi); 815668; 180m; EByz., LByz./Tur.; CEM, SP. Ca. 1 km sw. from Thermi, at the place named Karyes, stands the monastery of Agios Raphael, the origins of which date back to the 13C AC when the monastery was named Karyes (and was solely for nuns). In 1959, when foundations were being laid for a new chapel, architectural elements of an EByz. basilica were uncovered (along with a tomb of similar date), but no structural remains of such an early period were found. The only foundations located belonged to a much later LByz./post-Byz. church dated by

5

pottery associated with it. Also uncovered during the excavations were five tombs of the martyrs executed by the Turkish invaders on 9th April 1463 together with an older burial which was suggested to be that of the 13C leader of the original monastery.

Bibliography: Taxis, 94; Charitonidis, 1960, 236 and pl. 208α, γ, δ; Daux, 1960, 809 and fig. 4; Charitonidis, 1968a, 12-13, fig. 2 and pls. 4-5; Axiotis, 1992 I, 140-41.

*8. *Loutra Thermis* (Thermi); 8367; 10m; C., HL., R., Tur.; HAB(?), SP. At the mouth of the alluvial coastal plain above which (to the w.) rises the modern village of Thermi, is the small *skala* settlement (and harbour) of Loutra Thermis. The latter stands at the point where the road n. from Mytilene divides to head inland to Thermi (ca. 1.5 kms to the w.) or continues n. to Mystegna (ca. 4 km to the n.). There are hot springs near the shore (49°C) around which the settlement of Loutra Thermis still focuses.

In antiquity worship of Artemis Thermia was centred on this water source, and votives from the cult date from the 5C BC, with inscriptions from the C./HL.-R. periods. Architectural *membra* and tile fragments of varying date are scattered over the whole area surrounding the Turkish bath (a building later constructed on the springs themselves) and are apparent especially in the fields above to the w. where column bases are still visible *in situ*. When a trial excavation was carried out beneath the Tur. bath complex[4] a 1C AC bath building with a mosaic floor was discovered together with more structural remains of R. date. The magnificent two-storey Tur. hotel with enclosed gardens, the 'Sar-Litza' or 'Yellow Water' Palace (so-called after the colour of the springwater), was built in 1903 and stands in ruins beside the Turkish baths which are still in use.

In 1971 Chatzi located a possible extension of the cult place (or possibly one distinct from that at Thermi) half an hour further nw. at the spot known as 'Tis Geras to Seraï' ('The house of Gera') where ornate cuttings on a rock-face were suggested to represent an open-air shrine.

Bibliography: Newton I, 60-61; Koldewey, 42, 81; Taxis, 93; G. D. Kontis, "Η Θαμμένη Λέσβος', *Mytilini* 18/10/36; id., *Tachydromos* 18/10/36; B. G. Kallipolitis, ' Από τή λατρεία τῆς Ἀρτεμίδος στή Λέσβο', *Lesbiakes Selides* (1950), 206-11; Charitonidis, 1960, 236 and pl. 208β; id., 1963c, 267 and pl. 308α; id., 1965, 493, fig. 7; id., 1968b, 31-32; Chatzi, 1971, 457 and pl. 461α-β; Aupert, 697; Kontis, 1978, 235-38; Axiotis, 1992 I, 130-34 (and unnumbered photograph p. 134) and II, pl. 24.

9. *Epano Pyrgoi* (Thermi); 839669; 30m; LByz.; SP. In the hamlet of Epano Pyrgoi, 1 km ese. from the main village of Thermi, a branch w. from the main road leads to the LByz. church of the Panagia tis Troulotis (now the parish church of the community). In plan the church is in the shape of a cross, has a circular domed roof, and is constructed of mortared stone and tile (exhibiting many ancient blocks built into its walls, some of which come from the nearby shrine of Artemis, #8). The church lacks many features of EByz. structures and probably dates from the 14C or the 15C AC (see #3, #176, #241). Inside the church the wall paintings are now extremely faint and can

only be seen on the inside of the dome and on the e. side of the building.

Bibliography: Taxis, 92; Charitonidis, 1966, 72 and pl. IV; Axiotis, 1992 I, 128-30 and II, pl. 23.

10. *Treis Agioi* (Pamphila); 846664; 20m; EByz.; SP. Ca. 1.8 kms nw. from Pamphila near the hamlet of Pyrgoi Thermis a chapel dedicated to Taxiarchis stands to the w. of the main road. A few metres to the w. of this chapel are two ikonostases of the Panagia and Agios Theodoros. The former stands within the apse of a much older structure (probably the remains of an EByz. basilica). Also, a large wall (corresponding to the s. wall of the basilica) of mortared tile and unworked stone runs e.-w. to the s. of the Panagia shrine, separating it from the ikonostasis of Agios Theodoros. Scattered around the site are a number of EByz. architectural pieces including unfluted columns and column capitals, and the chapel of Taxiarchis also incorporates a large number of worked blocks.

Bibliography: Axiotis, 1992 I, 125 and II, pl. 22.

*11. *Pyrgoi Thermis* (Thermi); 849665; 5m; EBA., MBA., LBA., R.; HAB. Ca. 2 kms n. from the village of Pamphila on the road which leads from Mytilene to Thermi and Mystegna is the hamlet of Pyrgoi Thermis. To the e. of this main road (which runs directly through the hamlet) in the fields beside the shore Winifred Lamb excavated an extensive EBA.-LBA. settlement from 1929-1933 sited on what is now a high scarp (the Bronze Age coastline was further to the e. and has been eroded by the sea). Five main strata of settlement spanning the third millennium BC were distinguished; the site was then abandoned and later reoccupied in the MBA.-LBA., and from the latter period date imported Myc. wares (of LH II-IIIA date), local copies of similar style pottery, and bronze weaponry. The overall ceramic assemblage is very similar to that found both in nw. Anatolia (at Troy and Yortan) and also at the other Bronze Age sites in Lesbos on both the e. coast (sites #2 and #238) and around the Gulf of Kalloni (sites #84, #88, #91, #99, #108-09, #111-12, #114, #116, #131).

Basiakos also reported finding a semi-circular kiln and R. mosaic on the shore nearby.

Bibliography: Main references and comparanda are collected by Buchholz, 121-23, 133, 135-36 and figs. 36-37; see also Lamb, 1936; Bayne, 111-17, fig. 4.I, 4.V, 4.X, 13; Paraskeuaidis, 1976, 503; Chatzi 1972, 580; Kontis, 1978, 202-10; Basiakos, 210; Axiotis, 1992 I, 126-28.

12. *Gamila* (Aphalonas); 835638; 160m; Byz., 'MAge'; SP. On the s. slopes of the Gamila hill, 1.8 kms due w. from Aphalonas, Axiotis noted the remains of an older chapel beside the modern one of Agios Therapon. A number of architectural pieces (including an unfluted marble column and a threshold block of red trachyte) lie on the hillslope nearby. Beyond the e. end of the modern building are the foundations of a Byz. chapel constructed with unworked stone from which Axiotis suggested that the marble and trachyte *membra* originated. Axiotis also noted a dense scatter of 'MAge' tiles and sherds extending for some distance to the n..

Bibliography: Axiotis, 1992 I, 115-16 and II, pl. 20.

13. *Patia* (Aphalonas); 8463-8464; --; Byz., 'MAge', Tur.; HAB. To the nw., w. and sw. of the modern village of Aphalonas, an extensive area is covered with remains of the preceding Byz. and Tur. settlements which coalesced to

---

[4] A Tur. village at Thermi (or 'Ilica') is attested in Ottoman sources as far back as 1602, M. Kiel, pers. comm. (1995). An earlier Ottoman census list for the island dating from 1521 is preserved also, but as yet there is no published account of the settlements listed within it (ibid.).

form the modern village.[5] The n. part of the site lies around two old chapels, one known as 'Agioi Omologites' (at a spot called Kato Alonia[6]) and the other as the 'Panagia tin Armenopoula' to the nw. and w. of the modern village respectively. Near both chapels Axiotis reported dense scatters of 'MAge' sherds, tiles and rubble extending over a significant area. Ca. 0.4 km to the s. of the Panagia is a chapel of Agios Georgios near which Axiotis reported building foundations, worked blocks (including a marble statue base), unfluted columns, a scatter of Byz. tile and two press-stones of Tur. type.
Bibliography: Axiotis, 1992 I, 114-15 and II, pl. 19; id., 1994, figs. Δ and Z.

14. *Laka* (Aphalonas); 856634; 40m; HL., LR., EByz., Tur.; HAB. Ca. 0.5 km se. from Aphalonas, to the s. of the main road which leads up from Panagiouda to Aphalonas (at a spot known as Laka), tiles, sherds and structural remains of HL., LR. and EByz. date were uncovered on the slopes overlooking the Moria valley. A number of Byz. sherds were found on the same hillside together with worked blocks of trachyte. Nearby are stretches of a kalderimi which once formed the main communication route between Moria and Aphalonas.
Bibliography: Acheilara and Archontidou-Argyri, 1987, 486; Axiotis, 1992 I, 117.

15. *Katho* (Panagiouda); 859639; --; Tur.; HAB. Ca. 0.3 km w. from the village of Panagiouda, a track leaves the main road as it leads up to the village of Aphalonas and runs parallel to the road (to its n.) along the slopes overlooking the valley of the Kalamiaris River and Pamphila. In this area (known as Katho) are traces of old terraces covering the hillside together with foundations of houses, piles of stones and worked blocks. Associated with these remains is a concentration of tile and glazed sherds of Tur. date.

Local tradition suggests that this settlement was one of those from which the modern village of Aphalonas was formed (see also #13), and although this site of the Tur. period had been abandoned by the 19C the area was re-settled briefly after the severe earthquake in 1867. Stretches of a kalderimi nearby and a Tur. fountainhead built over one of the many water sources give further evidence for the existence of a former settlement.
Bibliography: Taxis, 92; Axiotis, 1992 I, 112.

16. *Kalamiaris* (Panagiouda); 864642; 10m; EByz.; SP. At the n. end of the Panagiouda village near the Kalamiaris River stands the chapel of Agios Georgios which exhibits a number of squared blocks and EByz. architectural *membra* either built into its walls or collected together at the chapel. Inside the chapel Charitonidis noted the foundations of an ancient structure constructed of large marble blocks which formed a right-angled corner. The architectural *membra* were thought to have originated from this building (probably an EByz. basilica). Similar worked blocks were found at the nearby chapel of Agios Konstantinos, probably originally from the same basilica.

Bibliography: Charitonidis, 1968a, 14; Axiotis, 1992 I, 111 and II, pl. 18.

17. Pamphila (village); 865648; 10m; C./HL., 'MAge'; HAB(?), CEM. At Pamphila a marble funerary statuette of a female figure was found in the Katsanou plot, comparanda suggesting a 4C date. Other scattered worked blocks and inscriptions have been reported in the area, some of which had been brought from the sanctuary of Artemis at Thermi nearby (#8). Axiotis noted also that at the e. edge of the settlement near the shore around the two small chapels of Agios Giannis and Panagiouda (which have both been rebuilt recently) are significant scatters of 'MAge' ceramics.[7]
Bibliography: Euangelidis, 1927-28, 18-19; Axiotis, 1992 I, 120-21 and II pl. 18.

18. *Augo Atsinganas* (Moria); 834617; 120m; R., Tur.; HAB, CEM, SP. The ruins of an isolated ancient building with an associated burial were reported by Axiotis on the hill named Augo Atsinganas ca. 1.9 kms wsw. from Moria. The hill rises to the s. of the road which leads w. from Moria to the shore of the Gulf of Gera near a fountain also named Atsinganas (constructed in 1891). On the hilltop Axiotis described foundations (with the line of the s. wall clearly preserved), a dense scatter of tiles, bones from a disturbed tomb, and plain ware sherds among which was the handle of a lamp dating to ca. 100 AD.

At the s. foot of the Augo Atsinganas hill on the shore of the Gulf of Gera (beside a ruined chapel of the Panagia Melani), stands a Tur. bath-house centred on warm springs (which Taxis thought to have R. foundations). The bath-house (of similar nature to the bath at Thermelia near Moria, #23) is still in use and comprises two large water cisterns with ducts leading into the cisterns from the n. and flowing s. into the Gulf of Gera.
Bibliography: Koldewey, 42; Taxis, 90; Axiotis, 1992 II, 721-22, pl. 145.

19. *Saliakas* (Moria); 837604; 170m; EBA., 'MAge'; HAB. The steep rocky hill named Saliakas rises above the n. shore of the Gulf of Gera ca. 2 kms sw. from Moria. On the peak of the hill Axiotis and Kophopoulos reported an extensive scatter of EBA. material including sherds from extremely coarse pottery, pithoi, brown-burnished pieces, handles and a dense scatter of lithics (including pieces of black stone similar to that found near Chydira [#180]). There were also fragments of trachyte millstones (a rock not naturally occurring in the se. of the island) and an especially large number of sea-shells including conches and scallops.

Below the peak to the se. are stretches of a kalderimi leading up from the main road onto the hill,[8] two fountains (now dry), and a scatter of sherds and tiles of 'MAge' date. Old terraces are apparent on this se. side of the hill and on a lower peak a large block from an olive-press lies disused.
Bibliography: Axiotis, 1992 II, 722-23 (and unnumbered photograph p. 723).

---

[5] A Tur. village at 'Afalona' is attested in Ottoman sources as far back as 1602, M. Kiel, pers. comm. (1995). Concerning an earlier 16C Ottoman census of the island, see n. 4 above.
[6] The nearby toponym of 'Epano/Apano Alonia' a little way up the hill is said to have been from where the modern village of Aphalonas took its name: from 'Απάνω αλώνια', to 'Αφάλωνια', to 'Αφάλωνας', see Axiotis, 1992 I, 114.

---

[7] A settlement here during the Tur. period is attested in Ottoman sources as early as 1602, M. Kiel, pers. comm. (1995). Concerning an earlier 16C Ottoman census of the island, see n. 4 above.
[8] This is probably part of the same kalderimi which is apparent further e. near the Lemonos chiftlik (#21) and which continues e., entering the former w. gate of the city of Mytilene near the ancient theatre.

20. *Kamares* (Moria); 852613; 50m; R.; SP. Ca. 0.4 km s. from the village of Moria stands a section of the R. aqueduct (probably of 2C AC date[9]) which carried water down from the area of the (now drained) Great Lake near Agiasos to Mytilene (see also #22). Twelve columns are preserved spanning the valley bottom with three series of arches between each pier (of which generally only the middle arch is preserved). The columns and spans of each arch are constructed of grey marble, with the spans of the top arch composed of mortared tile.
Bibliography: Newton I, 58 and pl. 3; Koldewey, 66-67, 81 and pl. 29.1; Taxis, 90-91; Paraskeuaidis, 1976, 502-03; Chatziioannou; Axiotis, 1992 I, 107-08.

21. *Outza* (Moria); 858610; 150m; EByz., 'MAge', Tur.; HAB. At the place known as Outza 1 km sse. from Moria stand the extensive remains of a Tur. (and possibly earlier Byz.) settlement.[10] The area is known to have been the chiftlik of a Mytilenean family named Lemonos and a number of ruins visible today attest the agricultural centre which once existed here: a building which housed an olive press, a paved aloni, a square cistern (used for the storage of wine), and a large number of foundations of buildings of mortared stone and tile.

Nearby to the s. are the remains of an EByz. basilica (the n., s. and e. walls are preserved together with the apse), architectural pieces from which are built into the chapel of Agios Giannis and a ruin known as the 'Panagia' which both stand near the remains of the chiftlik. A dense scatter of 'MAge' ceramics extending to the ne. as far as a chapel of Christos (where more EByz. elements are collected) indicates the extent of the settlement associated with the chiftlik. Before the current chapel of Christos was built the apse of an older structure was visible.
Bibliography: Taxis, 91; Charitonidis, 1968a, 14-15; Axiotis, 1992 I, 108-09 and II, pl. 17.

22. *Katolakos* (Moria) 868623; 60m; HL., R.; CEM, SP. Ca 1 km e. from the village of Moria immediately s. from the main road, at a point where it bends s. to head towards Mytilene, large excavated areas on the hillside indicate the remains of an extensive marble quarry at a place known as Katolakos. Ancient cuttings are still visible on a large number of ancient quarry faces (some of which have collapsed) and in the quarry hundreds of half-finished columns, capitals, bases, basins, altars and cut blocks are visible. It seems that the quarry was exhausted of marble at the time of its abandonment in late antiquity.

Sections of the R. aqueduct (see #20) which brought water from the (now drained) Great Lake near Agiasos to Mytilene and ran above the quarry on the same hill are still apparent. An empty (possibly R.) cist grave lined with limestone blocks lies beyond the e. edge of the quarry on the hill overlooking the main road to Mytilene.

Kontis added that in the Moria area a number of inscriptions of HL. and R. date have been found, the majority being funerary stelai.
Bibliography: Taxis, 91; Charitonidis, 1968a, 14; id., 1968b, no. 85 (p. 60); Kontis, 1978, 238; Axiotis, 1992 I,

101-02 and II, pl. 15; Pariente, 870; French, 1993, 65; Millar and Williams, 1993; id. 1994.

23. *Thermelia* (Moria); 869624; 50m; Tur.; SP. At the s. edge of the Moria plain (1 km e. from the village), between the fork in the main roads which lead either n. from Mytilene along the coast to Pamphila or inland (w.) to Moria, stands a chapel of the Panagiouda (painted yellow). The ruins of an old Tur. bath-house of mortared grey stone stand nearby, the main room being rectangular with an arched roof (and two air vents in the ceiling). A low sill exists around the wall on three sides (it is missing on the n. side where there are two openings for water-ducts). The main cistern is now full of earth but seems to have had steps leading down into it from the door, and from the extension of the e. wall towards the s. it seems that an entrance chamber of some sort once existed here. In the 19C Koldewey referred to both the bath-house and the warm springs at the spot[11] (the springs still flowed in 1905). Axiotis drew a comparison with the similar Tur. bath-house at Therma on the n. shore of the Gulf of Gera (#18).
Bibliography: Koldewey, 81; Axiotis, 1992 I, 102.

24. *Kara-Tepe* (Mytilene); 8762/8862; 30m; BA., C./HL.(?); HAB(?), CEM. On the promontory of Kara-Tepe, ca. 2 kms nnw. from Mytilene (now used as a military firing range), Charitonidis described a cist-grave oriented e.-w. (with the head of the body at the e. end) which contained a black-glazed bowl and a pair of iron scrapers. The lid-slabs of two other graves were also apparent. Axiotis reported a scatter of BA. pottery on the promontory but gave no more details of the finds (or their exact location).
Bibliography: Charitonidis, 1960, 236; Axiotis, 1992 I, 460.

25. *Agios Nikolaos* (Pyrgi); 856588; 120m; A., C., HL.(?), Byz.; HAB, CEM(?), SP. Ca. 2.5 kms wsw. of the town of Mytilene, on a spur overlooking the Gulf of Gera (between the villages of Kentron and Pyrgi), stands the chapel of Agios Nikolaos. On the n., nw. and s. slopes of the hill are worked blocks together with signs of quarrying activity and a scatter of plain ware sherds and tile. On top of the hill by the chapel are two unfluted columns (which may have been brought from Mytilene), and other architectural *membra* can be seen inside the chapel also.

Near the chapel, a cave faces w. towards the Gulf of Gera. The mouth of the cave is small (measuring 0.4 m x 0.8 m) but the walls open out inside to form probably the largest cave in Lesbos with five separate chambers. In the first chamber, the floor was found scattered with rocks, sherds of pottery, clay plaques, human bones, A., C. and Byz. coins, and figurines. The deposits seemed to be of votive nature and the sherds included black-figure, black-glaze and grey wares. A hoard of A. billon (silver alloy) and electrum coins was also found in the cave. The former exhibited two facing boars' heads on the obverse and an incuse square on the reverse. A number of electrum 'sixths' were also recovered and the obverse types included winged lions, a winged boar, lionheads, a griffin, the head of a calf, representations of Pan, Athena (the latter of Orientalising type), a Gorgon, Herakles with the Nemean lion, and the torso of a calf. The Byz. coins were of bronze.

---

[9] The aqueduct is probably of Hadrianic date at the earliest with some later repairs, H. Williams, pers. comm. (1994).

[10] A Tur. settlement at 'Moria' is attested in Ottoman records as early as 1602, M. Kiel, pers. comm. (1995). Concerning an earlier 16C Ottoman census of the island, see n. 4 above.

---

[11] Hence the toponym for the area, also known in the 19C by the alternative diminutive form 'Thermakia' ('Θερμάκια').

Bibliography: Charitonidis, 1965, 491; Kontis, 1978, 242; Axiotis, 1992 II, 724 and pl. 146.

26. *Ano Latomeia Kourtzi* (Aliphantas); 864587; 100m; C.(?), LR.; SP. On the plateau 0.3 km w. from the village of Aliphantas, before the road which leaves Mytilene to the w. descends to the shore of the Gulf of Gera, is a quarry area known as Ano Latomeia Kourtzi between the two toponyms 'Panagi' and 'Outza'. In this quarrying area iron tools, unfinished columns and a half-completed (C.?) relief of a male figure (probably Herakles) were recovered, testifying to the existence of an ancient quarry. Charitonidis dated some of the material to the LR. period also.
Bibliography: Charitonidis, 1961-62, 263, fig. 2 and pl. 318β-δ; Daux, 1962, 876, fig. 4; Charitonidis, 1963c, 268 and pl. 308δ; Axiotis, 1992 II, 723; Millar and Williams, 1993, fig. 1.

*27. Mytilene (town); 8858, 8859, 8860, 8958 (finds spread over all four squares); --; EBA., LBA., PG., G., A., C., HL., R., Byz., Ven., Tur.; HAB, CEM, SP. The earliest finds representative of settlement activity within the area of the modern town are EBA. sherds found in the area of the Medieval kastro. Trenches laid for the construction of the new museum also located Myc. sherds (the specific dating for this material awaits full publication). Earliest structural remains are of PG. date. The A. through R. periods exhibit domestic structures, the city wall (fig. 32), architectural *membra* from public buildings, a R. bath with mosaic floors, and tomb finds (including large C., HL. and R. cemeteries). Many EByz. architectural elements have been found. A fortress (possibly built originally in the 13C) was constructed on the ancient acropolis, rebuilt (and extended) in 1373 by Francesco Gattelusio (the founder of the Genoese dynasty who ruled the island from 1355-1462). After the Tur. conquest of Lesbos, large numbers of houses and mosques were built inside the castle walls, and a large number of Tur. remains (including mosques, bath-houses and fountains) are still visible throughout the town.
Bibliography (main): Koldewey, 3-12, pls. 1-3; Rouse, 147-49; D. Euangelidis, 'Λέσβου 'Επιγραφαὶ', *ArchDelt* 6 (1920-21), 99-114; id., 1927-28, 14-22; Charitonidis, 1960, 235-36, 239-43, pls. 206α-ε, 212-13δ, 214; id., 1961a, 207-14, pls. 168-71; id., 1961b, 211-15 and figs. 228-29; id., 1961-62, 261-63, fig. 1, pl. 318α; Moutzouris, 1962, 53, 55; Charitonidis, 1962a, 134-41 and pls. 140-42; id., 1962b, 155-59 and figs. 186-90; Bayne, 124 (and n. 233), 241-42 and figs. 17.1, 25B; Charitonidis, 1963a, 158-59 and pl. 141; id., 1963b, 157-59 and figs. 173-74; id., 1963c, 266-67 and pls. 306-07; id., 1964, 396-97 and pl. 464β, δ; id., 1965, 489, pls. 626-27; Petrakos, 1967c, 445-58, 460-62, figs. 1-11, 13, pls. 331-37α, 337γ-38; Charitonidis, 1968a, 15-20, figs. 4-11, pls. 6β-7; S. Charitonidis, L. Kahil and R. Ginouvès, *Les mosaïques de la maison du Ménandre à Mytilène* (AK supp. 6; Berne, 1970); I. Tsiribakos, ''Αρχαιότητες καὶ μνημεῖα τῶν νήσων Αἰγαίου - Λέσβος', *ArchDelt* 25 (1970) Chronika, 416; Chatzi 1971, 448-56, pls. 447-58; ead., 1972, 579-93, pls. 532-42; ead., 1973, 507-17, pls. 471-86; Kontis, 1973, 18 and fig. 12; Aliprantis, 1973, 557, pls. 527-29; I. Tsiribakos, ''Αρχαιότητες καὶ μνημεῖα τῶν νήσων Αἰγαίου - Λέσβος', *ArchDelt* 29 (1973-74) Chronika, 855-65, pls. 642-44; Buchholz, 123, 133, 136; B. Ch. Petrakos, 'Tὸ κάστρον τῆς Μυτιλήνης', *ArchDelt* 31 (1976) Meletimata, 152-65; Betancourt, 87; Kontis, 1978, 211-31; Williams and Williams, 1985, 225-

33; Acheilara and Archontidou-Argyri, 1986, 198-200, figs. 2-5, pl. 142β; Williams and Williams, 1986, 141-54; Acheilara and Archontidou-Argyri, 1987, 477-81, figs. 2-4, pls. 286-90; Williams and Williams, 1987, 247-62; id., 1988, 135-49; Archontidou-Argyri, 1988, 454-63, figs. 4-11, pls. 270β-279; Williams and Williams, 1989, 167-81; id., 1990, 181-93; id., 1991, 175-91; Axiotis, 1992 I, 19-69, 460, II, pls. 2-4; DAI sherd archive 'Mytilini, Kastro', unpublished.

28. *Limani tou Pyrgiou* (Pyrgi); 852577; 0m; HL(?), R.; HAB(?), SP. On the e. shore of the Gulf of Gera, ca. 0.4 km sw. from the hamlet of Pyrgi and 0.1 km s. from its small harbour, Axiotis reported the remains of walls on the beach (which also extended below sea level) of mortared, unworked stones ca. 0.5 m thick (Axiotis noted at least six walls in 30 m). Nearby, in addition to a dense tile scatter, a number of worked blocks were visible, and between two of the walls Axiotis and Basiakos reported traces of a mosaic floor. Both scholars also noted the remains of ancient kilns nearby (Basiakos counted two, Axiotis only one), which, together with the associated building, were suggested to date to the R. period.
Basiakos also described another ceramic production centre in the area known as Taxiarchis, 2 kms further nw. from the hamlet of Pyrgi, with material which dated to the HL. or R. periods.
Bibliography: Basiakos, 209; H. W. Catling, 'Archaeology in Greece, 1986-87', *AR* 33 (1987), 52; Axiotis, 1992 II, 725.

29. *Bigla* (Pyrgi); 858573; 30m; C./HL., LR./Byz.; HAB/SP(?). Ca. 0.5 km sse. from Pyrgi, Axiotis reported ancient remains on a rocky spur known as Bigla above a chapel of Agia Melani. The small outcrop falls steeply towards the coast, and on top of the spur to the w. of a modern *mandri* is an almost square foundation 5 m x 4.8 m. The walls of the foundations (associated with which are scatters of tile) are of mortared small, unworked stones (suggesting a LR./Byz. date), but the dense sherd scatter on the sheer w. side of the spur includes pieces of C./HL. black-glazed wares.
Kontis spoke of a tower of similar mortared small stones 0.6 km ne. from Pyrgi 'e. of the public road', but gave no dimensions and failed to mark the site on his map, so its relationship with (and possible similarity to) Axiotis' site is unclear.
Bibliography: Kontis, 1978, 242; Axiotis, 1992 II, 725-26 and pl. 145.

30. *Lakerdas* (Pyrgi); 864565; 5m; R., EByz.; CEM(?), SP. On the e. coast of the Gulf of Gera, ca. 2 kms sse. of the village of Pyrgi and 1 km before the junction with the tarmaced road from Mytilene to Loutra, stands a chapel of Christos. The chapel is near the shore to the w. of the road from Pyrgi, and a few metres to its s. Charitonidis noted the apse and architectural elements of an EByz. basilica. A R. funerary stele was built into the s. wall of the chapel, whilst inside was a Byz. epistyle with flower and other circular motifs in relief.
Bibliography: Charitonidis, 1963c, 268, 271; id., 1968a, 24 and fig. 16; Axiotis, 1992 II, 726.

31. *Phousa* (Ano Chalikas) 875562; 340m; 'MAge'; HAB. Ca 1 km ssw. from Ano Chalikas, on the w. slopes of the Prophitis Ilias hill, is an upland plateau at the place known as Phousa (the name of the lower peak of the

9

Prophitis Ilias hill). At the n. end of this plateau (where the ground rises slightly), Axiotis described a dense scatter of 'MAge' sherds and tile, and structural remains are visible at the plateau's w. edge. The finds were suggested to be the remains of a secluded, small habitation site.
Bibliography: Axiotis, 1992 I, 76.

32. *Agios Spyridon* (Ano Chalikas); 889573; 60m; C., LR., Tur.; SP. To the w. of the road which leads s. from Mytilene towards Taxiarchis (the inland branch of the main road away from the coast, see #33), ca. 0.7 km due e. from the village of Ano Chalikas, stands a chapel of Agios Spyridon. Nearby a small, older shrine (only 3 m x 3 m) once stood above the mouth of a cave 40 m in depth within which a (now exhausted) spring once flowed. Another small structure of Tur. date stands above the cave with an inscription dating its construction to 1791. Two unfluted columns and a large Ionic base lie near the cave's mouth, and a scatter of sherds and tile covers the area (possibly the remains of more ancient activity). During the digging of a channel for the springwater, a LR marble relief slab of three dancing maidens was unearthed inscribed with a dedication to the Nymphs. A sphinx and a marble lion (the latter of C. date) are also reported.
Bibliography: Charitonidis, 1965, 492 and pl. 629γ; Axiotis, 1992 I, 79 and II, pl. 8.

33. *Akleidios* (Mytilene); 892575; 20m; HL.; CEM. In September 1988 a small HL. cemetery was uncovered at the place known as Akleidios, ca. 0.4 km se. from the Chrysomalousa suburb beyond the s. edge of the town of Mytilene. The tombs were in the plot owned by the Kamatsos family, just to the s. of the point where the main road s. from Mytilene forks to head either inland to Taxiarchis or along the coast towards the airport (the plot lies between the two branches of the main road). The finds associated with two tombs were especially rich. Axiotis only gives details of the finds from one of these two burials (contained in a stone sarcophagus) which included a gold diadem, the remains of gold-coloured clothing, human figurines and a small knife. The other graves in the plot (the number of graves is not given) were poor by comparison, and Axiotis interpreted the latter as those of kinsmen or slaves in what he saw as a 'family' cemetery.
Bibliography: Axiotis, 1992 I, 78.

34. *Dyo Agioi* (Ano Chalikas); 888563; 250m; LR., EByz.(?), LByz./Tur.; CEM(?), SP. On the e. side of the Prophitis Ilias hill, 1 km se. from Ano Chalikas, the road which leads uphill from the village ends beside two chapels, one named Taxiarchis ('tou Myrintzou') and another dedicated to Agios Nikolaos. The location is known as the 'Dyo Agioi'. Into the wall above the door of the Agios Nikolaos chapel has been built a funerary stele of LR. date.

The Taxiarchis chapel is very old, exhibiting walls 0.8 m in thickness with many courses of tile immediately below the roof and one small window in the n. wall (where a very worn wall-painting is also just still visible). Axiotis compared the wall-construction to chapels of the Tur. period (the 17C AC), but the use of tile in the upper courses is also similar to Byz. examples. A number of EByz. architectural *membra* are present inside the chapel (including an inscribed arch dedicated to 'Agios Polykarpos') many of which are built into its walls. The existence of these pieces led Charitonidis to suggest that a basilica of similar date must have lain in the vicinity.

Axiotis reported the tradition that a monastery once existed nearby and proposed that the two nearby chapels had once marked the parish limits of a LByz./Tur. settlement in this area.
Bibliography: Charitonidis, 1968a, 20-22 and figs. 12-15; Axiotis, 1992 I, 75-76 and II, pl. 7.

*35. *Agios Bartholomaios* (Taxiarchis[12]); 888548; 190m; LN./EBA.; HAB, CEM(?). High above the e. coast of the island, on the e. slopes of the Amali range of hills, are located the villages of Agia Marina and Taxiarchis. A dirt road leaves the village of Taxiarchis and heads w., climbing even higher over the elevated ground just below the summit of the Amali range and subsequently descending in a sw. direction to the village of Loutra. As the road approaches its highest point, ca. 1 km w. of Taxiarchis, it follows the contours of the Strobolas hill and there is a deep ravine immediately to the n.. The chapel of Agios Bartholomaios is clearly visible across this ravine, perched high on a rocky spur of the Prophitis Ilias hill. Ca. 15 m below the chapel, in the s. face of the hill, is the small mouth of a cave (measuring 1.5 m x 0.7 m). A noteworthy feature of the topographical location is that the cave possesses a rare view over both the shores of the Gulf of Gera to the w. and also the e. shores of the island and Turkey to the e..

(S.) Paraskeuaidis discovered complete hand-made LN./EBA. vessels in the cave (which have never been published fully), and later Koumarelas collected a large number of smaller sherds in the first chamber of the cave which were also presented to the archaeological Ephoreia. Charitonidis suggested that the large proportion of whole vessels represented a use of the cave for burial, whilst Kontis and Axiotis thought that the lack of skeletal remains rather pointed towards the interpretation of the site as a shelter for shepherds. Recently (1993), excavations have been started by the island's archaeological Ephoreia but still await publication.
Bibliography: Charitonidis, 1960, 235 and pls. 206ς-07; Buchholz, 122; Kontis, 1978, 210; Axiotis, 1992 I, 89 and II, pl. 11.

36. *Agia Kyriaki* (Agia Marina); 904536; 160m; EByz.; SP. Ca. 0.7 km s. from the village of Agia Marina, along the track which leads s. and then se. along the e. side of the Kouteri and Amali hills, stands the chapel of Agia Kyriaki just s. of the village cemetery. The present chapel is newly built (in 1979), but under a large oak nearby are the ruins of an EByz. basilica. Axiotis reported a dense concentration of tiles and sherds around traces of building foundations, and a large number of grey marble architectural blocks from a basilica (including three unfluted columns).
Bibliography: Axiotis, 1992 I, 91 and II, pl. 11.

*37. *Agia Euprepeia* (Pligoni); 919547; 10m; HL./R., EByz.; CEM, SP. At the se. corner of the large enclosed garden of the 'Lesbos Beach' hotel, ca. 4 kms s. from Mytilene along the coast, is the small chapel of Agia Euprepeia. Around the chapel the foundations of the older structure are visible (which dwarf the existing chapel), and the immediate surrounding area is covered by a dense scatter of late antique ceramics. A number of worked EByz. blocks are visible built into nearby *spitakia*.

The area was excavated in 1931 by Euangelidis and revealed an EByz. basilica 26.1 m in length by 17 m in width. The building was part of a complex which included

---

12 The modern village is known also by the name of Kagiani.

10

a baptistry built onto the w. end of the basilica, a long structure which Euangelidis termed a 'Hotel' built onto the s. side of the basilica, and a separate building which included martyrs' graves a short distance to the sw.. The excavation dated the whole complex to the beginning of the 5C AC.

Nearby, to the nw. of the modern airport runway at a spot known by its Tur. name of 'Hasan Aga', Charitonidis reported an ancient fountain-head (still flowing in 1961-62) constructed of well-fitted isodomic masonry (probably of HL./R. date).

Bibliography: Sotiriou, 190; D. Euangelidis, 'Πρωτοβυζαντινὴ βασιλικὴ Μυτιλήνης', *ArchDelt* 13 (1930-31), 3-33 and figs. 1-24; Iakobos, 35-36; Charitonidis, 1961-62, 263 and fig. 3; id., 1968a, 22; Axiotis, 1992 I, 94 and II pl. 13.

*38. *Kalamies* (Agia Marina); 922536; 10m; C., HL., R., EByz.; HAB(?), CEM, SP. Ca. 6.5 kms s. along the coast from Mytilene, beside the modern airport runway (the latter was constructed in 1951), a small chapel of Agia Paraskeui once stood at the sw. corner of the site now occupied by the 'Kalamies' restaurant. When building work for the airport was taking place, a number of items of gold jewellery and silver holy relics, together with gold and bronze coins, were uncovered 60 m to the n. of the chapel. There were four gold coins and a number of bronze issues of Phokas (602-10 AD), 28 gold coins of Heraklios (613-50 AD), and bronze coins of Justinian and Sophia (565-66 AD).

A rescue excavation carried out in 1954 at the site of the chapel itself revealed architectural remains and foundations of superimposed structures dating from C. to EByz. times. The EByz. basilica (which included two tombs without grave goods and a baptistry) was dated by some of the incised monograms on the architectural *membra* to the 6C or 7C AC. Beneath the basilica were found older remains including a roof antefix of the 5C BC, a 4C BC Doric capital (associated with sherds of similar date), later HL. and R. sherds, heads of clay votives, parts of a lamp, and a coin of Justinian.

Axiotis also noted that, towards the s. end of the airport runway, cultivation work brought to the surface sherds from C./HL. black-glazed vessels and amphorae, and that near the main road which runs along the shore in this area a number of burials in stone sarcophagi (of similar date to the sherd material) were uncovered in 1989.
Bibliography: A. K. Babritsas, ' Ἀνασκαφὴ Κρατήγου Μυτιλήνης', *PAE* (1954), 317-29 and figs. 1-15; M. S. F. Hood, 'Archaeology in Greece, 1954', *JHS* 75 (1955) supp., 16 and pl. Ig; Charitonidis, 1968a, 22 and fig. 1; Axiotis, 1992 I, 94-95 and II pl. 14.

39. *Myloi* (Agia Marina); 910524; 300m; C./HL., Tur.; HAB(?), SP. On the n. spur of a narrow, rocky valley which descends the e. side of the Amali hill, 2 kms sse. from Agia Marina, stand the remains of an ancient structure with associated C./HL. pottery in the region known as Myloi. A pile of stones, tiles and pottery represents the remains of a ruined, small building and amongst the sherds were black-glazed pieces and fragments of amphorae. Two nearby chapels (of the Panagiouda and Agios Nikolaos), lower down the n. spur of the valley, both exhibit squared blocks built into their walls which may come from the building. The view from the spur on which the ruined structure stands is spectacular, over the whole coastal plain where the modern airport runway now lies. Axiotis suggested that these remains near to a number of abundant water sources were those of a small shrine (perhaps to the Nymphs, see also #32).

In the narrow valley itself are the remains of a number of Tur. watermills and traces of a Tur. aqueduct system (the latter comprising mortared stone sections), wells up to 3 m deep, and underground channels. The system was built originally in the late 18C by Hasan Pasha I to improve the water supply to Mytilene and was subsequently remodelled in 1822 to take in the waters from another nearby spring.
Bibliography: Axiotis, 1992 I, 96-97 (and unnumbered photograph p. 99).

40. *Koukkaki* (Agia Marina); 932507; 20m; HL./R.; CEM, SP(?). Ca. 4.3 kms sse. from Agia Marina, to the w. of the main road s. from Mytilene (just before the end of the tarmaced section), the old Koutsoukidis Hotel stands at a spot known as Koukkaki. Nearby, at the w. edge of the narrow coastal plain, Charitonidis and Axiotis both reported that a number of (possibly R.) rock-cut tombs were located (no details of any associated finds are given) together with the upper part of a funerary monument (also undated). An inscribed HL./R. funerary stele is built into the chapel of Agios Ioannis ca. 0.3 km to the se., immediately w. of the end of the main road. Associated with this chapel are elements of an older structure; three unfluted columns of red trachyte and cut blocks with holes for clamps and dowels.
Bibliography: Charitonidis, 1965, 492; Axiotis, 1992 I, 98 and II, pl. 14.

41. *'Aja Tschiftlik'* (Agia Marina); 9350; 20m; A./C.; HAB(?), SP. In 1885 Koldewey found a very large ancient site (possibly a shrine) with high quality finds including black-figure pottery on the n. slope of a protruding small hill half an hour n. from the chapel of Agios Georgios (see #42). Beside this scatter, on the hill near the beach, were the remains of decaying copper-coloured pieces of metal, suggested to be either from votive metal containers or fragments of weapons.
Bibliography: Koldewey, 41, 75.

42. *Agios Georgios* (Agia Marina);[13] 933489; 20m; A., C.; HAB. Near the very se. tip of the island at Cape Malea, low down near the shore, stands the newly re-built chapel of Agios Georgios. A short distance from this chapel, on the coast, Kontis reported a sherd and tile scatter representative of a 'significant' settlement. These surface remains included material of the A. and C. periods. Kontis proposed that the site functioned as a small fishing community, but the good harbour which would be necessary seems to be lacking, at least in modern times.
Bibliography: Kontis, 1978, 239; Axiotis, 1992 I, 98.

43. *Panagia tis Amalis* (Agia Marina); 904509; 400m; Byz.; SP. Ca. 3.3 kms due s. from the village of Agia Marina (but ca. 4.4 kms by following the sinuous trackways), near the s. end of the long ridgetop of the

---

[13] It is impossible to know whether the site found by Koldewey near the Agios Georgios chapel (here catalogued as #41) and that found by Kontis (here #42) are one and the same. Kontis merely refers to his large site in this area as being 'a short distance from the chapel' whilst Koldewey states that the site at 'Aja Tschiftlik' was 'a half hour north of the chapel of Agios Georg[ios]'. Both are suspiciously similar in their finds, including A. and C. ceramics, and the metal fragments to which Koldewey refers on his visit of 22nd April 1885 (Koldewey, 75, excursion 1) could of course have disappeared by the time Kontis traversed the area nearly a century later.

Amali hills, stands an old, narrow chapel known as the 'Panagia tis Amalis'. On the site there are clear traces of a much older building: a number of worked blocks of Byz. date scattered around the present structure and built into the walls; two small Ionic capitals (found by Koldewey which he suggested probably had come from two different buildings); and a dense scatter of tiles and plain ware pottery sherds. Architectural *membra* of very similar nature to those found beside the chapel were also noted by Axiotis in the village of Agia Marina at the church of the same name (Grid Ref. 904543). Axiotis proposed that these pieces, now in the village, had been removed from the chapel of the Panagia tis Amalis and that the site of the original Byz building was at the latter location, but it is impossible to offer a definitive judgement without excavation.

Bibliography: Koldewey, 41; Charitonidis, 1968a, 22 n. 30; Axiotis, 1992 I, 98-99 (and unnumbered photograph p. 70) and II pl. 11. (For the architectural pieces at Agia Marina thought to have been removed from the site see Axiotis, 1992 I, 90-91 and II, pl. 11).

*44. *Tsesmedes* (Loutra); 880515; 60m; HL.(?), EByz.; SP. Ca. 2 kms s. from Loutra, the road which leads towards Agios Ermogenis and Charamida passes through a narrow valley. In this valley, at the place known as Tsesmedes,[14] a small hamlet is centred upon a strong perennial spring (to the e. side of the road). Slightly to the w. of the road is a chapel of Taxiarchis, and it was near here (probably in 1932[15]) that Euangelidis uncovered part of a mosaic floor and the foundation inscription of an EByz. basilica. EByz. architectural pieces formerly beside the Taxiarchis chapel have now been gathered together at the roofed shelter which was set up over the mosaic. Charitonidis and Axiotis also proposed that a building of HL. date had once stood at the site, but only one block is preserved.

Taxis and Charitonidis noted more Byz. remains (including another possible basilica and gold Byz. coins) to the right (w.) of the same road towards Agios Ermogenis and Charamida, ca. 1 km to the s. of Tsesmedes (at locations known as 'Palioloutro' and 'Palia Klisia'), and also still further s., immediately sw. of the chapel of Agios Stylianos (Grid Ref. 888505).

Bibliography: Taxis, 89; Orlandos, 1937, 115 n. 1; Iakobos, 1959, 36; Charitonidis, 1961-62, 263; id., 1963c, 271 and n. 15; id., 1965, 489 and pl. 625γ; id., 1968a, 23-24 and pls. 8α-γ, 9α, γ; Axiotis, 1992 II, 730-31.

*45. *Dibolon* (Skala Loutron); 8652; --; C., HL., R., Byz.; HAB, CEM, SP. Brief excavations in 1965 on the slopes of the Dibolon ('Twin Peaked') hill, immediately nw. from the settlement of Skala Loutron, detected a C. cemetery (comprising cist graves of different orientation), supporting Taxis' earlier report of sarcophagus burials in the same area. Associated pottery of the 1965 excavation dated to the late 5C and early 4C BC, whilst Taxis also listed amongst the finds 'ancient Greek coins'.

On the steep rocky ridge to the se. of the modern *skala*, dry rubble walls of irregular stones were reported also, with which were associated tile fragments. The walls lie on the w. and s. sides of the ridge. Kontis proposed that the remains dated to the C. period, possibly influenced by the date of the nearby graves, but no finds to support this supposition have been reported. Kontis also reported general surface scatters of (mainly) HL. and also R. sherds and tiles over the whole *skala* area.

At the se. foot of this rocky ridge were traces of ancient quarry working (for the good quality limestone). Worked blocks (including half-carved columns and EByz. architectural *membra*) were found being used as counterweights for launching ships at the harbour, pieces which were said to have been dredged from the sea originally at Tarti (see #59).

Offshore to the nw. (beyond the steep 'Oros' hill), on the tiny islet where a chapel of Agios Isidoros now stands (Grid Ref. 846537), Charitonidis described the remains of a small Byz. defensive enclosure.

Bibliography: Taxis, 89; Charitonidis, 1961-62, 263; id., 1965, 490-91, figs. 1-3 and pls. 628γ, 629α; Kontis, 1978, 241; Axiotis, 1992 II, 728.

46. *Skala Dipiou* (Kato Tritos); 789593; 5m; BA., C.-EByz.(?), 'MAge'(?); HAB. At the base of the Ippios plain, on the nw. shore of the Gulf of Gera, Koldewey and Kontis both reported ancient remains at Skala Dipiou. Kontis dated the finds to the BA. and also indicated on his maps that there was habitation activity in the area from the C.-EByz. periods, although no mention is made of finds specifically dated to these periods in the text. Koldewey noted lime-mortared ruined walls near the shore which he tentatively suggested were of 'MAge' date.

Bibliography: Koldewey, 40, 76; Kontis, 1978, 247, n. 469, and figs. 21-30; Axiotis, 1992 II, 722.

47. *Agios Georgios* (Kato Tritos); 789584; 0m; HL., R.; HAB. On the shore beside the chapel of Agios Georgios, ca. 1.5 kms ne. of Kato Tritos, the remains of a HL. and R. habitation site dated from the 3C BC-3C AC were noted by Basiakos. The majority of the remains are now inundated, but still visible is a sherd scatter comprising fragments of amphorae.

Bibliography: Basiakos, 209.

48. *Phousa* (Mychou); 774569; 100m; HL.; CEM. Axiotis reported that to the n. of the road leading wsw. from Mychou[16] (ca. 0.4 km from the village) a group of graves were uncovered which included idols of HL. date.

Bibliography: Axiotis, 1992 II, 699.

49. *Taxiarchis* (Kato Tritos); 778569; 100m; Byz.; SP. Ca. 0.2 km ssw. from Kato Tritos, on a plateau overlooking the village, is the Byz. church of Taxiarchis, the remaining part of a now deserted monastery which once stood on the spot but was dissolved before 1600 AD. Inside the church are fading frescoes badly in need of protection which clearly have two phases, the earliest dating from the end of the 15C. The foundations of the monastery are still visible around the church, and the toponym 'Metochi' which is associated with the area immediately e. of Kato Tritos probably originates from the monastery's former estate.

---

[14] The toponym comes from the Turkish word 'Tsesmes' meaning 'spring'. On the British Army Map the hamlet is named 'Thafto Nero' ('Buried Water').
[15] The chronological details of Euangelidis' exploration of the area are unclear, see Charitonidis, 1968a, 24 n. 43.

[16] The small village of Mychou was Turkish before the exchange of Greek and Turkish populations (initiated by the Treaty of Lausanne in 1923). Its mosque subsequently became a chapel of Agios Dimitrios and also still visible is a large olive press built in 1902 which belonged to Mustapha Bey.

12

Bibliography: Taxis, 99; Iakobos, ''Η ιερὰ μονὴ τῶν Ταξιαρχῶν εἰς Κάτω Τρίτος', *Lesbiaka* 6 (1973), 5-21 and pls. 1-9; A. Pariente, 'Chronique des fouilles et découvertes archéologiques en Grèce en 1991', *BCH* 116 (1992), 923; Axiotis, 1992 II, 699.

50. *Manosados* (Kato Tritos); 784571; 60m; EByz.(?); HAB, SP. Ca. 0.5 km se. from Kato Tritos, at the place known as Manosados, Taxis noted the extensive remains of an ancient settlement (including houses, a bath-house, fountains and cisterns), of which only the apse of a single building (with little associated material) was preserved when Charitonidis visited the site. The abundance of EByz. material found in the vicinity (including a number of pieces during the renovation of the Panagia Galousa chapel) persuaded Charitonidis, however, that the apse was the remaining part of an EByz. basilica.[17] During the renovations of the Panagia chapel, Axiotis also noted the finding of part of an ancient altar with Aiolic cymation decoration (the date of which is unclear) and both Axiotis and Petrakos described a small statuette of a seated figure of Kybele 0.36 m in height (the head and hands of which were missing).

Bibliography: Taxis, 99-100; Petrakos, 1967c, 462; Charitonidis, 1968a, 24-25; Aupert, 697; Axiotis, 1992 II, 695.

51. *Paliokastro* (Mesagros); 778532; 405m; Byz., 'MAge', Tur.; HAB, SP. On the peak of the steep, rocky hill known as Paliokastro, ca. 1.5 kms nw. from Mesagros, are the extensive ruins of a kastro said by Axiotis to date originally to the Byz. period and to have been taken by Cattaneo in ca. 1300 AD. A kastro in this area was shown on the maps of Lesbos drawn by Buondelmonti in 1420 AD and Zamberti in 1485 AD.

The ruins on the hilltop comprise sections of the 2 m thick outer walls (of mortared small stones) with external, semi-circular towers on the w. side (where the gate is also located). Inside, a large water cistern is apparent together with the foundations of other buildings. Axiotis described a scatter of glazed 'MAge' sherds on the hilltop, a coin (of which he gives no details), and more 'Byz.' debris on the lower slopes of the hill. More Medieval remains (of Tur. date) can be found nearby in the village of Mesagros itself where a well-preserved mosque stands.

Bibliography: Newton II, 13; Taxis, 102; Moutzouris, 1962, 54, 56-57; Charitonidis, 1964, 399-400 and pl. 466α-γ; Axiotis, 1992 II, 691.

52. 'Sti Manna' (Papados); 790531; 170m; C., HL., ER.; EByz., 'MAge', Tur.; HAB(?), CEM, SP. Above the w. edge of the Perama plain, at the place known as 'Manna' or 'Sti Man(n)a'[18] (0.8 km nw. of the village of Papados), a number of marble blocks were noted by travellers in Lesbos from the mid-nineteenth century onwards. Newton and Conze were the first to comment upon them, the latter finding a number of grey marbles scattered over the properties of different landowners in the area, some very finely worked and six of similar dimensions. One was still

in situ, and Conze's conclusion was that a R. villa of Augustan date had once stood on the spot. Koldewey agreed with Conze's ER. dating, but thought that the building had been an elaborate fountainhead for the nearby spring. Other blocks (probably originating from the site) were noted built into later structures in the nearby villages of Papados, Plakados, Mesagros and Palaiokipos.

An earlier component to the site was represented by the sculpture of a marble lion dating to the second quarter of the 4C. A HL. wall and an undated sarcophagus have also been noted (exact position not recorded), and both Charitonidis and Axiotis spoke of EByz. architectural *membra* at the site together with 'MAge' and Tur. remains (including a rock-cut olive press, probably of Tur. date[19]). Kontis suggested there had once been cult activity linked to the spring, and a cemetery nearby lining the road which approached it.

Bibliography: Newton II, 14-15; Conze, 51-52; Koldewey, 64-65, 76 and pl. 28.18-25; Taxis, 103; Charitonidis, 1968a, 26; Kontis, 1978, 252-54; Axiotis, 1992 II, 689-90 (and unnumbered photograph p. 690); id., 1994, 34 and fig. Z.

53. *Agia Paraskeui* (Papados); 793526; 140m; 'MAge'; SP. On the hill of Agia Paraskeui, ca. 0.2 km nw. from the village of Papados (above the old Gymnasio of the village), Axiotis described the ruined towers, surrounding wall and cistern of a 'MAge' kastro. No further details (or illustrations) are given and it is unclear whether the site should be dated to the Byz., Ven. or Tur. periods.

Bibliography: Moutzouris, 1962, 56-57; Axiotis, 1992 II, 685.

54. *Chalatses*[20] (Perama); 8352; --; MBA, LBA., R.; HAB, CEM. On the w. coast of the Gulf of Gera, ca. 0.8 km n. along the coast from modern Perama, Cook discovered a MBA.-LBA. site which was subsequently revisited by Bayne. Cook described 'an extensive stratified prehistoric site of about the end of the BA. a little n. from Perama on the w. shore of the Gulf of Gera' whilst Bayne added some topographical detail, saying that the site was 'an extensive low mound on the w. shore of the Gulf of Hiera (Gera) near the narrows'. The precise location is unclear today (it is possible that the mound has since been destroyed since cultivation in the coastal plain is intense). If one takes these two reports in unison, however, the only place where the gulf 'narrows' to the n. of Perama is opposite the Dibolon Hill of Skala Loutron (see #45 above) in the area known as Chalatses.

The analyses of Cook and (especially) Bayne indicated that the site is of extreme importance in terms of the transition from the LBA. to the EIA. in Lesbos since the material collected was of LH IIIB-C date with LH IIIC prevailing (periods similar to those represented at Emporio on Chios). Bayne suggested that the significant Myc. influence on the ceramics indicated that this settlement had

---

[17] It is difficult to know whether these EByz. remains are to be equated with those visited by Chatzi (1971, 457-58) which were described as lying in the plain of Ippios at a spot known as 'Panagia'.

[18] Conze called the site 'S ti mana' ('ς τὴ μᾶνα'), Koldewey 'Sti Mana'. Today it is generally termed simply Manna ('Μάννα').

[19] There is documentary evidence from the early travellers who visited Lesbos that olives had been grown in large numbers in this area during the Tourkokratia. The Gulf of Gera is specifically named as the region of the island from where oil was exported to European markets in the early nineteenth century, and oil was the largest of the island's export trades from the mid-eighteenth century at least. See P. S. Paraskeuaidis, Οι περιηγήτες για τη Λέσβο (Athens 1983, 2nd ed.), 62, 97-99.

[20] The alternative toponym Chalakies ('Χαλακιές') is also used for this area, see Kontis, 1978, 250.

been composed of a group of poor refugees from mainland Greece fleeing the destructions of LH IIIB. MBA (Minoan style[21]) bowls and mugs together with LBA. sherds (from the visits of Cook and Bayne) were brought back to Athens and are now stored in the BSA sherd archive.

In the same area, slightly n. from Perama, Koldewey, Kontis and Axiotis all reported a number of historic surface remains. Koldewey saw scatters of sherds and tile along the coastline in the region and was told by local inhabitants that many architectural blocks had been built into the walls of a factory at Perama. Kontis noted that a number of (mainly R.) tombstones and inscriptions had also been found in this area (including *IG* XII.2.484), whilst Axiotis spoke of surface ceramic scatters, foundations and a kiln.[22]

The material was equated by Koldewey and Kontis with 'Hiera' or 'Ira', a city in Lesbos possibly referred to by Alkaios (Lobel-Page, D11.3; Page, 227) and which Pliny the Elder stated had been abandoned before his own day (Plin. *HN*. 5.39.139).
Bibliography: Conze, 53 and pl. Ia, 17; Koldewey, 40, 63, 76; J. M. Cook, 'Archaeology in Greece 1949-50', *JHS* 71 (1951), 247; Charitonidis, 1963c, 268; Bayne, 122-25, 139-40 and figs. 14B-15A; Buchholz, 123, 136; Paraskeuaidis, 1976, 503; Kontis, 1978, 249-50; Axiotis, 1992 II, 682-83; BSA sherd archive <u>Perama</u>, unpublished.

55. *Agios Georgios tis Kourkoutas* (Perama); 829516; 10m; EByz., LByz.(?); SP. Ca. 1.2 kms wsw. from Perama, immediately s. of the road from Perama to Skopelos, the chapel of Agios Georgios has parts of an earlier building surviving at its sw. corner which include the feature of false external windows (extremely rare in Lesbos). More material from an older structure is built into other parts of the modern chapel, and all around are scatters of ancient ceramics. Column capitals and other window elements suggest an EByz. date for the earlier centre of worship but Axiotis also proposed that a later Byz. church had existed at the site.
Bibliography: Charitonidis, 1965, 494; id., 1968a, 27; Axiotis, 1992 II, 682.

56. *Brachonisi* (Pyrgoi); 865496; 3m; Byz.; SP. On the small Brachonisi rock at the entrance of the Gulf of Gera, ca. 0.2 km offshore from the hamlet of Pyrgoi, a group of ruins have been equated with the Byz. Monastery of Aristoi attested in the 12C AC. Axiotis described the remains of a church and other structures, noting also that the waters which separate the island from the w. coast of the gulf are so shallow that the islet once may have been larger.
Bibliography: Axiotis, 1992 II, 681.

57. *Monastiraki*[23] (Pyrgoi); 860488; 50m; A., HL., R.; HAB, CEM. Sw. from the coastal hamlet of Pyrgoi, on the w. coast of the Gulf of Gera, is a small coastal plain where the Aulonas River empties into the sea. Kontis reported surface sherds of HL. and R. date in the area, and the cutting of terraces on the e.-facing slopes to the n. of this

plain (at a place named Monastiraki) brought to light sections of mortared schist walling, pithoi and potsherds including grey wares and an Attic lekythos dating to ca. 500 BC (probably from a disturbed tomb).
Bibliography: Charitonidis, 1964, 396; Kontis, 1978, 250-51; Axiotis, 1992 II, 681.

58. *Kabourolimni* (Pyrgoi); 873472; 5m; --; HAB. On the s. tip of the Kabourolimni promontory, ca. 2 kms sse. from the coastal hamlet of Pyrgoi, Taxis noted an 'ancient' cistern and Axiotis described a site with remains similar to those found at many points around the Gulf of Gera (which he listed as dating to the HL., R., 'MAge' and Tur. periods). No specific details are given, however, concerning the nature of the remains on the promontory itself.
Bibliography: Taxis, 101; Axiotis, 1992 II, 680-81.

59. *Tsaph* (Tarti); 832450; 40m; C., HL., R., EByz.; HAB, CEM, SP. Above the e. edge of the small bay at Tarti, in the region named 'Tsaph', the remains of an ancient quarry are visible, including the ancient quarry faces, a large spoil heap and three unfinished columns. Axiotis dated this quarry to the 5C BC and noted that nearby (not far from the chapel of Agioi Saranda) were more traces of ancient quarrying activity. The scatter of HL. and R. sherds and tiles (ca. 0.4 km to the n.), together with a rock-cut tomb, indicate that there was an accompanying small settlement. It was from the quarry at Tarti that the half-worked columns and EByz. architectural *membra* had originated which were being used as counterweights at Skala Loutron (see #45).
Bibliography: Charitonidis, 1963c, 269 and pl. 308ε-ς; id., 1965, 490-92; Kontis, 1978, 255; Axiotis, 1992 II, 680.

60. *Osios Grigorios* (Skopelos); 813479; 130m; HL./R., EByz., LByz.; SP. Ca. 2.5 kms s. from Skopelos, along the main road which leads to Plomari, a dirt road leaves the main road heading se. and later due s. to the coastal hamlet of Tarti. 2 kms along this dirt road is a right turn which leads to the remote valley in which the ruined 13C Byz. monastery of Osios Grigorios stands, near a chapel dedicated to the same saint. Both are located near a spring which gives the spot an abundant water supply. Amongst the ruins, Charitonidis reported the e. end of a building (probably an EByz. basilica) which gave indications of many different building phases. EByz. architectural *membra* were found nearby, and an ancient altar with cowhead motifs (probably of HL./R. date) was built into the chapel.
Bibliography: Charitonidis, 1968a, 28 and pl. 10α; Axiotis, 1992 II, 680.

61. *Kastri* (Plagia); 795452; 150m; Byz.; SP. On the hill known as Kastri, ca. 4.5 kms e. from Plagia,[24] a chapel of Agios Georgios stands near the remains of a small kastro, said to be of Byz. date by Koldewey (who described a pillar exhibiting a Byz. inscription 'ΑΓΑΘΗ ΤΥΧΗ'[25]). Axiotis added few details about the site apart from noting that a large cistern was incorporated into the complex and two reliefs were found near the chapel (which has the foundations of an older chapel underneath it).

---

[21] The nearly complete small open bowls and mugs of coarse orange clay in the BSA sherd archive are probably of MM III date, Susan Sherratt, pers. comm. (1995).
[22] Other kilns (of HL. and R. date) were found elsewhere on the gulf of Gera at Agios Georgios (near Kato Tritos, see site #47 above), Marmaro (to the south of Perama), Skala Loutron, and Taxiarchis (near Pyrgi, on the ne. coast), see Basiakos, 209.
[23] Known locally as 'Monastireli' ('Μοναστηρέλι'), see Section 2.1 (b) at the beginning of the catalogue.

---

[24] The overall area is known as 'Metia': see Koldewey, 39; Axiotis, 1992 II, 678.
[25] *IG* XII.2.485.

Bibliography: Koldewey, 39, 77; Taxis, 101; Moutzouris, 1962, 68; Axiotis, 1992 II, 678.

62. *Ypapanti tou Christou* (Plagia); 748457; 50m; BA(?), LHL., R., EByz.; HAB, CEM, SP. On the e. edge of the village of Plagia a number of ancient remains have been reported since the 19C near the Ypapanti tou Christou, the chapel associated with the village's main cemetery. In addition to a significant scatter of ancient tile and sherds (which Kontis dated to the LHL. and R. periods), Conze and Koldewey noted a number of worked marble blocks and inscriptions (some, such as *IG* XII.2.488, built into the chapel itself). Most of the worked blocks and inscriptions are of R. date and comprise a column capital, unfluted column drums, a tombstone, sections from a black marble exedra (whose ends were in the form of lions' feet), and a relief of Artemis. There are also a few EByz. pieces including an architectural element of 5C AC date. During the renovation of the chapel, Taxis reported that the remains of an old bath-house, tombs and a mosaic floor had been uncovered inside. Nearby in Plomari (Grid Ref. 7245), the single worn marble block with a cymation decoration which once lay in the dockyard may well be from the site at Plagia, and also near the shore (ca. 2 kms ese. from Plomari) a cave in the sheer cliff above the chapel of Agios Isidoros (Grid Ref. 740441) was said by Taxis to have human burial remains inside (possibly of BA date).
Bibliography: Newton II, 12; Conze, 49-51 and pl. XVI; Koldewey, 39; Taxis, 109-10; Charitonidis, 1968a, 28; Kontis, 1978, 256-57; Axiotis, 1992 II, 669-70.

63. *Glyphia* (Drota); 645486; 5m; EByz.; HAB, CEM, SP. Ca. 8 kms wnw. along the almost impenetrable cliffs which form the coastline w. of Plomari, a very small coastal plain has been formed where the Prionas River empties into the sea, 1 km sw. from the hamlet of Drota. In May 1960 a monolithic, unfluted column (now broken into three pieces) was uncovered during digging work near the chapel of Agios Isidoros. The column probably came from an EByz. basilica, and immediately to the w. of the church were traces of a late antique (probably EByz.) settlement including associated tombs.
Bibliography: Charitonidis, 1968a, 28; Kontis, 1978, 257; Axiotis, 1992 II, 619-20.

64. *Mitoilia* (Kato Stauros); 634516; 80m; EBA.; CEM. Ca. 0.7 km ssw. from Kato Stauros,[26] on the road which leads down the Bourkos gorge to the s. coast of the island, Axiotis described a number of highly significant finds which were found at the junction with a track leading e. along the Mitoilia valley to Akrasion. Pithoi with bones inside were said to have been discovered a number of years ago, and more recently fragments of more pithoi (of coarse red fabric) were recovered together with the beaked neck-fragment of a jug with cutaway spout (similar to many found at Yortan and Thermi, cf. Lamb, 1936, fig. 26.3-4; pl. XII.116) and a whole EBA. vessel with lid and base also paralleled at Thermi (*ibid.*: pl. XVII.173). There were also reports of bronze items including jewellery, but none of these pieces now survive.
Bibliography: Axiotis, 1992 II, 604 and pl. 136.

65. *Mesa Rongada* (Ano Stauros); 635553; 310m; --; HAB, CEM. At the location known as Mesa Rongada, ca. 2 kms nnw. from Ano Stauros, Axiotis reported a scatter of grey wares (which could date at any time from the BA.-HL. periods) on the n. slopes of a rocky knoll[27] to the e. of the road which leads n. to a chapel of Agia Kyriaki. Stretches of a crudely built wall (possibly part of an enclosure) run across the saddle of the knoll nearby. At the chapel itself (an area known as 'Palaiochori') an inscription on a marble stele was found, and nearby was a rock-cut tomb and a scatter of ceramics (no details of which are given).
Bibliography: Axiotis, 1992 II, 605-06.

66. *Agios Basilis* (Kato Stauros); 658527; 80m; LR., Tur.; CEM. Ca. 2 kms e. from Kato Stauros, on the n. side of the road to Ambeliko, stands a chapel of Agios Basilis. Near this chapel Axiotis described a LR. tile-grave inside which was a lamp of 4/5C AC date with a representation of a winged sphinx.
   In this area between Kato Stauros and Ambeliko, Axiotis stated also that there are a number of remains of the Tur. period (including more graves) without giving specific details: a group of tombs (possibly Tur.) were found ca. 0.5 km e. from Kato Stauros (approximate Grid Ref. 6452[28]); another single tomb (along with more cuttings in the bedrock) was located a similar distance from Kato Stauros to the n. of the Ambeliko road in the area known as Strongylos (a toponym which does not appear on the British Army map); and yet another tomb which had a small ceramic vessel inside was uncovered beside the chapel of Agios Georgios further ne. (Grid Ref. 668531). Near this chapel of Agios Georgios there are also stretches of a kalderimi which presumably is part of the old road up to Ambeliko.[29]
Bibliography: Axiotis, 1992 II, 606.

67. *Kambia* (Ambeliko); 6654/6754; --; ER./MR., LR., EByz.(?); HAB, CEM. To the w. of Ambeliko, on a plateau above the w. bank of the rema which possesses the same name as the village, Axiotis reported that a LR. grave (dated to the 3C-4C AC by a coin found within it) was uncovered when villagers were levelling the area for a sports ground. More graves without grave goods were uncovered later in the same area and 50 m further downhill, during the laying of a new road, sherds (including fragments of pithoi, *terra sigilata* and pieces with yellow glaze) together with yellow-glazed tiles, were located. Walls of buildings and foundations were also apparent, many constructed with unworked stones and suggested by Axiotis to be of LR. or EByz. date.
Bibliography: Axiotis, 1992 II, 610.

68. *Agios Christophoros* (Ambeliko); 676531; 450m; --; SP. Ca. 1.2 kms sse. from Ambeliko, along the road s. towards Akrasi, a kalderimi leads se. upslope to the small chapel of Agios Christophoros. Near this chapel Axiotis reported a large marble quarry (the date of which is unclear),

---

[26] The two villages in this area labelled as Ano and Kato Bourkos on the 1943 British Army maps are now known as Ano and Kato Stauros, see Axiotis, 1992 II, 601-04.

[27] This knoll may be part of the hill called Arbylos which Axiotis states is to be found in this area, but his description is ambiguous.

[28] The description by Axiotis does not allow a more accurate placing of the site on the British Army map.

[29] In the village of Ambeliko the ruin of a mosque and a Tur. tower indicate activity during the Tourkokratia, and the village is also referred to in a Mitropolitan codex of 1567 as 'Ambelikon' ('Ἀμπελικῶν'). For the tower see Taxis, 120.

still with squared blocks of stone lying beside the quarry faces.
Bibliography: Axiotis, 1992 II, 612.

69. *Dede Kambous* (Ambeliko); 6955; --; Tur.; CEM, SP. Ca. 2 kms to the w. of Olympos, in an area known as Kambeia (or 'Dede Kambous', 'Ντέντε Κάμπους'), Axiotis reported what seem to be the remains of the Tekke (or dervish convent) of Ibrahim, a member of the liberal Bektashi order. The convent is attested in Ottoman archives from the 17C until the 19C.

Axiotis described a square building of dry stone, made of small schist blocks without any joining material. The outside dimensions are 5.5 m x 5.13 m, the outside height is 1.8 m and the walls 0.75 m thick. The entrance lies to the e. (although no trace of the door remains) and on the w. side there is a small window. A smaller two-storey structure which once stood inside this building may have been the remains of the leader's grave. Skleparis stated that this inner structure was dedicated to Ibrahim and that it had links also with the religious practices (including a nearby cemetery) of the mountain-dwelling 'Yoruks' who lived in the forests of the island.
Bibliography: D. Skleparis, 'Ντέντε Κάμπους', *Lesbiaka* 6 (1973), 171-77; Axiotis, 1992 II, 719; M. Kiel, pers. comm. (1995).

70. *Xylokastro* (Agiasos); 7352/7353; --; 'MAge'; SP. To the w. of the road which leads s. from Agiasos to Megalochori, ca. 4 kms sse. from Agiasos, are the remains of a substantial, irregular-shaped enclosure at the location known as Xylokastro. A turning to the w. of the main road leads to the chapel of Agios Phanourios which stands beside a (now dry) well inside the n. edge of the enclosure wall. In addition to this new track, a kalderimi approaches the enclosure from the e.. Stretches of the dry-stone walls are preserved 2 m in height and are 2 m thick (constructed with two faces of larger outer blocks and a rubble fill). Sections of the nw. side of the structure have been destroyed by recent quarrying work. Axiotis gives no details of associated sherd scatters but dates the kastro to the 'MAge' period.

The view from the kastro is panoramic, including both gulfs (Gera and Kalloni), and its location is strategic in watching over the main routes n. from the area of Plomari and Megalochori towards Agiasos.
Bibliography: Moutzouris, 1962, 68; Axiotis, 1992 II, 719 (and unnumbered photograph p. 717) and pl. 144.

71. *Pitsilia* (Agiasos); 739555; 500m; Byz., Tur.; HAB, CEM. Ca. 2 kms along the road which leaves Agiasos heading s. to Megalochori, one reaches the area known as Pitsilia (or Pitzilia), a narrow spur jutting w. from the road and overlooking the e. slopes of Olympos. This toponym has traditionally been equated with 'Penthili' (stated by Stephanus of Byzantium to be a *polis* of Lesbos, St. Byz. s. v. 'Πενθίλη') and thereby also linked to the 'Penthilidai', the aristocratic *genos* of Archaic Mytilene (Lobel-Page, D17.10, R1.ii.5; Arist. *Pol.* 1311b.26-30).

No visitors to the spot, however, have ever given reports of remains dating from before the 'MAge' period. Kolaxizelis and Kontis both stated that no ancient remains were visible. Axiotis only saw five undiagnostic marble blocks built into the two chapels which stand on the site (of Taxiarchis/Astratgos and the Panagia), together with a scatter of Byz./Tur. tiles and sherds in the area between the two chapels. In 1861, however, Braniadis reported that the

foundations of buildings, tombs, potsherds and tiles were apparent and that during the nights illicit digging was taking place searching for hidden 'treasures'. Subsequently, the ceramic material from the site was transported to Agiasos, broken up and used in building work, whilst the foundations at Pitsilia were destroyed by cultivation. Tombs came to light during renovation of the Panagia chapel in 1935 (no dating for them has been given).

Kolaxizelis thought that the Byz. and Tur. site consisted of two small villages, Ano Penthilis centred upon the Panagia chapel, and Kato Penthilis centred on the chapel of Taxiarchis/Astratgos. It is more likely, however, given the scatter of material between the two chapels seen by Axiotis, that the village was a single one defined at its n. and s. edges by the two centres of worship.[30] Kolaxizelis also suggested that the inhabitants of both villages had then abandoned the site, forming the settlement of Agiasos nearby (attested for the first time in 1567 as the village 'Agia Sion', ''Αγία Σιών'), a re-location which had taken place in the 15C according to Axiotis.[31]
Bibliography: Taxis, 96, 98 and n. 1; S. P. Kolaxizelis, Θρῦλος καὶ ἱστορία 'Αγίασου τῆς νήσου Λέσβου (Mytilene[32]) I, 79-80; Kontis, 1978, 260; Axiotis, 1992 II, 716 and pl. 144.

72. *Kastelli* (Agiasos); 721572; 400m; Byz.; SP. On the hill named Kastelli, ca. 0.3 km wnw. from Agiasos, a small kastro (originally of Byz. date) is constructed on the plateau of the peak of the hill near a chapel of Taxiarchis. Stretches of a kalderimi are visible on the slopes leading up to the kastro, and within the mortared stone walls are the remains of two cisterns (only one of which is now well-preserved). Axiotis dated the site (especially the e. side) to the 9-10C AC and stated that extensions built later are referred to in 13C sources.
Bibliography: Taxis, 96; Moutzouris, 1962, 68; Axiotis, 1992 II, 717.

73. *Karini* (village); 744609; 80m; HL.; HAB, SP. On the main road from Mytilene to Agiasos, the village of Karini lies in an especially fertile narrow valley (possessing a freshwater spring) ca. 1 km w. from the edge of the Ippios plain.[33] Koldewey noted the remains of an ancient

---

[30] Such definition of settlements with the location of chapels on their periphery is known elsewhere in Greece during the Medieval period.

[31] This tradition of relocation in the Pitsilia/Agiasos area during the Tourkokratia is not unlikely if one supports the hypothesis of Paraskeuaidis that one result of the Turkish administration of the island from the 15C onwards was the abandonment of some small villages and localised synoikismos into larger 'komopoleis' nearby. See P. S. Paraskeuaidis, 'Η Λέσβος κατὰ τὴν Τουρκοκρατία (Mytilene, 1991), 18. The archives of the Ottoman administration of Lesbos do indeed suggest that many small villages on Lesbos were abandoned, or re-grouped into larger units, from around 1600 AD onwards, although other scholars have attributed this change more to the spread of olive-tree monoculture than to the effects of Ottoman taxation (D. M. Karidis and M. Kiel, pers. comm. [1995]). For the possible derivation of the village name 'Agiasos' from Agios Grigorios of Assos, see Rouse, 151-54.

[32] No date is given for publication, but Vol. II was published in 1947.

[33] Kontis (1978, 245) suggested that the topographical location of the hamlet was the reason for its name, deriving Karini ('Καρίνη') from 'κρήνη' ('fountain'/'spring').

building complex at Karini (which he called a 'villa'), with walls of small stones joined with mud, 0.43 m thick. In the corner of one room Koldewey found a well-fired buff vessel filled with ca. 100 bronze coins. The character of the whole hoard was very similar although some of the coins exhibited different obverse and reverse types. Amongst these types the head of Apollo was common, with a four-stringed lyre on the reverse. Some were inscribed 'MYTI' and there were also monograms on each side ' ⋈ ', ' ⊠ '. The hoard dated to the 3C BC or slightly later. In the vicinity, Taxis described an ancient cistern and Kontis also noted the remains of quarries, the majority of which were said to show signs of working in antiquity.

Bibliography: Koldewey, 40-41; Taxis, 96-97; Kontis, 1978, 245.

*74. *Agios Phokas* (Brisa); 552493; 20m; EBA., LG., A., C., HL., ER., EByz., MByz.; HAB, SP. On a narrow, irregularly-shaped promontory, 4.5 kms ssw. from Brisa, stands the chapel of Agios Phokas which gives its name to this coastal location. Stephanus of Byzantium (St. Byz. s. v. 'Βρῖσα') refers to the promontory, saying that the site was the focus of a cult to Dionysos, testimony which has been backed up by a HL. (probably 3C) inscription found at the site dedicated to 'Dionysos Brisagenis' (*IG* XII.2.478) and another noted by Taxis which read 'ΔΙΟΝΝΗΣΙΩι ΤΩι ΒΑΚΧΩι' (not in the *IG* collection).

The earliest traces of habitation activity were those noted by Chatzi in 1972 on both the downward slope s. of the promontory and along its s. cape. Surface inspection in this area located EBA. sherds (of coarse red/buff fabric) and incised LG. grey wares. Ca. 0.1 km se. from the modern chapel, a series of possible foundations encouraged Chatzi to carry out a trial excavation. In this excavation a rectangular structure was uncovered, suggested to be a watchtower by Chatzi, ca. 1 m below which were A .and C. sherds (including a black-figure fragment with a representation of Silenos), grey wares and more EBA. material. This sequence (and especially the presence of stratified fine ware pottery) strongly suggests an A. predecessor of the Dionysos cult which the epigraphical evidence testifies from the HL. period (see above).

In the ER. period a small Doric *in antis* temple was built on the site (thoroughly investigated by Koldewey after an initial report of the presence of antiquities by Newton). An EByz. basilica was later constructed near the temple, into which many of the Doric fragments were built, and two coins (one of the 6C AC and another of the 10C AC) indicate later MByz. activity at the site.

At the e. shore of the promontory in the 19C Pottier and Hauvette-Besnault reported the remains of a silted-up granite harbour mole together with other worked blocks and broken columns lying submerged. Subsequently Taxis and, much more recently, Axiotis noted this ancient harbour mole also, which now underlies the blocks of the small (modern) harbour construction. Furthermore, the shore near the harbour is densely scattered with ancient sherds, and even more were found below the surface recently when foundations were being dug in the area.

Bibliography: Newton II, 12-13; E. Pottier and A. Hauvette-Besnault, 'Inscriptions de Lesbos', *BCH* 4 (1880), 446; Koldewey, 63-64 and pl. 28.1-17; Taxis, 119; J. D. Quinn, 'Cape Phokas, Lesbos - site of an archaic sanctuary for Zeus, Hera and Dionysus?', *AJA* 65 (1961), 391-93 and pls. 128-29; Paraskeuaidis, 1963, 1418-20; Chatzi, 1972, 596-99, fig. 14 and pls. 548-50; Kontis, 1973, 88-91; Paraskeuaidis, 1976, 503; Touchais, 1977, 624; Catling,

58; Kontis, 1978, 364-65; Axiotis, 1992 II, 599-600 and pl. 135.

75. *Achilopigado* (Brisa); 558504; 15m; LR./EByz.(?); HAB, CEM, SP. Ca. 2.7 kms ssw. from modern Brisa (and ca. 1.5 kms w. from the coastal resort of Batera), just beyond the bridge which crosses the Almiropotamos River, is a place known as Achilopigado. The spot was linked by Mantzouranis to the Homeric legends of the (allegedly Lesbian) maiden Brisa taken by Achilles (Hom. *Il.* 9.128-32).

On the w. side of the mouth of the Almiropotamos River there is an (originally late 19C) chapel of Agia Katerini rebuilt in 1940 near a stone-headed well. Taxis had seen ancient remains near the chapel, and more recently to the w. of it Axiotis reported worked marble and trachyte blocks, a large stone sarcophagus and a column. Another column which now stands on the shore at Batera also came from this spot.

Charitonidis noted that beside the modern chapel older walls were visible in 1968 which he ascribed to a late antique basilica. The basilica walls were said to be 0.5 m thick by Tselekas, and in the next field beside the chapel a paved floor was uncovered. Charitonidis proposed that the associated finds nearby, including a tomb (possibly the sarcophagus described by Axiotis) from which came a number of lamps now in Mytilene museum, were the remains of an 'extensive' settlement of similar date, and the dense scatter of tiles and sherds reported by Axiotis all over the immediate area support this hypothesis.

Bibliography: Taxis, 119; D. P. Mantzouranis, Οἱ πρῶτες ἐγκαταστάσεις τῶν Ἑλλήνων στὴ Λέσβο (Mytilene, 1949), 28; Paraskeuaidis, 1963, 1420; Charitonidis, 1968a, 28; Axiotis, 1992 II, 598-99.

76. *Paliopyrgos* (Brisa); 5652; --; BA.(?), Ven.; HAB(?), SP. A track heading w. just before crossing the bridge and entering the village of Brisa leads (in ca. 1 km) to the remains of a Ven. tower similar to those found at Pyrgi in Chios (possibly the 'Kastro of Brisa' referred to by the early traveller Legrand[34]). The tower is square, its walls constructed of mortared small stones 12.6 m in length and 2.1 m thick, and inside a dividing wall runs from n.-s. creating two rectangular rooms. A basement (possibly also serving as a cistern) was dug out below ground level. The n. outer wall (where the gate once was) has nearly completely collapsed, but the s. wall stands to ca. 15 m and on the outer wall is a slab with the Gattelusi crest. All around the tower Axiotis reported scatters of ceramics (possibly indicating an associated settlement) and to the e. an old stone-built well may date to the same period.

On the hill to the n. stands a chapel of Christos around which Axiotis described worked blocks and ceramics, possibly including some of BA. date, a scatter of lithics and a millstone.

Bibliography: Taxis, 118-19; Moutzouris, 1962, 55; Axiotis, 1992 II, 593-94 (and unnumbered photograph p. 593) and pls. 133-34.

77. *Brysi tou Deligianni* (Brisa); 5553; --; EBA., C./HL.; HAB. On the w. side of the track which runs along the w. bank of the Almiropotamos River, opposite the Ven. tower (#76), is a fountain known as the Brysi tou Deligianni (repaired by the Forestry Commission). Above the fountain is a scatter of grey wares (including pieces of open

34 For this hypothesis, see Moutzouris, 1962, 55.

vessels), sherds of red pithoi, black-glazed pieces and a mass of tiles (including one whole tile).

Axiotis also reported from the same location a number of pieces of cruder pithoi, burnished sherds and a millstone, all probably the remains of EBA. activity at the spot.
Bibliography: Axiotis, 1992 II, 594-95.

78. *Strongylos* (Polichnitos); 553559; C./HL., Byz., Tur.; HAB, CEM, SP. Ca. 1 km sw. from Polichnitos at the w. foot of the Oxys hill are four chapels (dedicated to Agia Marina, Agia Paraskeui, Agios Georgios and Agios Charalambos) and other ruins which are the remains of the Byz. village of Strongylos attested in texts from the late 9C-early 10C AC. Charitonidis dated the Agios Georgios chapel, which has a number of marble and trachyte architectural blocks inside it, to the early Tur. period. Under the s. wall were found tombs of children, and over the whole area were a scatter of sherds and tiles, millstones and a number of worked blocks (a disused aloni is apparent beside the chapel of Agia Marina. Coins of the 4C BC and the 6C AC are reported to have been found at the site.
Bibliography: Charitonidis, 1964, 399 and fig. 5 (p. 400); Charitonidis, 1968a, 33-34; Axiotis, 1992 II, 586-87 and pl. 132; Mason, 1993, 237 and n. 50.

79. *Traperia* (Polichnitos); 533551; 190m; R., Byz.; HAB, CEM, SP. Immediately s. of the large Taxiarchis tis Traperias church, 3.3 kms sw. from Polichnitos, are the ruins of a chapel of Agios Dimitrios amongst a cluster of *mandria* and ceramic scatters. Pithoi sherds were found amongst those near the chapel, and Axiotis described also the remains of a square structure (possibly a tower), R. *terra sigilata* and later Byz. wares. EByz. architectural pieces are visible near the Taxiarchis church.

Around the (now deserted) chapel of Agia Paraskeui close by to the s., and also near the chapel of Agios Isidoros 0.5 km to the n., tombs have been reported but no details given. During the laying of trenches near the latter chapel, building foundations were revealed, and there is a tradition that a monastery once stood on the site.
Bibliography: Axiotis, 1992 II, 584-85 and pl. 132.

80. *Garbias* (Polichnitos); 474569; 8m; C.-EByz.(?), 'MAge'; HAB. On the small island of Garbias at the mouth of the Gulf of Kalloni, ruins were first noted in the 18C. In the 19C Koldewey described a wall of 'MAge' date around the outside of the island and stated that only short sections of walling to the s. and w. (and scatters of tiles) seemed ancient. Kontis indicated habitation activity from the C.-EByz. periods including structural remains, but no more details of these finds were offered by Axiotis who merely repeated the earlier reports.
Bibliography: Pococke, 19; Koldewey, 42; Kontis, 1978, figs. 21-30; Axiotis, 1992 II, 536.

81. *Bougazi* (Polichnitos); 499572; 140m; C./HL.; HAB. Ca. 6 kms w. from Polichnitos, on the e. side of the rema which descends the s. slopes of the Bougazi hill, Kophopoulos noted the remains of buildings on two levels and associated retaining walls around which were grey ware and black-glaze sherds, amphora handles and tiles.
Bibliography: Axiotis, 1992 II, 583.

82. *Louta* (Polichnitos); 504587; 10m; C./HL., R., LR.-Byz.; HAB. In the narrow bay of Louta, 5.8 kms wnw. from Polichnitos (the promontory to the e. is known as Perama), Axiotis noted significant traces of ancient settlement activity. The remains lie near an old well and rock-cut trough for animals located over a spring. Foundations of buildings (and possibly the remains of kilns) are visible near the shore amongst a mass of tiles and sherds including amphorae handles and bases, and also LR.-Byz. 'combed' wares. Further inland are scattered C./HL. black-glazed sherds, grey wares and R. *terra sigilata*.
Bibliography: Axiotis, 1992 II, 582.

83. *Peribola* (Polichnitos); 533581; 20m; A./C., R., EByz., 'MAge'; HAB, SP. In the property of Moutaphis at the place named Peribola, 2 kms wsw. from Skala Polichnitou and immediately s. of the promontory of Chalakies (see #84), the floor of an EByz. basilica was uncovered during cultivation. In the same plot (and also in the adjoining properties to the n. and sw.) were many architectural *membra* including unfluted columns, column capitals, an inscribed plaque and other worked blocks. Amongst these pieces there were also elements from an early 5C BC Ionic order building (the foundations of which have not been located).

Axiotis reported that more finds made in the area have included a coin of Tiberius I (574-82 AD), 'MAge' surface material, and (to the w. of Peribola) sherds of R. date.
Bibliography: Daux, 1960, 809 and fig. 3; Charitonidis, 1960, 237 and pls. 208στ, 209ε; Paraskeuaidis, 1966, 203; Charitonidis, 1968a, 32-33 and pls. 11-13; Paraskeuaidis, 1976, 503; Kontis, 1978, 362; Axiotis, 1992 II, 580-81.

84. *Chalakies* (Polichnitos); 532589; 5m; LN., EBA., C., R.; HAB, CEM. On a tongue-shaped promontory being eroded by the sea (similar in form to Kourtir, #91), 2 kms wsw. from Skala Polichnitou, is a small, but extremely significant, prehistoric site at the location known as Chalakies.[35] An old *spitaki* stands on top of the site near the seaward side of the eroding scarp. Recent resurfacing and banking of the road which passes over the promontory leading to the coastal resort of Nyphida further to the sw. has seriously disturbed the strata of ancient material once visible on the exposed side of the scarp facing the sea, and the construction of a new two-storey house ca. 20 m to the s. has led to further disturbance. The surface scatter is said to consist of black, red and buff sherds (including some burnished pieces) together with a scatter of lithics, and Charitonidis dated the material to the LN. and EBA. periods (comparable to that from Agio Gala in n. Chios). When a well was dug at the site a large closed vessel of LN. date was found complete (the pot is now on display in Mytilene museum). LN. and EBA. sherds and lithics from the site are also stored in the DAI in Athens.

Remains of later date reported at Chalakies include C. marble architectural elements, a R. sarcophagus and 16 graves of various dates (which were not given by Axiotis) but would be of extreme significance if any belong to the LN.-EBA. settlement.
Bibliography: Charitonidis, 1960, 237 and pl. 209γ; Hood, 23; Buchholz, 122-23; Paraskeuaidis, 1976, 503; Kontis, 1978, 359; Axiotis, 1992 II, 580; DAI and BSA sherd archives Chalakies, unpublished.

85. *Ara* (Polichnitos); 5659/5660; --; C.(?), HL., R., EByz.; HAB, CEM. In the area known as Ara, immediately e. and ne. from Skala Polichnitou, are the remains of a settlement and associated cemetery of long

---

[35] The toponym given to the spot originates from the mass of tiles and sherds visible.

18

duration. A number of EByz. architectural pieces are scattered in the fields at the n. foot of the hill immediately e. from the Polichnitos-Skala Polichnitou road beside the *skala* settlement, and during the construction of the road more similar broken pieces were uncovered. Two R. tombstones were found nearby (*IG* XII.2, 489-90) together with the head of a HL. female idol and a 4C BC coin. Worked blocks and ceramic debris from HL. and R. occupation were described by Charitonidis, many of the former built into the cistern in the Kallias property, and a mosaic floor was reported in 1938 in the plot of Theodorellis nearby (no longer visible) with worked blocks and marbles.

Axiotis noted tombs (which he did not date) near three chapels to the e. and ne. of Skala Polichnitou: a large trachyte coffin beside the chapel of Christos (three others had once existed but were now destroyed); a cover slab from another coffin (also of trachyte) near the Agios Georgios chapel; and more undefined tombs around a chapel of the Panagia.

Bibliography: Charitonidis, 1968a, 31; Paraskeuaidis, 1976, 503; Axiotis, 1992 II, 560-61 and pls. 124-25.

86. *Agios Ioannis* (Lisbori); 579594; 50m; HL., R. (?), EByz., MByz., Ven., Tur.; CEM, SP. At the warm (69°) springs beside the chapel of Agios Ioannis, ca. 1.5 kms wsw. from modern Lisbori, is a Tur. fountain-head and the remains of a Tur. bath-house, some of the walls possibly dating back to a R. predecessor.[36] In 1959, when a decision was taken to build a new chapel slightly to the sw. of the older one, the foundations of an EByz. basilica were uncovered. The floor of the basilica was constructed with large clay tiles, and at the sw. corner of the structure an EByz. cist grave with 3 skeletons inside was uncovered (2 of which were children). Architectural elements of grey marble from the basilica (including four Doric column capitals) are built into the n. part of the peribolos around the modern chapel at the site and also into the old schoolhouse in the village of Lisbori.

From the area around the springs a number of coins have been found, two of the 3C and 2C BC (one showing the type known from Mytilene of Apollo and a lyre, the other from Sardis), five of Byz. date (4 of the 10C AC, one of the 11C AC), one of the Gattelusi period, and a Tur. coin of 1687 AD.

Bibliography: Charitonidis, 1960, 237; Daux, 1960, 809; Paraskeuaidis, 1963, 1419; id., 1966, 212-13; Charitonidis, 1968a, 30-31 and fig. 17; Kontis, 1978, 362; Axiotis, 1992 II, 563-64 and pl. 126.

87. *Kaukara* (Lisbori); 580597; 55m; A., EByz.; CEM, SP. At the point where the roads from Lisbori to Skala Polichnitou and Agios Ioannis to Skamnioudi cross, 1.8 kms w. from Lisbori, is the chapel of 'Panagiouda tis Routis'.[37] Into the upper part of the chapel is part of an

A. altar, compared by (M.) Paraskeuaidis to the A. Kroisos altar at Ephesos. The altar exhibits a Lesbian cymation, is curved at the top, and has a maximum length of 0.48 m. Kontis noted that in the area of Kaukara there were also EByz. remains and 'even older' sherds, adding that the local inhabitants in the area frequently uncover tombs (of which he gave no details).

Bibliography: Paraskeuaidis, 1966, 211-12; id., 1970, 261; Kontis, 1978, 362-63.

88. *Prophitis Ilias* (Lisbori); 589590; 170m; EBA., MByz., 'MAge'; HAB. On the n. side of the main road from Mytilene to Polichnitos, ca. 1 km ssw. from the modern village of Lisbori, a dense EBA. pottery scatter covers the twin-peaked hill of Prophitis Ilias (also known as 'Katapyrgos'). Charitonidis compared the material at the site to that visible at Chalakies (#84) and Kourtir (#91) nearby. A particularly heavy concentration was reported on the saddle between the two peaks, and Axiotis found much material on the terraces of the w. slope. In addition to EBA. ceramics, the debris of lithic production (including stone flakes and broken blades) has been reported together with shell middens and trachyte millstones. Around the n. peak where the (recently rebuilt) chapel stands, house foundations and some 'MAge' sherds are apparent, and near the chapel a MByz. coin (dated to 945-959 AD) was found. At the s. lip of the hilltop, a once substantial wall of irregularly shaped andesite blocks has now collapsed down the slope, but these traces of an enclosure seem too insubstantial to equate the site with the (still unlocated) 'Kastro Basilikon' to which a number of early travellers to the island make reference (Moutzouris suggested that this Kastro was to be equated with the site of ancient Pyrrha, see #99).

Bibliography: Moutzouris, 1962, 54, 58-61; Paraskeuaidis, 1963, 1419; Charitonidis, 1965, 489-90 and pl. 628α; Buchholz, 122-23; Axiotis, 1992 II, 550-51.

89. *Damandri* (Polichnitos); 597574; 160m; HL./R.(?), Byz.(?), 'MAge', Tur.; HAB, SP. Ca. 3 kms ne. from Polichnitos along the main road to Basilika, just before the turning left (n.) to Lisbori, a sign indicates a right turn to the Monastery of Damandri. The *terminus ante quem* for the monastery's existence is a codex of 1567, and according to tradition it was founded when the nearby monastery of Agios Georgios ('Palaiomonastira', which lies ca. 1 km to the s.) was dissolved. The Monastery of Damandri gradually declined in numbers, however, and in 1863 there were only four monks remaining. From 1958 the complex was used as a home for the infirm, but the monastery even lost this function in 1989 when the home was closed.

At the monastery itself there are 18C wall paintings in the chapel of the Panagia, and in the vicinity of Damandri a number of early modern chapels and ancient remains suggest that the monastery was the focus for significant habitation and religious activity, both in antiquity and also later during the Byz./Tur. periods until early modern times. On the ridge to the n. of the monastery are the foundations of an old chapel (at a place worshipped now as Agios Georgios), worked marble blocks, unfluted columns and a mass of tiles and sherds of 'MAge' and later date. Charitonidis also noted the lowest course of an ancient enclosure of large blocks, some of which were clearly well-fitted together. In this same area threshing floors and the

---

[36] Ottoman records attest a Tur. village at 'Lisvori' in 1602, M. Kiel, pers comm. (1995). Concerning an earlier 16C Ottoman census of the island, see n. 4 above. More warm springs said to have medicinal properties lie ca. 1.5 kms ese. from Polichnitos at the place known as 'Therma' (Grid Ref. 579564), see Taxis, 116.

[37] The exact location of this chapel, and the toponym 'Kaukara', is hard to work out since no such chapel (or toponym) is marked on the detailed maps of either the British Army or Axiotis, and the latter makes no reference to the chapel or the altar despite extensive research in the area. The

grid reference provided here gives the location of the cross-roads described by Paraskeuaidis.

remains of an olive press are apparent, and slightly further n. from Agios Georgios are more worked blocks and scattered ceramics around the chapels of Agia Anastasia, Agios Basilis, Agia Paraskeui and Agia Marina.

Close by to the e. and se. of the monastery, Charitonidis and Axiotis noted more ancient components to the site. Charitonidis reported 'clear traces of an ancient settlement' (including worked blocks and carvings on the rocks) to the e. around the chapel of Taxiarchis, and immediately to the sw. of the main monastery complex (at a spot known as Myrophores) Axiotis described rock-cut niches and the foundations of a structure (possibly a fortification).

Bibliography: Koldewey, 78; Taxis, 117-18; Daux, 1960, 808 and fig. 2; Paraskeuaidis, 1963, 1419; Charitonidis, 1965, 490 and pl. 628β; Kontis, 1978, 361; Axiotis, 1992 II, 546-49 and pls. 123-24; id., 1994, fig. E.

90. *Astratgos* (Lisbori); 575617; 10m; EByz., LByz.(?); SP. Ca. 2.7 kms nw. from Lisbori, slightly to the s. of the coast road which runs between Skala Polichnitou and Skamnioudi, the apse of an EByz. basilica is preserved at the ne. corner of the modern chapel known locally as Agios Stratis or 'Astratgos'. An extremely heavy scatter of sherd and tile (the date of which is not reported) lies further to the n. in the same field. This spot has been associated with the Monastery of Archistratigos mentioned in a patriarchal document of 1324 and said to be 'in the vicinity of Basilika', the remains of which have never been found.

Bibliography: Charitonidis, 1963c, 271; id., 1968a, 31; Axiotis, 1992 II, 564-65.

*91. *Kourtir* (Lisbori); 588629; 5m; LN., EBA., MBA., LBA., G., C., R., E-LByz., Ven., Tur.; HAB, CEM, SP. At the coastal location known as Kourtir, 3 kms due n. from modern Lisbori and at the e. edge of the hamlet of Skamnioudi, lies probably the most important prehistoric site in Lesbos, and potentially the most important in the whole ne. Aegean. A tongue-shaped promontory, 5 m in height, and now covered with a field of cereal crops and a small *spitaki* is being eroded by the sea, and all over the top of the promontory and in the eroding scarp a stratified mass of material including structural remains indicates long-lived settlement activity dating from the LN. period.

A surface survey was carried out by Chatzi at the site in 1970 and a trial excavation in 1972. In the eroding scarp, ca. 0.3 km in length, Chatzi counted 3 strata of settlement (at least) associated with which were LN. sherds (the only sizeable assemblage of such a date in Lesbos); a large proportion of EBA. wares similar to those from Thermi; a not insignificant amount of MBA. material; Lesbian red and grey wares; and large numbers of imported Myc. sherds. Also recovered was a human skeleton (precise context unclear). The size of the BA. site was estimated by Kontis to be five times as large as Thermi. G. sherds were noted by (M.) Paraskeuaidis, whilst Hood, Daux, Megaw, Christomanos, Paraskeuaidis and Axiotis spoke of submerged harbour works and buildings.[38]

To the sw. of the N.-BA. site, near a chapel of Agios Nikolaos, Axiotis described the ruins of a tower of mortared stones with a dense tile scatter, and near the chapel were a number of sarcophagus lids and EByz. architectural blocks. Built into the chapel is a block bearing the monogram of Manuel Palaiologus (the Ven. ruler of Lesbos, 1391-1425) which is said to have been brought from the tower. In the area around the tower, and Kourtir in general, a number of other (mainly numismatic) finds have been reported: a seal of Pope Eugenius IV; a coin of the 4C BC; another of ca. 100 BC; 7 of the 4C AC; one of the 9C AC; another of the 11C; 7 Ven coins; and a lead one of 15C date.

Bibliography: Charitonidis, 1960, 236-37 and pl. 208ε; G. Daux, 'Chronique des fouilles et découvertes archéologiques en Grèce en 1960', BCH 85 (1961), 835; Hood, 22-23; A. H. S. Megaw, 'Archaeology in Greece, 1962-63', AR 9 (1963), 29; Paraskeuaidis, 1963, 1419; id., 1966, 208, 217; Charitonidis, 1968a, 30 and pl. 10β; Chatzi, 1971, 457 and pl. 461γ; Paraskeuaidis, 1970, 259; id., 'Τὰ νέα προβλήματα τῆς ἔρευνας τῶν προϊστορικῶν οἰκισμῶν τῆς Λέσβου', Lesbiaka 6 (1973), 128-29, 131; Buchholz, 122-23; Aupert, 697; H. W. Catling, 'Archaeology in Greece, 1975-76', AR 22 (1976), 28; Paraskeuaidis, 1976, 502-03; Kontis, 1978, 359-60; Axiotis, 1992 II, 565-67 and pl. 126; French, 1994, 67; BSA sherd archive Skamnioudi, unpublished.

92. *Aspres Petres* (Lisbori); 595624; 5m; LR.(?); HAB, CEM. Ca. 2.5 kms n. from Lisbori (and 1 km se. from Kourtir, #91), on either side of the road which runs along the coast from Skala Polichnitou ne. to Skala Basilikon, a dense scatter of ceramics was noted by Axiotis in the region known as the 'Aspres Petres' or 'Leukades'. Tombs (the dating of which is unclear) have been uncovered from time to time in the area and clearance cairns at field boundaries include large slabs and worked blocks.

This toponym recalls that mentioned on the LR. inscription linked to the toponym Temenos (the 'λευκὴ ἀκτὴ σὺν τεμένει', see Appendix 1). With regard to this association, it is interesting that nearby are the large salt pans at Skala Polichnitou, a resource which could well have been exploited in antiquity and gives the term 'white coast' added meaning.

Bibliography: Kontis, 1978, 361; Axiotis, 1992 II, 569.

93. *Temenos* (Lisbori); 593618; 40m; HL., R., Byz., Ven.; HAB, SP(?). Ca. 2 kms n. of Lisbori, at the n. foot of the hill known as Temenos, stands the chapel of Agios Isidoros beside an old kalderimi leading to Lisbori. The toponym 'Temenos' is known from the LR. census inscriptions associated with a piece of coastline known as the 'λευκὴ ἀκτὴ σὺν τεμένει' (see #92 and Appendix 1).

Newton reported ancient remains and red-coloured pottery beside the chapel in the 19C, and today two unfluted columns and the marble base of a perirrhantirion remain. A number of ancient coins were found nearby: a Mytilenean one dating from the 2C BC, three R., one Byz. and one Ven.. Despite the toponym and epigraphical evidence, however, there is no proof yet for any centre of worship at the site although Kontis assumed that this must be the case.

Close by to the s., contiguous with the remains around Agios Isidoros, is an area known as Tuda (another of the names on the LR. census inscriptions, see Appendix 1) and a number of ancient remains have been noted here around the chapel of Phrankokklisia: HL. sherds, Byz. coins and a lead seal of the end of the 12C (of the Byz. family Katakalon).

Bibliography: Newton I, 92; Charitonidis, 1968a, 29-30; Kontis, 1978, 361-62; Axiotis, 1992 II, 567-69.

---

[38] In a visit to Kourtir with Prof. J. Coleman on 8th June 1973 (reported in the local paper *Dimokratis* on 22/6/73) Paraskeuaidis stated that Coleman had swum around offshore from the site and defined some of the submerged structural remains as being of LN. date.

94. *Loutzas* (Basilika); 608626; 20m; R., LR.(?), Byz., 'MAge', Tur.; HAB. On the w. bank of the Loutzas stream, ca. 2.8 kms nnw. from Basilika and on the s. side of the road which runs e.-w. parallel to the shore of the gulf, are the ruins of a chapel dedicated to Agios Dimitrios. The fields all around the chapel (especially towards the sea) are covered in a dense scatter of tiles and sherds including 'MAge' glazed sherds, LR.-Byz. 'combed' wares and R. *terra sigilata*. Worked marble blocks are apparent near the ruined chapel together with large stones from olive presses (probably of Tur. date[39]). Axiotis also reported that Byz. coins of the 7C AC and 10C AC were found nearby.
Bibliography: Axiotis, 1992 II, 569.

95. *Plaka* (Basilika); 6163; --; C./HL., HAB. At a place known as Plaka, ca. 3 kms due n. from Basilika on the flat coastal plain near the shore, Axiotis described tiles and sherds including the bases of amphorae together with black and brown-glazed C./HL. sherds.
Bibliography: Axiotis, 1992 II, 569-70.

96. *Xiro* (Achladeri); 624641; 10m; A., LR.-EByz.(?); HAB, CEM, SP. On the shore of the Gulf of Kalloni, 2.5 kms wsw. from Pyrrha, is the small bay and harbour of Skala Basilikon to where until recently the magnesite mined further inland near Basilika was transported and loaded onto ships for export.[40] Near the shore, at a place named Xiro, a chance tomb find was reported by Charitonidis near the chapel of Agios Paulos. The pottery from the tomb included a black-painted phiale and a bucchero kantharos, the latter of which was compared to the 6C BC inscribed kantharos from Antissa (Lamb, 1930-31, pl. 28.3).

Axiotis reported that a surface scatter of grey wares and foundations of buildings are also apparent on the w.-facing slopes to the e. of the small plain near the shore (possibly the same material reported in the 19C by Koldewey[41]). On the low ridge ('Gaidourorachi') 55 m high and ca. 0.3 km to the e., six rock-cut tombs (probably of LR.-EByz. date) and further cuttings are also visible.
Bibliography: Koldewey, 39; Charitonidis, 1964, 398; Kontis, 1978, 363; Axiotis, 1992 II, 570-71 and pl. 127.

97. *Pastourmas* (Achladeri); 631636; 30m; R., Tur.; HAB, SP. Ca. 2.2 kms sw. from Achladeri is the Makri stream which flowed down from the Mikri Limni (or 'Small Lake') to the s. and sustained the water mills of the Georgantinis family built in 1850 (still visible as ruins nearby[42]). On the e. side of this stream, Axiotis noted the

foundations of buildings associated with which was a scatter of rubble, tiles and sherds (including pieces of R. *terra sigilata*). A worked marble block from an ancient structure is visible built into the mill-house with two cuttings. This area at the s. edge of the coastal plain is known as Pastourmas.
Bibliography: Axiotis, 1992 II, 571.

*98. *Agios Dimitrios* (Achladeri); 653652; 10m; EByz.; SP. Near the shore, at the n. foot of the Geniotos hill (on the sw. side of the acropolis of Pyrrha), are a large number of marble elements and the foundations of a large EByz. basilica (comprising a nave and two flanking aisles) excavated in preliminary fashion in 1939 by the Mytilenean Iakobos and later partly published by Orlandos. It is probably this basilica from which come the architectural *membra* seen by Koldewey at the church of Agios Dimitrios between the acropolis of Pyrrha and the village of Achladeri. The apse was well preserved and the e. wall (which was complete) measured ca. 20 m. In the middle of the s. side, parts of a mosaic floor with geometric patterns were uncovered subsequently.
Bibliography: Koldewey, 28; Iakobos, 37-38; Orlandos 1952-54, 403-04 and fig. 363.3; Charitonidis, 1968a, 29 n. 65; Axiotis, 1992 II, 576 and pl. 128.

*99. *Pyrrha* (Achladeri); 656654; 77m; EBA.(?), MBA.(?), LBA., PG., G., A., C., HL., R., LByz./Tur.; HAB, CEM, SP. The earliest grey wares found on the acropolis of Pyrrha by Boehlau during his excavations of 1906-07 may date settlement activity there from the EBA.. Buchholz was of the opinion that the LBA. was the most strongly represented phase of the prehistoric period (including a large number of grey wares, coarse wares and some LH IIIA/B Mycenaean sherds). The cemetery to the sw. of the acropolis (at the foot of the Geniotos hill) dates from the PG. period, and the earliest structural remains on the acropolis are of the 8C. The acropolis was walled from the A. period. An A. building complex (possibly with a centre of worship beside it) lies on the acropolis, and architectural *membra* together with tombs of A., C. and HL. date are known also. The historically-attested *proasteion* (Str. 13.2.4) which survived Pyrrha's destruction (probably by the earthquake of 231 BC) seems to have lain on the s. slopes of the earlier acropolis (where foundations of buildings are apparent together with a dense concentration of HL., R. and LByz./Tur. pottery). Two kilns (the dating of which are unclear) were also found at the foot of the acropolis and a LR. village dating to the reign of Diokletian is attested epigraphically (see Appendix 1).

Moutzouris proposed that the hill of ancient Pyrrha, with its late/post-antique pottery, took the name 'Basilika' in the Byz. period and was the site named by early travellers as the 'Kastro Basilikon' (see also #88), a fortified settlement later abandoned when the inland village of Basilika was founded ca. 7 kms ssw. (probably in the 15/16C).[43]

Axiotis reported that 0.6 km ne. from the acropolis is an outcrop of trachyte which showed signs of ancient quarrying activity, but offered no further details.

---

[39] A Tur. settlement is attested in Ottoman records nearby at 'Vassilika' in 1602, M. Kiel, pers. comm. (1995). Concerning an earlier 16C Ottoman census of the island, see n. 4 above.

[40] All the loading facilities and landing stages of this once important industry (which supported 50 families) have now fallen into disuse and stand in ruins near the shore. As recently as 1937 the British summary of the island's industry noted that the magnesite mined near Basilika was extremely significant, forming the sole mineral export of the island; see Naval Intelligence Division, *Greece: Regional Geography* (London, 1945) III, 504.

[41] Koldewey, 39, merely stated that ancient material was apparent 'south of Pyrrha on the beach'.

[42] The water mills are marked on the British Army map nearby, Grid Ref. 626630.

---

[43] As support for this thesis Moutzouris (1962, 60) noted that in a Mitropolitan codex of Mytilene dating to the 16C there were two villages in the area with similar names, 'Basilika' and 'Basilikiotis'. His interpretation of this phenomenon was that the coastal site of Pyrrha ('Basilika'/'Kastro Basilikon') was slowly being abandoned and the movement to the inland site of modern Basilika ('Basilikiotis') had not been completed.

Bibliography (main); Conze, 44-46 and pls. III, XVI.3; Koldewey, 27-29 and pls. 11-12; Rouse, 147; Lamb, 1932, 1-12 and figs. 4.1, 4.7 and 4.12; Moutzouris, 1962, 58-61; Bayne, 245-46 and fig. 25D; Paraskeuaidis, 1963, 1403-16, 1418; Charitonidis, 1964, 398; Petrakos, 1967c, 459, fig. 12 and pl. 337β; W. Schiering, 'Zweihundert Jahre Göttinger archäologische Sammlungen', *AA* (1967), 432-33 and fig. 28; H. Walter, *Samos V: Frühe samische Gefässe, Chronologie und Landschafsstile ostgriechischer Gefässe* (Bonn, 1968), 128 and pl. 131; E. Walter-Karydi, *Äolische Kunst* (*AK* supp. 7; Olten, 1970), figs. 1-2 (p. 4); Paraskeuaidis, 1970, 262; Buchholz, 123, 133, 136 (and index s. v. Pyrrha); Kontis, 1973, 20-21, figs. 16-20; id., 1978, 346-50; W. Schiering, 'Ein Tierfrieskessel aus Pyrrha auf Lesbos', *Anadolu* 22 (1981-83), 201-10; Touchais, 1985, 831; Acheilara and Archontidou-Argyri, 1986, 203; Archontidou-Argyri, 1986-87, 59; Basiakos, 209; Schiering, 339-77; Axiotis, 1992 II, 573-78 and pls. 128-30.

100. *Tokatia* (Achladeri); 667657; 10m; EByz.; SP. At the edge of the small plain to the ne. of ancient Pyrrha (#99), near the storehouse in the Tsoukaladellis property, wall foundations and worked blocks of an ancient structure are preserved, probably part of an EByz. basilica. The worship of Agios Nikolaos is practised at the spot, although no modern chapel is mentioned either by Charitonidis or Axiotis. Amongst the ancient material associated with the ruins is part of an EByz. unfluted column and a column capital.
Bibliography: Charitonidis, 1968a, 29; Axiotis, 1992 II, 578.

101. *Mesintziki* (Achladeri); 6667; 25m; 'MAge'; HAB(?), SP(?). In a small coastal plain known as Mesintziki,[44] 2 kms nne. from ancient Pyrrha to the e. of the main road along the coast from Achladeri to Messa, stands a small chapel of Agios Nikolaos. In the vicinity of the chapel both Kontis and Axiotis reported a dense scatter of tiles and sherds brought to light by the repeated ploughing of the olive groves, including Lesbian grey wares (which could date from any time within the BA.-HL. periods) and 'MAge' sherds.
Around the lip of the plateau immediately above the chapel (to the s.) is the enclosure and inner tower which Kontis first described,[45] constructed of large, unworked blocks. Axiotis also stated that near to the central 'tower' structure (founded on the bedrock) were a number of light, slate-like stones, probably the remains of the tower's roof. The enclosure was noted as being more strongly defended on its n. side.
Bibliography: Kontis, 1978, 357-58; Axiotis, 1992 II, 578-79.

102. *Kryo Neri* (Achladeri); 684685; 60m; C., HL., R., LR.-Byz., 'MAge'; HAB, SP. Immediately s. of the asphalt road from Mytilene to Kalloni, 0.9 km se. from the Temple of Messa (#103), is the spring known as 'Kryo Neri', from which the immediate surrounding area is named. Kontis reported that the spring itself showed signs of artificial cutting, possibly ancient, and that 0.3 km to the se. of the spring were worked blocks which he suggested to be an altar. A scatter of C. and HL. sherds together with structural remains (comprising walls made of small stones joined with mud) lay 0.4 km to the w. of the 'altar'.

Axiotis added more detail and definition to the site, noting that ca. 0.2 km n. from the spring, on the low rocky rise immediately n. of the road, the apse of an old chapel, other foundations (including a possible tower) and a significant scatter of sherds and tile (comprising grey wares, R. *terra sigilata*, LR.-Byz. 'combed' wares, and glazed 'MAge' sherds) were apparent, stretching e. as far as a small chapel of Agios Nikolaos.

Axiotis also suggested that the toponym may be that referred to in a decree of the Patriarchal Synod of 1331 which spoke of a 'Monastery of Agios Georgios of Kryo Nero', but the precise location of the monastery is unclear.
Bibliography: Kontis, 1978, 357; Axiotis, 1992 I, 365 and II, pl. 79.

*103. *Messa* (Achladeri); 675693; 1m; A., LC.-EHL., EByz., LByz.; CEM, SP. As the main road from Mytilene to Kalloni descends from the pine forest covering the 'Pyrrhaion Oros' into the Arisbe plain, ca. 1 km before the turning s. to Achladeri, a track heads n. serving the small hamlet of Messa. To the e. of this track, after ca. 0.5 km, some tall poplar trees stand beside the fenced enclosure of the large late-4C pseudo-dipteral temple known as the Temple of Messa.[46]

During Koldewey's excavations under the e. end of the 4C temple, two rows of smaller blocks were found which were the remains of an earlier structure subsequently encompassed within the larger LC.-EHL. building. The date of this earlier structure could not be determined. No earlier architectural elements have ever been found at the site (or nearby), but A. graves were uncovered by Petrakos n. of the temple and A. fine ware pottery was located in the same season nearer to the cella walls. An open-air A. centre of worship is possible even if no temple existed (the site probably represents Alkaios' 'τέμενος μέγα ξῦνον' of the Lesbians, see Lobel-Page, G1.2-3; Page, 161-69).

On top of the LC.-EHL. Ionic temple an EByz. basilica was constructed, using many elements from the temple itself (especially column drums) in its walls. The walls of the basilica still stand to ca. 1.5 m, including the apse, and worship to Taxiarchis still continues. Columns, column bases and relief plaques are amongst the finds at the site, and in the stone surface of the temple's stylobate tombs have been hewn, probably also of EByz. date.

Other finds which have been made near the temple include a kiln and a hoard of 48 gold Byz coins dated to 1330 AD.
Bibliography (main): Koldewey, 36, 47-61 and pls. 18-26; Rouse, 147; Taxis, 125; Orlandos, 1937, 129 n. 2; Iakobos, 36; Paraskeuaidis, 1963, 1418; Petrakos, 1967a, 96-102 and pls. 74-84; id., 1967b, 72-75 and figs. 73-76; id., 1967c, 458-59; id., 1968a, 84-86 and pl. 63; id., 1968b, 80-82 and figs. 84-87; Charitonidis, 1968a, 46-49, figs. 22-26 and pl. 86; Kontis, 1973, 87-88 and figs. 49-50; id., 1978, 350-57, figs. 62-63; H. Plommer, 'The temple of Messa in Lesbos' in L. Casson and M. Price (eds.), *Coins, culture and history in the ancient world*

---

[44] 'Μεσιντζίκι' is the Turkish diminutive of 'Messa', a link which prompted Kontis (1978, 357) to suggest a link of this site to the shrine at Messa (#103) in antiquity.
[45] Kontis' toponym for this enclosure was 'Kalogera', but this name is imprecise since it is applied to all the hills on the w. edge of the pine forest in this region.

---

[46] The latest analysis of the temple suggested a date of 340-20 BC, see F. Rumscheid *Untersuchungen zur kleinasiatischen Bauornamentik des Hellenismus* (Mainz, 1994) II, 43.

(Detroit, 1981), 177-86; M. Pfrommer, 'Bemerkungen zum Tempel von Messa auf Lesbos', *Ist.Mitt.* 36 (1986), 77-94 and pls. 23-27; Axiotis, 1992 I, 362-64 and II, pls. 78-79; F. Rumscheid, *Untersuchungen zur kleinasiatischen Bauornamentik des Hellenismus* (Mainz, 1994) I, 59-70 and II, 43 (where a full list of references to the temple is given).

104. *Chiftlik* (Achladeri); 673699; 15m; Tur.; HAB. Ca. 0.7 km nw. from the Temple at Messa (#103), beyond two *spitakia*, are the remains of an extensive Tur. chiftlik. A dense scatter of tile and sherds (including pithos fragments) is visible, together with two large millstones of a ruined olive press and the remains of a bath-house.
Bibliography: Taxis, 125; Axiotis, 1992 I, 364.

*105. *Agios Georgios Chalinadou* (Agia Paraskeui); 683728; 70m; EByz., 'MAge'; HAB, SP. Further e. from the Taxiarchis chapel (#106), along the road from Agia Paraskeui to Komi and Pigi (in total ca. 4 kms se. from the village), are the remains of an EByz. basilica now worshipped as a shrine to Agios Georgios. Orlandos excavated and restored the basilica in December 1937, and considered that the building had been the central chapel of a small monastery which once stood at the spot. Possible evidence for the latter was found to the s. of the basilica where the remains of the walls of cells were visible. The associated architectural fragments dated the building to the second half of the 6C AC (a coin of 567-68 AD was also found within the chapel).
In the fields further to the s., traces of foundations, tiles and sherds (including pithoi) of 'MAge' date gave further indication of habitation activity in the immediate area around the two nearby chapels of the Panagia and Agios Dimitrios (both of which had EByz. architectural *membra* from Agios Georgios associated with them).
Bibliography: Orlandos, 1937, 115-26; Iakobos, 37; Paraskeuaidis, 1963, 1417; Charitonidis, 1968a, 52; Axiotis, 1992 I, 359-60 (and unnumbered photograph p. 359) and II, pls. 76-77.

106. *Taxiarchis* (Agia Paraskeui); 6674; --; EByz.; SP. Ca. 3 kms ese. from Agia Parakseui, on the road which leads eventually to Pigi and Komi on the e. coast of the island, is an old chapel of Taxiarchis. The chapel stands 0.1 km below the road to the s. and is founded upon the apse of an EByz. basilica. A large number of architectural *membra* from the basilica, including column capitals and bases, are scattered inside and around the modern chapel together with some pieces from the temple at Klopedi (#111).
Bibliography: Charitonidis, 1968a, 51-52; Axiotis, 1992 I, 358 and II, pl. 75.

107. *Agios Dimitrios* (Agia Paraskeui) 663754; 100m; Tur.; HAB, SP. Ca. 1.3 kms along the road e. from Agia Paraskeui (which leads eventually to Nees Kydonies on the e. coast of the island) stands a chapel of Agios Dimitrios, built in 1874. The fragments of an earlier structure, including EByz. architectural *membra*, are visible beside the chapel, and these ruins are thought to be the parish church of an Agios Dimitrios settlement which lay in the vicinity of the modern village of Agia Paraskeui, referred to by Gabriel of Methymna in 1636-41.[47] The location of the

old settlement associated with the chapel is placed nearby at a place known as Chalasmata, where the finds included a number of large pithoi.
Bibliography: Charitonidis, 1968a, 52; Chatzi, 1971, 458 and pl. 461δ; Axiotis, 1992 I, 358.

108. *Mosyna* (Napi); 6576-6676; --; BA.(?); HAB. On the Mosyna hill, ca. 1 km s. from Napi (exact location unspecified), Axiotis reported that many years ago a pithos and three large (possibly BA.) lithics were uncovered during agricultural work in the plot of Chatzigiannis. One stone was grey/beige in colour, 11.5 cm x 5.5 cm x. 4 cm (the latter its thickness), and two others were of a 'heavy, black stone' (possibly obsidian), one 18 cm x 6 cm x 5 cm and another 9.5 cm x 5.5 cm x 4 cm.
Bibliography: Axiotis, 1992 I, 349.

109. *Taxiarchis tou Troulotis* (Napi); 6477; --; BA.(?), EByz.; HAB, SP. Ca. 1.5 kms w. from Napi, near the chapel of Taxiarchis tou Troulotis, Koldewey found a number of Aiolic capitals and column drums brought from Klopedi, supposing the temple from which they had come to be near the chapel itself. Koldewey also discovered the apse and walls of an EByz. basilica nearby, and Charitonidis and Axiotis noted architectural *membra* built into the chapel itself. A chapel of Agios Georgios (0.2 km to the sw.) also preserved EByz. pieces from the basilica.
On the hill of Troulotis, to the n. of the basilica, Axiotis described a scatter of lithics and sherds which he considered were representative of BA. habitation activity.
Bibliography: Koldewey, 44-46, pl. 16.8, 16.15; Taxis, 125; Charitonidis, 1968a, 51 and pl. 25α-γ; Kontis, 1978, 293; Axiotis, 1992 I, 348-49 (and unnumbered photographs pp. 350, 366) and II, pl. 73.

110. *Agios Therapon* (Napi); 631781; 80m; EByz.; SP. After leaving Agia Paraskeui and heading n. on the road to Napi, a fork to the left after ca. 0.75 km leads nw., reaching after ca. 3 kms the single-arched Tur. (or possibly Ven.[48]) bridge over the Tsiknias River at Kremasti. As well as the elements from the temple at Klopedi built into the bridge (#111), there are also a number of EByz. architectural *membra* incorporated. Just beyond the bridge to the w. of the river, on the n. side of the road, is a newly built chapel of Agios Therapon. Beside the modern chapel, however, are the overgrown remains of an EByz. basilica of which the apse, wall foundations and door jambs are preserved.
A large number of architectural blocks from the basilica (and even a few from the temple at Klopedi) are scattered in the vicinity together with a dense concentration of tiles and sherds (including a large number of pithoi). More pieces of the basilica (including column capitals) can be found at the shrine of Agios Stathis, ca. 0.5 km wsw.

---

[47] Agios Dimitrios and Gerna (#114) were two earlier settlements which coalesced to form the village of Agia

Paraskeui. For this dating of the description of Lesbos written by Gabriel of Methymna, see I. Phountoulis (ed.), Γαβριήλ Μητροπολίτου Μηθύμνης, Περιγραφὴ τῆς Λέσβου (Athens, 1960).
[48] The date of the original bridge is unclear. Makistos suggested that it had been built by the Venetian company which began to exploit the alum deposits further north near Stypsi (literally 'Alum') in 1437. To facilitate this exploitation a communication system was established to link the production centre both with other regions of the island and also outside markets, see Axiotis, 1992 I, 347 (and unnumbered photograph p. 348).

from the Kremasti bridge, beside a spring on the e. slopes of the Petsophas hill.

Bibliography: Taxis, 125; Charitonidis, 1968a, 50-51 and pls. 23-24; Axiotis, 1992 I, 345-47 and II, pls. 71-72.

*111. *Klopedi* (Agia Parakseui); 624765; 100m; EBA., LG., A., C.(?), HL.(?), R.; HAB(?), CEM, SP. At the location known as Klopedi, ca. 2 kms wnw. from Agia Paraskeui and w. of the Prini bridge over the Tsiknias River, the remains of two temples stand on an e. plateau of the Skepasto hill. Architectural elements from the temples, especially the distinctive Aiolic column capitals, were known to Koldewey (see #109), but the precise location of the temple from which the elements came was not discovered until the 1920s[49] when the first excavations were begun by Euangelidis, later supplemented by Chatzi's brief resumption in 1972.

Euangelidis uncovered an A. peripteral temple (possibly dedicated to Apollo Napaios, see St. Byz. s. v. 'Νάπη') with another smaller (probably older) temple beside it. To the e. of the two temples, Chatzi found traces of another structure (possibly an altar) together with LG. bucchero pottery. Only the stylobate of the larger (peripteral) temple was preserved when excavated, with two column bases *in situ* in the nw. corner. Inside this larger temple was found a square structure of Lesbian polygonal masonry (also incorporating isodomic blocks, see Appendix 2, sections 2.3-2.5), suggested by both Euangelidis and Betancourt to be either the base of a cult statue or the remains of an older shrine.

Regarding the precise dating of the temples, Euangelidis unfortunately devoted almost no space to the associated ceramics, stating only that the pottery seemed to indicate continuation of the cult until the R. period (presumably meaning therefore that C. and HL. sherds were present also). Descriptions were offered of some small finds: bronze fibulae and a bronze buckle (of G. date), a small bronze vase, and 5C BC female idols. The large peripteral temple was dated to the late 6C BC by the fragments of the terracottas which survived (which Åkerström concluded had all come from the same building). There are no other remains of the superstructure, suggesting that it was of wood. The date of the smaller temple is unclear, mainly due to its thorough destruction. From its plan, Betancourt proposed a date in the late 7-6C BC, but as yet there is no evidence to support the claims of Kontis that there were 'three or more' building phases of either temple or that cult practice at the site dates back to the early first millennium.

A much earlier phase of activity at the site was detected between the two temples where Euangelidis uncovered the semi-circular section of a building constructed of small stones inside which was a whole EBA. pyxis of reddy-black fabric.

Charitonidis also reported briefly that very near to the temples, and to the n. at a spot known as Pigadia, tombs were uncovered (no details were given), and Chatzi described

the remains of a trachyte quarry 20 minutes to the w. from where at least some of the material for the temple was hewn.

Bibliography: Koldewey, 1890, 44-46 and pl. 16; Euangelidis, 1924-25, 41-44; id., 1927, 57-59 and figs. 1-3; id., 1928, 126-37, figs. 1-17 and pl. I; Bayne, 246-47; Paraskeuaidis, 1963, 1417; Charitonidis, 1965, 492 and n. 13; Åkerström I, 27-33 and II, pl. 11; Chatzi, 1971, 457 and pl. 460α-γ; H. W. Catling, 'Archaeology in Greece, 1971-72', *AR* 18 (1972), 20; D. Chatzi, 'Εἰδήσεις ἐκ Λέσβου', *AAA* 5 (1972), 43-46; J.-P. Michaud, 'Chronique des fouilles et découvertes archéologiques en Grèce en 1972', *BCH* 97 (1973), 363 and figs. 233-34; Kontis, 1973, 45-46 and figs. 25-26; Buchholz, 123; Aupert, 697 and fig. 267; Paraskeuaidis, 1976, 503; Betancourt, 82-87; Kontis, 1978, 295-99; Axiotis, 1992 I, 343-44 and II, pl. 70.

112. *Prophitis Ilias* (Agia Paraskeui); 642759; 170m; EBA., MBA., LBA., A., C./HL.(?), LR., 'MAge'; HAB, SP(?). At the nw. edge of Agia Paraskeui, the church of the same name and the village cemetery lie at the foot of the small hill on which stands an old chapel of Prophitis Ilias. Kiepert first visited the hill in 1841 and both he and Koldewey stated that there were sherds and tiles on the hill which were not modern. Koldewey also noted a polygonal wall on the same hill 'which could be ancient', but gave no more details.

In 1975 (M.) Paraskeuaidis and Kalaitzis returned to the site and published details of a large number of EBA., MBA., LBA. and LR. sherds, a collection of lithics, and also a loomweight. The assemblage was similar in nature to that at Kourtir (#91), and the BA. material was especially dense on the e. slope of the hill facing the village. Axiotis also found material of later periods (largely around the peak of the hill) including grey wares, black-painted sherds and glazed sherds of 'MAge' date to add to the BA. (and also LR.) material reported by Paraskeuaidis. On the e. slope of the hill, Axiotis added that in association with the concentration of BA. material eroding out of the hillslope were the foundations of (probably BA.) houses of small, unworked stones.

Bibliography: Koldewey, 35, 81; Paraskeuaidis, 1978, 161-81; G. Touchais, 'Chronique des fouilles et découvertes archéologiques en Grèce en 1978', *BCH* 103 (1979), 596; M. Paraskeuaidis, ' 'Ο προϊστορικός οἰκισμός τοῦ λόφου Προφήτη 'Ηλία 'Αγίας Παρασκευῆς Λέσβου', *To Bima* (16/2/79); Axiotis, 1992 I, 340-41; BSA sherd archive Prophitis Ilias, unpublished.

113. *Agia Photia* (Agia Paraskeui); 650733; 190m; C./HL.(?); SP. On a narrow ridge which lines the w. bank of the Mylopotamos River, ca. 2 kms s. from Agia Paraskeui, stands a small, newly-constructed chapel of Agia Photia built inside the remains of an ancient tower. The foundations of the tower measure 9 m (e.-w.) x 7 m (n.-s.) and were described by Axiotis as having coursed polygonal masonry (suggesting, therefore, a construction date in the C. or HL. periods). On the s. side of the tower a retaining wall is preserved, possibly constructed to support the small plateau on which the tower was built. No associated ceramics were mentioned by Axiotis. The hill is one of highest points in this part of the plain, commanding the passes inland (n.) along the Mylopotamos River from the head of the gulf.

Bibliography: Axiotis, 1992 I, 332 and II, pl. 69.

---

[49] The exact date when the excavation at Klopedi was started is unclear from the published reports. Euangelidis (1924-25, 41) stated that he had been searching for the site of the temple since 1919 and that after failing to locate the temple near the chapel of Taxiarchis tou Troulotis (#109, where Koldewey had presumed the temple lay) he began to examine other possible locations. Euangelidis omits to say exactly when the work at the correct location was begun, however, and the first report is simply grouped in the supplement to the *ArchDelt* 1924-25 volume which covers work carried out between 1922-25.

114. *Gerna* (Agia Paraskeui); 634738; 20m; N., EBA., EByz., Tur.; HAB, CEM, SP. On the s. slopes and at the s. foot of the Phaskari hill, ca. 2 kms ssw. from Agia Paraskeui, are the extensive remains of the village of Gerna attested in the Tourkokratia. Kalderimia, the piers of an old bridge, wells, a large number of building foundations, five chapels and dense ceramic scatters mark the area of the village referred to in the Leimonos Monastery records (#119) from 1578 and by the Methymnaean Gabriel in his description of Lesbos dated 1636-41.[50] Amongst these remains, beside a chapel of Taxiarchis, is the apse and part of the s. wall of an EByz. basilica, and architectural pieces from the building are incorporated into a nearby enclosure wall. More material from the basilica (together with a tombstone) is apparent at the chapel of Agios Athanasios to the ne.. Other elements were moved to the chapel of Taxiarchis in the village of Agia Paraskeui in 1856.

The remains on the s. slopes of the Phaskari hill also include a few EBA. sherds as well as the large number of 'MAge' pieces and house foundations. At the spot nearby known as 'Phkolides' a small N. axehead was found before World War II.

Bibliography: Taxis, 123; Charitonidis, 1966, 76; id., 1968a, 49-50; Paraskeuaidis, 1978, 166; Axiotis, 1992 I, 332-34 and II, pl. 68.

115. *Agios Giannis* (Arisbi); 615728; 44m; EByz., 'MAge'; HAB, SP. A shrine of Agios Giannis stands on the low rise (known by the shrine's unabbreviated named of Agios Ioannis[51]) in the Plain of Kalloni, ca. 3 kms ese. of modern Arisbi to the s. of the main Mytilene-Kalloni road. Near the s. end of the low ridge, the apse and architectural *membra* of an EByz. basilica are visible, and on the sw. slope of the hill is a dense scatter of 'MAge' tiles and sherds. A cistern (of similar 'MAge' date) lies some 30 m to the n. of the shrine constructed of mortared tile and stone and an old well stands at the e. foot of the hill near a *mandri*.

Bibliography: Charitonidis, 1963c, 271; id., 1968a, 45-46 and pl. 27α-β, δ; Axiotis, 1992 I, 329 and II, pl. 68.

*116. *Palaiokastro* (Arisbi); 605742; 40m; EBA., MBA., A., C., HL., R., Byz./Ven.(?), 'MAge'; HAB, SP. Leaving the village of Arisbi on the main road towards Mytilene, after ca. 0.15 km a track leaves the road to the left (as the road bends sharply right) and heads n. to the low rocky hill which forms the acropolis of ancient Arisbe or Palaiokastro. Arisbe is mentioned by Herodotos (Hdt. 1.151.2) as one of the six original *poleis* of Lesbos, one which had been conquered by Methymna before his time. The site has been known since the 19C when Conze, Kiepert and Koldewey all visited the hill, and subsequently there have been surface surveys by Bayne, Kontis and Axiotis together with brief excavations by Chatzi in 1972.

The earliest traces of habitation activity on the acropolis are the EBA. and MBA. sherds found in a surface inspection by Bayne and during the excavations of Chatzi.

Stretches of a very substantial 2 m wide Lesbian (polygonal) masonry wall encircling the acropolis still exist on the e., n. and w. sides of the hill up to 1.5 m in height (see Appendix 2 and fig. 21). Inside the e. part of this wall, on the plateau of the acropolis below the small kastro, are traces of many houses. Koldewey mapped some of the house remains in the 19C when they were better preserved, at which time 'megaron' plans could be determined. Chatzi could not define the period to which either the houses or the enclosure wall belonged in 1972. Coarse ware pottery (red and grey wares) are scattered over the whole acropolis area. Chatzi reported C. pottery on the w. and s. cheeks of the acropolis and Bayne noted HL. and R. sherds also.[52]

Koldewey noted that many of the 'MAge' remains at the site (said to date from the 11C AC) were on the nw. side of the acropolis (where Axiotis reported the foundations of 5 chapels). The first reference to the kastro on top of the acropolis (inside which a cistern was constructed) is made in 1336, agreeing with the assessment of Axiotis who considered parts of the walls (of tile and mortared stones) to be of Byz. date. Both the acropolis and kastro (the location of the Byz.-Ven. settlement known by the name 'Kalloni') were destroyed in 1444 AD in an attack by the Tur. renegade Balta Oglou. Most of its inhabitants who were not killed or captured immediately fled, but others stayed at least until the start of the 17C at which point they dispersed to nearby villages. Even before this final abandonment, the hill with the ruined kastro had already assumed the name of 'Palaiokastro' (at the latest by the 16C since this is the name given to the area in the archives of the Leimonos Monastery [#119] which date from this period).[53]

The location of the site's cemeteries is not known, since not a single tomb has ever been found in the vicinity of the acropolis. Koldewey did note on his map two scatters of ancient tile and sherds to the n. and nw. of the acropolis respectively, but he gives no details of his finds in the text, and the intense cultivation in both these areas now makes it impossible to corroborate these earlier reports.

Bibliography: Conze, 41-43 and pl. III; Koldewey, 29-30, 35 and pls. 13.1, 14.1-5; Rouse, 147; Moutzouris, 1962,

---

[50] In Gabriel's text of 1636-41 (see n. 47), the village of Gerna was referred to jointly with Agia Paraskeui as if a localised synoikism had taken place between the late 16C and the 17C (Axiotis, 1992 I, 333). The village of 'Aya Paraskevi' is listed at an earlier date also, in the Ottoman records for 1602, M. Kiel, pers. comm. (1995). Concerning an earlier 16C Ottoman census of the island, see n. 4 above.

[51] Charitonidis also calls the shrine on top of the hill Agios Ioannis.

[52] When Bayne inspected Palaiokastro (Bayne, 118, 246), he was so disappointed at the lack of obviously A. material and the predominance of EBA., HL. and R. sherds that he even began to question whether the hill was, in fact, ancient Arisbe. A few fragments of A. grey wares, however, together with the lack of a suitable alternative, led him to conclude that this site must be the ancient acropolis.

[53] Later, in the mid-nineteenth century, Newton (II, 2) stated that there were seven villages in the plain lying close together: Daphia, Keramia, Papiana, Sumaria, Achyrona (modern Kalloni), Argenna and Agios Cosmas (or Tzumali), that Achyrona was the most important, and that the name 'Kalloni' was given to the whole group (in the same way that the name 'Gera' is given today to all the group of villages at the head of the Perama plain on the Gulf of Gera). At the beginning of the twentieth century, in addition to Achyrona, Taxis (120-23) recorded Daphia, Soumouria, Tzoumaili, Argiana, Kerami and Papiana as existing villages, stating also that others which had existed previously included Pharanx (#117), Phkiolia, Ambeliotis, Trianta (#120), Agios Leptis and Gerna (#114). Of these 19C and 20C settlements, three are attested much earlier in the 1602 Ottoman records for the island: 'Kerami', 'Papiani' and 'Ayo Kozma', M. Kiel, pers. comm. (1995). Concerning an earlier 16C Ottoman census of the island, see n. 4 above.

52, 54, 61-63; Bayne, 246; Paraskeuaidis, 1963, 1417; French I, 232 fig. 29a, b1; Chatzi, 1972, 593-95 and pls. 543-45, 546α-στ, 547α; Kontis, 1973, 16, 61-62 and fig. 35; Paraskeuaidis, 1976, 503; Touchais, 1977, 624; Catling, 58; Kontis, 1978, 288-91; Moutzouris, 1983, 22; Axiotis, 1992 I, 325-28 and II, pl. 68; BSA sherd archive Arisbi, unpublished.

117. *Pharanx* (Daphia) 5975-5976; --; Tur.; HAB. On either side of the main road which leads n. from Kalloni to Petra and Methymna, ca. 1.5 kms ne. from Daphia, are the remains of the village of the Tur. period attested in archival sources as Pharanx. The remains are scattered on the s. slopes of the hills which form the edge of the Kalloni plain (where the main road climbs sharply). To the w. of the road, near the ravine after which the village was named, stands an ikonostasis to Taxiarchis amongst a pile of rubble, the remains of the parish church of the Archangeloi attested in the 17C. E. from the road, the slopes near the chapel of Agios Dimitrios are covered with tiles and sherds of Tur. date.

The village (birthplace of Agios Ignatios of Agallianos) is first attested in 1548 in the archives of the Leimonos Monastery (#119) and in 1636-41 Gabriel of Methymna referred to the village (situated 'on the slope') as possessing 25 Christian households.[54] Moutzouris suggested that the site was one of those in the Kalloni area abandoned in the later 17C.
Bibliography: Taxis, 123; Moutzouris, 1983, 19-20, 25-26; Axiotis, 1992 I, 321.

118. *Monastiri tis Myrsiniotissas* (Daphia); 586759; 30m; Byz., Tur.; SP. On the slopes which limit the Kalloni Plain to the nw., ca. 1 km n. from Daphia on the w. side of the main Kalloni - Methymna highway, stands the (originally Byz.) monastery of Myrsiniotissa first attested in 1331 AD (then known as 'Myrsini'). Although abandoned immediately after the Tur. conquest in 1462,[55] the church continued to function and the site was re-established as a monastery in the early 16C, continuing until the present day despite a serious fire in 1862 and the destructive earthquake of 1867.

The complex of buildings includes a number of cells, a water-mill, a cheese-making factory and the church of the Panagia (comprising a nave and two flanking aisles). For a long period this church housed the tomb of Agios Ignatios who revived the monastery in the 16C (see #117; the tomb has now been moved to the nearby Leimonos Monastery, #119). A number of old wells are apparent also, fed by a spring on the hillslope near the monastery.
Bibliography: Newton II, 3-4; Taxis, 122 and n. 3; Moutzouris, 1973, 92-104; Axiotis, 1992 I, 322-24 (and unnumbered photograph p. 323).

119. *Moni Leimonos* (Daphia); 564758; 150m; Byz., Tur.; SP. The large complex of the Leimonos Monastery lies to the s. of the main road from Kalloni to Philia, ca. 2.2 kms wnw. from Daphia. The original Byz. monastery was abandoned after the Tur. conquest of the island in 1462,

but was revived in 1526 and has continued to the present day. In the 16C a 'Leimonos School' was founded in the monastery which flourished much later in the 19C. The current church of the Archangel Michael (with a nave and two flanking aisles) dates from 1795 but incorporates parts of the older 16C structure (some of the wall paintings also date from the 16C).

The large complex of buildings includes an olive press, cells for the monks and a collection of manuscripts and vestments now on show as a museum (with manuscripts dating from the 9C). From this central area a kalderimi leads s. to the buildings of the monastery's metochi ca. 2 kms away at the sw. foot of the Parthenis hill (see #121).
Bibliography: Newton II, 3-5; Koldewey, 83; Taxis, 121-22 and n. 1 (p. 121), 140; Aliprantis, 1972, 617; id., 1973, 557; Moutzouris, 1973, 92-104; Axiotis, 1992 I, 369-73 (and unnumbered photograph p. 370) and II, pl. 80.

120. *Trianta* (Kalloni); 573731; 5m; C., HL., LR.-Byz., Tur.; HAB, CEM. At the place known as Trianta, ca. 2 kms sw. from Kalloni, are the remains of a 'MAge' village (probably of Byz. origin) which survived into the Tourkokratia. Trianta is attested in the archives of the Leimonos Monastery (#119) in the 15C and was still in existence in the 17C (when there were 20 Christian households). The village was said to have originally taken its name from the 30 churches which stood within it (some of which are still visible as ruins).[56] The dense surface scatter of ceramics attests to the Tur. village, but there are also older components to the site. A 5C BC grave was discovered in 1964, Kontis spoke of other C. and HL. tombs 'often' being found in the area, Axiotis noted LR.-Byz. 'combed' wares and a press-stone, whilst Koldewey reported an ancient well with a Byz. inscription.
Bibliography: Koldewey, 35; Taxis, 123; Charitonidis, 1964, 398; id., 1968a, 44; Kontis, 1978, 294; Moutzouris, 1983, 18, 20, 25; Axiotis, 1992 I, 305-06; id., 1994, fig. Δ.

121. *Prophitis Ilias* (Kerami); 564722; 70m; A.(?); HAB/SP. Traces of an ancient enclosure stand on the hill of Prophitis Ilias, 3 kms sw. from Kalloni on the n. side of the Potamia River. On the oval hilltop, the traces of a substantial enclosure wall of polygonal masonry are visible around the chapel, well preserved especially on the n. side where two external towers are apparent. A scatter of amphora, pithos and other sherds lie on the slopes below the summit outside the enclosure wall, and on the peak of the hill are traces of foundations and a dense scatter of ceramics.[57]

The position of the enclosure is significant topographically in that it stands on the n. side of the river valley through which the Potamia River enters the Plain of Kalloni, opposite the enclosure at Xirokastrini to the s. of the river (#122). This enclosure must be the 'fort' referred

---

[54] For the dating of Gabriel's text, see n. 47.

[55] In the later 15C the name of the monastery is recorded as 'Stauropigiaki', but with the re-establishing of the monastery proper in the early 16C the name Myrsiniotissa was restored (the latter is clear from the testimony of Gabriel of Methymna [in 1636-41, see n. 47] who knew the monastery as 'Myrsiniotisa'), see Axiotis, 1992 I, 323-24.

[56] An alternative hypothesis for the origin of the village name is that it may have been linked to the number of serfs working the village land in Byz. times, since a number of similar placenames are known, 'Okto' ('Eight'), 'Ennea' ('Nine') and 'Deka' ('Ten'), which are said to have originated in a similar fashion. See Moutzouris, 1983, 25.

[57] Basiakos, 209, also reported traces of a R. settlement in this area '2 kms w. from Skala Kallonis', on the w. bank of the 'Ennea Kamares' rema. The remains included parts of a kiln (probably for amphora production in the view of Basiakos), but it is impossible to place this site on the maps of the British Army or Axiotis.

to by Kontis as being 'near to Metochi', namely, the area around the metochi of the Leimonos Monastery (which lies ca. 2 kms n. of the Prophitis Ilias site).

Another noteworthy feature of the hill recorded by Axiotis is that at its e. foot are the traces of old (possibly ancient) quarry working.

Bibliography: Kontis, 1978, 291; Axiotis, 1992 I, 301-02 and II, pl. 65.

122. *Xirokastrini* (Kerami); 547716; 220m; A., HL., Byz., Ven.(?), 'MAge', Tur.(?); HAB, SP. The high rocky outcrop of Xirokastrini rises above the modern Kalloni-Parakoila road, ca. 4 km sw. from Kalloni and immediately s. of the Potamia River. Across the top of the ridge is a cross-wall, originally of Lesbian polygonal masonry (see Appendix 2 and figs. 25, 27), with later (probably Byz./Ven.) additions above the ancient masonry comprising mortared tile and stone courses and two external towers. The wall is some 80 m long, 2.5 m thick, and its irregular course is determined by the desire to take advantage of the natural rocky outcrop at the top of the hill which gives extra height. At the n. side of the hilltop the wall ends when the natural rock offers protection. A rectangular tower of isodomic masonry 8.2 m x 7.1 m stands 0.13 km further up from the cross-wall at the peak of the hill just beyond a chapel of the Panagia.

From the central gate in the ancient wall, a kalderimi leads uphill towards the Panagia and the foundations of an older chapel to the e. of it which are probably the remains of the fortified 'Xirokastro Monastery' attested in a Patriarchal Synod of 1331. Koldewey and Axiotis both noted an enormous number of 'MAge' sherds and tile scattered all over the hilltop (from both the monastery and an associated settlement) and the latter also reported a number of ancient worked blocks, some with holes for clamps. By the 17C the settlement which accompanied the monastery had been abandoned and only the church remained.

Bibliography: Conze, 43 and pl. II; Koldewey, 30-31, 88, pls. 13.2, 14.6-7; Rouse, 147; Taxis, 121; Moutzouris, 1962, 63-64; Kontis, 1978, 312-13 and figs. 53-55; Axiotis, 1992 I, 298-300 (and unnumbered photograph p. 302) and II, pls. 63-64; Spencer, 1994, 210 and figs. 1, 5.

123. *Palaiokastro Issas* (Parakoila); 5370; --; A./C.(?), Byz./Tur.; HAB, SP. Ca. 2.5 kms due n. from Parakoila on the lower e. slopes of the mountain named Issa, is a small plateau known as Palaiokastro, naturally fortified by cliffs on its se. and e. sides. Along the sw. lip of the plateau is a substantial wall 1.5 m thick constructed of two outer faces and a rubble fill. A set of stairs has been cut in the s. edge of the cliff to allow an easy approach. On the plateau inside the wall is the complex of small rooms first seen by Koldewey (with walls ca. 0.8 m thick which were constructed in a polygonal masonry style). Both Koldewey and Axiotis felt unable to date the structure by the accompanying sherd and tile scatter (although Kontis gave a vague report of pottery being found from time to time, the majority of which was 'pre-Hellenistic'). A separate large, circular enclosure (with large 2 m thick walls) stands at the sw. corner of the plateau, and two alonia on the e. and w. sides indicate that this upland area was once under cultivation. The latter is further indicated by the large numbers of terraces on the surrounding slopes which supported cereal crops until recently.

Slightly to the w. of the Palaiokastro site, further up the slopes of Issa, Koldewey noted the terraces of old vineyards and an old press-stone at a spot known as

Pigado.[58] Axiotis added that at this latter location were a large number of thick (probably Byz./Tur.) tiles and potsherds (including pieces of pithoi) and again the whole hillside was covered in old, abandoned terraces.

Bibliography: Koldewey, 39 (with sketch plan), 88; Kontis, 1978, 314-15; Axiotis, 1992 I, 296-98 and II, pl. 63.

124. *Kastrelli* (Parakoila); 531668; 20m; 'MAge', Tur.; HAB, CEM, SP. The ruins of a Tur. settlement which preceded modern Parakoila[59] are visible s. of the present-day village, to the e. of the main Agra-Kalloni road. One focus of the remains is on the rise known as Kastrelli where Axiotis reported that beside a chapel of Agios Georgios was a dense scatter of 'MAge' tiles, potsherds and foundations of old buildings. An aloni is preserved at the nw. foot of the low hill. Nearby stands a ruined mosque with its minaret intact (the lower of two mosques which had existed in the Tur. village), a Tur. cemetery, and a small bath-building of similar date. A kalderimi, preserved for a considerable distance, approaches these remains from the ne., passing over a three-arched Tur. bridge near the mosque.

Bibliography: Moutzouris, 1962, 55, 64-65; Axiotis, 1992 I, 289-90 and II, pl. 62.

125. *Nipos* (Parakoila); 525665; 130m; C./HL.; HAB. On the narrow peak of the Nipos hill, ca. 0.7 km sw. from Parakoila and exactly opposite the remains of the Tur. mosque (#124), Axiotis located a scatter of black-glaze sherds and grey wares, together with fragments of pithoi and amphorae.

Bibliography: Axiotis, 1992 I, 290.

126. *Aetos* (Parakoila); 5066; --; C./HL.; HAB/SP(?). On a plateau of the hill named Aetos, ca. 2.5 kms wsw. from Parakoila, Axiotis described traces of building foundations and defensive walls associated with which were ceramics including black-glazed sherds. This site is not to be confused with that at Bigla also on a hill named Aetos near Agra (#187).

Bibliography: Axiotis, 1992 II, 537.

127. *Chontro Bigli* (Agra); 4864; --; C./HL.; SP. At the place known as Chontro Bigli on the s. slopes of the Mala mountain, ca. 2.5 kms se. from Agra, Axiotis described an extensive area of ruins. A group of substantial, irregularly-shaped walls surround a rocky outcrop on the w. side of the rema which descends the s. side of the mountain, partly built into a modern *mandri*. The walls create a platform on the outcrop, inside which cuttings are apparent on some rocks together with small terrace walls and foundations of more structures, perhaps the remains of a small rural shrine. Over the whole area a scatter of black-glazed sherds, grey wares and tiles were apparent, and a C./HL. female

---

[58] This toponym 'Pigado' may be the spot near Parakoila where Rouse saw ancient remains, which he knew by the name 'Páleo-páti, or the Old Wine-press' (Rouse, 147). Koldewey, 39, also noted similar terrace walls and pieces from press-stones to the n. of Parakoila, one of the latter exhibiting a inscribed cross of Byz. date.

[59] Moutzouris, 1962, 64-65, also suggested that the hill of Kastrelli was where the kastro of 'Parachila' (attested on the map of Lesbos published by Legrand) should be located. These remains at Kastrelli are possibly those spoken of by Taxis, 124.

figurine head was found in the lower section of the enclosure. Slightly to the sw., built into another *mandri*, is the votive stele of two carved footprints (known elsewhere in the region of Eresos, see Conze, 32-33, pl. XIII[60]), and Axiotis also reported more foundations to the w. (with undiagnostic tiles and sherds in association).
Bibliography: Axiotis, 1992 II, 528-29 and pl. 62β.

128. *Lapedia* (Agra); 477644; 270m; HL.; SP. Ca. 2.5 kms se. from Agra, to the w. of the main road which descends to the coast, is the hill of Prophitis Ilias crowned by an old chapel of the same name. On the e. slopes of the hill, just to the w. of the road, is the place known as Lapedia where Koldewey noted the rectangular blocks of a tower near a *mandri*, with dimensions of 11.04 m x 9.2 m. Koldewey reported that some blocks had fallen down the slope and were built into a chapel of Agia Kyriaki in an area known as 'Kudicha'. Five of the blocks at the chapel (four of which formed the door-frame) exhibited holes for clamps on their ends, suggesting to Koldewey that they once formed the window jambs of the tower.
Bibliography: Koldewey, 62, 87 and pl. 27.6; Rouse, 147; Kontis, 1978, 331; Axiotis, 1992 II, 527.

129. *Listis* (Parakoila); 5063/5163; --; C.(?); HAB(?). On the w. side of the Koukmos Bay, ca. 4 kms ssw. from Parakoila, Axiotis described building foundations and a concentration of sherds on a small plateau which descends steeply to the main Agra-Parakoila road running below it to the e.. Amongst the ruins on the plateau (known as Listis), Axiotis described a wall ca. 3 m thick and 2 m high (he gave no details regarding its style of construction). Kontis also marks this site on his settlement pattern maps as dating to the C. period but offered no description of finds in the text.
Bibliography: Kontis, 1978, figs. 21-22; Axiotis, 1992 II, 536-37.

130. *Apothiki* (Agra); 496612; 15m; A., C., HL., R., 'MAge'; HAB, SP. At the small bay of Apothiki, 6 kms sse. from Agra and ca. 4 kms by road n. from Makara (#131), a large rectangular structure (oriented ne.-sw.) stands on the e. slope of a low ridge at the innermost (n.) side of the bay. The main feature of the structure is the massive terrace wall of very large Lesbian polygonal masonry blocks (known locally as 'Kaloktisto' or 'Rodotoicho', see Appendix 2 and figs. 19, 24, 28) 58 m in length and in places over 5 m high which forms the se. wall of a rectangular platform 58 m x 42.2 m. Koldewey and Kiepert visited the site in 1841, and later twice in the 1880s, and their plan indicated a ramp at the sw. end of the structure (also of polygonal masonry) leading up to the artificial platform created by the terrace wall. Divisions of four internal rooms were mapped by Koldewey, the last two extending ne. beyond the end of the terrace wall. Another polygonal wall (possibly part of an altar) lay ca. 40 m further to the sw. directly in line with the ramp of the platform.

A large proportion of the pottery found near and upon the platform is fine ware: black-figure and black-glazed sherds from the site are in the archives of the BSA, and Axiotis spoke of HL. and R. material together with black-glazed tiles. The colossal scale of the terrace wall (very similar to the terrace wall of the temple of Apollo at

Delphi) led Koldewey to suggest that the structure was an A. temple, and the large platform and ramp, together with the ceramics assemblage (and especially the large fragments of glazed tiles), seem conclusive support of this assertion.

Kontis reported that there were other ancient walls higher up the slopes from the main structure including the foundations of houses and also a tower of isodomic masonry which watched over the bay and the entrance to the gulf. Squared blocks from this tower were first seen by Koldewey built into a *mandri* a little upslope from the large platform, and he was also of no doubt that both these blocks, and some others ca. 0.4 km to the ne. of the *mandri*, were from the tower. The similar ancient squared blocks seen by Axiotis built into the Panagia chapel to the sw. of the platform presumably also come from this tower, and near this chapel Koldewey reported a scatter of ancient tiles.

Regarding later activity in the area, Axiotis spoke of 'MAge' ceramics near the Lesbian masonry structure, a report which is of little surprise given the remains of kalderimia which were traced over the hillside near the bay.
Bibliography: Koldewey, 38, 43-44, 62, 87 and pl. 15.1-4; Rouse, 147; Bayne, 247; Kontis, 1973, 81-82 and figs. 45-46; id., 1978, 331, 336-38; Axiotis, 1992 II, 534-36 (and unnumbered photograph p. 524) and pls. 62, 122; id., 1994, fig. Δ; Schaus and Spencer, 416-17 and figs. 2-4; BSA sherd archive Apothiki, unpublished.

131. *Makara* (Agra); 4658/4758; 40m; EBA., LBA., A., C(?), HL., Byz., Tur.; HAB, CEM, SP. Around the small coastal plain of Makara at the w. mouth of the Gulf on Kalloni, a whole series of remains indicate prolonged habitation activity from the EBA.. Sherds dating to the latter period were distinguished by French in the BSA collection from the site, and on the se. arm of the bay (known as Koukkos) Charitonidis noted 3 large cist tombs constructed with massive crudely-worked slabs which were compared with similar LH IIIC tombs on Psara, Chios (at Emporio) and at Eleusis. The tombs stand either side of the road as it turns sharply w. at the mouth of the plain, today appearing as small, open tumuli.

Lower down, on a low ridge immediately w. of the seasonal flow in the middle of the valley, stands one of the two towers of isodomic masonry reported by Koldewey (dimensions 9 m x 9.34 m). On this w. side of the valley Axiotis reported that more graves together with building foundations and an ancient well were discovered previously. Koldewey's other isodomic masonry tower is built into a *mandri* on the hill which overlooks the valley from the w.. Only the n. wall and part of the w. wall survive, the former being 8.59 m in length. A significant scatter of sherds (including grey wares and pithoi) are visible nearby.

More remains are apparent ca. 0.2 km further nw. from this *mandri*, including a tower and associated enclosure of polygonal masonry described by Boutan, Kiepert, Newton and Koldewey in the 19C and more recently by Charitonidis, Kontis and Axiotis. The polygonal walls seem to have been altered significantly since the 19C, however, and it is difficult to reconcile all these reports spanning some 150 years. Kiepert gave the measurements of some Lesbian polygonal masonry walls in the area as ca. 200-250 feet (ca. 66-82 m) in a n.-s. direction, and 70 feet (ca. 23 m) e.-w. (see Appendix 2, section 2.2 and fig. 26); Newton described one wall as 60 paces e.-w. and 14 ft in height, with another wall at right angles to the first 49 paces long. The enclosure noted by Charitonidis in 1961-62, however, was only ca. 25 m x 13 m with the remains of a tower inside, and of this structure today only the

---

[60] The illustration of carved feet in Axiotis (1992 II, pl. 62β) is most similar to those shown in Conze, pl. XIII.1.

enclosure is apparent (of approximately the same dimensions which Charitonidis gives) with no trace of this inner tower. The cistern of polygonal masonry uncovered in 1972 and reported by Kontis also lies amongst this group of remains on the w. side of the valley.

On the rocky ridge which forms the e. arm of the bay (known as Pithos), Axiotis reported an irregular shaped enclosure (ca. 16 m in diameter) with substantial 1.5 m thick walls preserved in places up to 2 m in height. The walls, crudely rebuilt in places, appear to use ancient blocks and are based on foundations formed of two large outer faces of blocks with an inner fill of rubble. A 1 m wide gate is apparent on the nw. side and traces of a less substantial inner wall are apparent on the s. side. A scatter of grey wares is associated with the structure, which may be another tower designed to watch over the e. side of the bay and the entrance to the gulf.

Traces of later (Byz.) and early modern activity in the area are also apparent. Further n. from the spot known as Pithos, Axiotis found worked blocks and walls of mortared tile and stone. In the 19C Anagnostis reported watermills in use at Makara (which are still visible today), whilst Axiotis noted disused alonia in the valley to the n. of the modern hamlet. The extensive areas of terracing all around (observed first by Koldewey and still apparent today) also testify to the previous intense cultivation in an area now devoted nearly entirely to pasturage.

Bibliography: Newton I, 101 and n. 42; Koldewey, 38, 62, 87 (and unnumbered sketch), pl. 27.3 and 27.5; Rouse, 147; Charitonidis, 1960, pl. 210α, δ; id., 1961-62, 265; Paraskeuaidis, 1963, 1416-17; French I, 232 fig. 29a, b1; Buchholz, 123-24, 133-34, 136; Kontis, 1978, 333-35; Axiotis, 1992 II, 529-34 (and unnumbered photographs pp. 532, 537) and pls. 62, 62α, 122; French, 1994, 67; Schaus and Spencer, 415-16 and nn. 26-27; BSA sherd archive Makara, unpublished.

132. *Seistria* (Mesotopos); 420624; 40m; EBA., MBA.(?), EByz.; HAB, SP. At the n. end of the Podaras valley, 1.2 kms se. from Mesotopos, the remains of an EByz. basilica are preserved near a shrine of Agios Eustratios at the place known as Seistria. A *spitaki* on the low slopes nearby has an EByz. architectural block built into it, and near a neighbouring hut are the remains of a mortared tile and stone wall. An apse of similar construction lies in bushes to the e., and other foundations and scattered architectural blocks (of local trachyte and marble) are visible nearby together with ceramics and fragments of ancient glass. More similar worked blocks are apparent both in the valley further to the s. (at the Agios Kyrikos chapel) and also in the village of Mesotopos itself, some of the latter gathered at a small museum and others built into the Panagia church in the village. Probably all the pieces come from the basilica at Seistria. Kontellis and Axiotis reported what may be the accompanying settlement immediately to the e. near the Panagia Trouloti shrine, where house foundations, old cisterns and worked blocks were associated with a dense scatter of EByz. ceramics including sherds from pithoi.

At Palialona, near the EByz. basilica, EBA. (and possibly some MBA.) ceramics, including two nearly whole closed vessels reminiscent of Thermi Class A wares, pithoi fragments and spindle whorls, were found together with a lithic scatter in the property of Papabasileios.

Bibliography: Charitonidis, 1968a, 34; Kontellis, 63-64, 79-81 (and unnumbered illustration p. 79); Axiotis, 1992 II, 519, 522 and pl. 121.

133. *Tabari* (Mesotopos); 398610; 5m; BA., HL., ER., 'MAge'; HAB, SP(?). At the small coastal settlement of Tabari, 2.5 kms ssw. from Mesotopos, traces of older habitations are apparent to the e. of the modern houses near the shore. Over the whole area Axiotis and Balabanis reported sherds of HL., ER. and 'MAge' date including two large pithoi found near the mouth of the seasonal river in the plain. A large aloni nearby is constructed of ancient squared blocks of trachyte exhibiting holes for clamps, and many other similar pieces can be seen built into the *spitakia* near the shore. Axiotis also reported traces of BA. settlement in the plain, but gave no details.

Bibliography: Kontellis, 82-84; Axiotis, 1992 II, 518-19.

134. *Krousos* (Skala Eresou); 370610; 10m; EBA./MBA., C., HL., LR., Byz.; HAB, CEM, SP. Remains of a tower constructed with isodomic blocks were noted in the 19C by Newton and Koldewey at the w. edge of the Krousos plain, 3.5 kms se. from Skala Eresou. The tower measures 9.25 m x 8.7 m and today stands three courses (1-1.5 m) high with a large number of squared blocks scattered around and built into nearby *spitakia*.

Further to the e. in the plain, a ruined chapel dedicated to Agios Georgios exhibits more ancient squared blocks with cuttings for clamps, an unfluted column and a dense scatter of tile and sherds. At this chapel (already ruined and deserted in the 19C), Newton saw a column inscribed with a LR. dedication to Constantine the Great and his sons (now in the village of Mesotopos) together with 'the foundations of an ancient structure'. Presumably the blocks visible today built into the chapel were still *in situ* 150 years ago, and this whole assemblage may therefore be the remains of a small LR. building of similar date to the inscription. Axiotis reported that near these remains on the e. side of the narrow plain, the remains of a Byz. chapel and associated cemetery were located by Balabanis.

Other brief reports of finds in the plain include the following: an amphora of 5C AC date near the shore; other amphorae dating to the C. and HL. periods from the sea near Cape Kopanos (the promontory which forms the plain's w. edge); and during drilling in the plain in 1984, pottery similar to that found at Seistria (#132) of EBA./MBA. date was located 6 m below present ground level.

Bibliography: Newton I, 100-01, Koldewey, 62, 87 and pl. 27.4; Kontis, 1978, 333; Kontellis, 71-73, 85; Archontidou-Argyri, 1986-87, 73; Axiotis, 1992 II, 514-15 and pl. 119.

*135. *Bigla* (Skala Eresou); 352638; 60m; A., C., HL., R., EByz., Ven.; HAB, CEM, SP. The acropolis of ancient Eresos is the rocky hill named Bigla near the shore, immediately se. of the modern settlement of Skala Eresou. Habitation activity on the hill is indicated from the A. through to the EByz. eras, including a R. hypocaust building and the remains of houses found terraced on the steep slopes (one of which exhibited a mosaic floor very similar to that of Agios Andreas, see #136). There are traces of an A. Lesbian polygonal masonry enclosure wall around the hill, including monolithic gate jambs on the e. side (see Appendix 2, sections 2.1, 2.3 and fig. 22) and stretches of later C. and HL. isodomic and pseudo-isodomic walls. The earliest dated surface pottery finds from the acropolis are A., and other sherds of C.-R. date have been reported by the various scholars who have visited the site since the 19C. C., HL., and R. epigraphical evidence is also preserved, and much of the material now has been collected together at the small museum in Skala Eresou.

A capital from an A. votive column or temple was found recently on the beach to the s. of the acropolis (presumably it had fallen from the acropolis' peak).[61] An EByz. basilica may have stood at the nw. foot of the acropolis where part of a curved wall lies near a number of reused EByz. architectural pieces now built into a house (although the latter could conceivably have come from the Agios Andreas basilica, #136).

The approximate location of the town cemeteries is given by Conze, Koldewey and Laskaris, who noted tombs to the nw., n., e. and se. of the acropolis. The majority of these were undiagnostic sarcophagus burials, but one was an A. pithos burial uncovered 0.15 km nw. from Bigla. The harbour of the town lay to the sw. of the acropolis, but the sea has since regressed, masking the harbour's location. The latter was elucidated by the finding of an *in situ* R. block with a large mooring ring to the nw. of the acropolis, now a long way from the sea.

The kastro on the peak of the acropolis (of Byz. origin) is attested by travellers from the early 14C AC.[62] It has both rounded and rectangular external towers and a cistern dug out in the centre of the hilltop.

Bibliography (main); Conze, 27-39 and pls. II, XII-XV; Koldewey, 22-26 and pls. 8-10; Rouse, 147; Taxis, 140; K. Lehmann-Hartleben, *Die Antiken Hafenlagen des Mitelmeeres* (*Klio* supp. 14; Leipzig, 1923), 76-78 and plan 13; Euangelidis, 1925-26, 154-56 and figs. 6-8; Orlandos, 1929, 42 and fig. 45; G. D. Kontis, 'Capitello Eolico di Eresso', *Annuario* 24-26 (1946-48), 25-36; Laskaris; Charitonidis, 1960, 237-39 and pls. 209δ, 210β, 211α; Moutzouris, 1962, 52; Bayne, 246 and fig. 25E; Charitonidis, 1963c, 269 and pl. 311; id., 1964, 397-98, fig. 4 and pl. 464γ; id., 1968a, 34-36, 38-39; Kontis, 1973, 19-20 and fig. 15; Betancourt, 88; Kontis, 1978, 324-29; Papazoglou, 20-42; Acheilara and Archontidou-Argyri, 1986, 200-02 and fig. 6; Archontidou-Argyri, 1986-87, 58, 71, 73; Acheilara and Archontidou-Argyri, 1987, 481 and fig. 5; G. Touchais, 'Chronique des fouilles et découvertes archéologiques en Grèce en 1986', *BCH* 111 (1987), 559; Axiotis, 1992 II, 503-06 (and unnumbered photograph p. 507) and pls. 115-16; Schaus and Spencer, 421-24.

*136. *Agios Andreas* (Skala Eresou); 350640; 5m; EByz., LByz., Tur.; CEM, SP. At the nw. foot of the Bigla hill which formed the acropolis of ancient Eresos (#135) stand the remains of an EByz. basilica dedicated to Agios Andreas. Tradition claims that the worship of Agios Andreas began in 740 AD when Bishop Andreas of Crete died on a voyage back from a synod in Constantinople. The ship carrying him was forced by a storm to put in at Eresos where he was buried beside a large basilica already in existence. A small Byz. chapel was founded above his grave and subsequently became the focus for worship after the basilica fell into disuse in the LByz. and Tur. periods. It was this small chapel dedicated to the saint which Conze reported in 1865, and after the construction of the large church beside both the chapel and the remains of the

basilica in 1936, the older Byz. chapel served simply as a 'mausoleum' for the sarcophagus of the saint.

The EByz. basilica (which stands next to both the 'mausoleum' and the modern church) was first uncovered in 1884 and 1885 by the monks of the Hypsilo and Pithari Monasteries and subsequently was excavated by Orlandos in 1928. Excavations revealed a large two-storey building with a nave, two aisles, mosaic floors and large numbers of architectural pieces. Some scholars have dated the basilica to the first half of the 5C AC on the strength of an inscription found in the excavations,[63] but an older basilica underneath the one excavated equally could be that to which the inscription refers.

Bibliography: Conze, 28; Koldewey, 25; Orlandos, 1928, 325-30 and figs. 4-6; id. 1929, 29-41, figs. 30-34 and pl. II; Sotiriou, 188-89 and fig. 20; Iakobos, 33-34; Charitonidis, 1963c, 269, fig. 2 and pls. 309-11; A. H. S. Megaw, 'Archaeology in Greece, 1963-64', *AR* 10 (1964), 24; Charitonidis, 1968a, 36-38, figs. 19-20 and pls. 14-15; Papazoglou, 81-88; Axiotis, 1992 II, 500-01.

*137. *Aphentellis* (Skala Eresou); 337646; 10m; EByz.; SP. Ca. 1 km w. from Skala Eresou the Prophitis Ilias hill forms the w. limit of the coastal plain, and at the e. foot of this hill Orlandos excavated an EByz. basilica in 1928 in the plot of Aphentellis. The basilica comprised a nave and two flanking aisles (measuring in total 33.77 m x 19.15 m) with a mosaic floor preserved in the nave, and was dated by Euangelidis to the second quarter of the 6C AC on the evidence of an inscription found in association, together with the style of the mosaic.[64] A large number of marble architectural *membra* were excavated with the building. Some of these pieces have now been removed and another piece was reused in the hall of the Agios Konstantinos church in Eresos. Noteworthy small-finds included a small bronze amphoriskos (now in the museum at Skala Eresou).

Bibliography: Orlandos, 1928, 330 and fig. 7; id. 1929, 43-71, figs. 46-79 and pl. III; Sotiriou, 189-90, 237 and figs. 21, 69; Iakobos, 34-35; Charitonidis, 1968a, 38; G. Mastoropoulos, 'Ἀνασκαφικές ἐργασίες', *ArchDelt* 37 (1982), 362-65 and pl. 242; A. Pariente, 'Chronique des fouilles et découvertes archéologiques en Grèce en 1989', *BCH* 114 (1990), 805-06; Papazoglou, 88-95; Axiotis, 1992 II, 508-09.

138. 'Plain of Eresos' (Eresos); --; EBA., A., HL.; CEM, SP. Throughout the plain of Eresos a number of finds have been reported by different scholars without giving precise locations for the findspots. A burnished EBA. body sherd from 'Eresos' (but apparently not from the C. acropolis, Bigla [#135]) exists in the archives of the BSA. Also, Koldewey sketched some marble architectural *membra*, grave stelai and three pieces of small statuary from 'the plain'. Large Doric column drums were found *in situ* near Agios Andreas (#136) in 1931, and at a spot named 'Kapasoula' near Skala Eresou (the precise location of which remains unclear) ancient architectural pieces were incorporated in the modern buildings, including a Doric capital. Two reliefs of Kybele were also noted not far from

---

[61] S. Roumeliotis, pers. comm. (1990). The capital is now on display in Mytilene museum.

[62] The kastro at Eresos is one of those which the Phocaean commander Dominikos Katanis failed to capture in his attack on Lesbos in 1334, and it is also represented on the map of Buondelmonti, where it is shown as having four towers. See Moutzouris, 1962, 52; Axiotis, 1992 II, 505.

[63] The inscription (Orlandos, 1929, 38 [inscription 1]; Axiotis, 1992 II, 500) mentions a bishop Ioannis, equated by some scholars with the bishop of the same name who represented Lesbos at the Synod of Ephesos in 431 AD.

[64] Charitonidis (1968a, 38 and n. 92) placed the basilica slightly earlier at ca. 500 AD.

the ancient acropolis; one, in low relief, near a chapel of Agios Paulos ne. from the acropolis; the other at the chapel of Christos, specifically said to be an 'early' relief. A. architectural remains apparently lie in the private fields and estates in the plain, and tombs with HL. fine ware pottery were once found by Euangelidis 'in the plain'.
Bibliography: Koldewey, 26; Euangelidis, 1925-26, 156; Laskaris, 71; French I, 232 fig. 29a, b1; Archontidou-Argyri, 1986-87, 58, 61, 73; Acheilara and Archontidou-Argyri, 1987, 482 and pl. 290β; Pariente, 872; BSA sherd archive Eresos, unpublished.

139. *Tholos* (Eresos); 335679; 100m; R.; HAB. Ca. 1.5 kms w. from Eresos on the road to Sigri, just before the road turns sharply s., a spring lies to the left (s.) from the road near a large plane tree. The area is known as Tholos after the knoll nearby. Throughout the olive grove is a dense scatter of sherds including grey wares (which could date to any point from the BA.-HL. periods), R. *terra sigilata* and tile fragments. Foundations of a narrow structure are visible nearby together with other worked blocks and alonia. The surrounding area also exhibits the remains of old, disused terracing.
Bibliography: Axiotis, 1992 II, 488; Schaus and Spencer, fig. 11.

140. *Blitsi* (Eresos); 314682; 40m; HL.; SP. Heading e. in the valley of the Tsichliontas River along the road from Sigri to Eresos, the road crosses the river 3 kms w. from Eresos (an older ruined bridge stands beside the new one). As the road continues to the e., six old alonia stand on the lower slopes of the Blitsi hill to the s. of the road (indicating that cultivation was once practised in this now barren valley). Amongst these alonia and associated *mandria* are the foundations of two (probably HL.) towers of isodomic masonry, and a number of the well-cut blocks have been re-used in modern structures nearby. The threshold block of the lower tower is built into the *mandri* which stands in front of it. A dense scatter of undiagnostic plain sherds and tiles is associated with the structures.
Bibliography: Axiotis, 1992 II, 487 and pls. 109-10.

141. *Spilios* (Eresos) 311687; 10m; A; HAB, SP. At the n. edge of the Tsichliontas plain, low down on the s. slopes of the Chamandroula hill, a boustrophedon inscription (probably of 6C date) was found on a stele of grey trachyte at a place known as Spilios. The surface is badly damaged and very few words can be read. Further upslope on the same hill (to the n.), Koumarelas noted an enclosure of large unworked stones inside which were the foundations of houses, one of which exhibited the 'megaron' plan seen on the Lesbados hill closeby (#144). No associated finds were reported.
   A short distance to the sw., the neighbouring spur of the Chamandroula hill (known as Kopetri) has the remains of a rectangular structure 18 m x 15.5 m constructed with coursed polygonal masonry. The s. and w. walls are best preserved (width 0.7 m) and the blocks exhibit cuttings for clamps still with traces of lead inside. Walls creating internal divisions are visible within the outer rectangular wall.
Bibliography: Charitonidis, 1964, 397 and fig. 3; G. Daux, 'Chronique des fouilles et découvertes archéologiques en Grèce en 1966', *BCH* 91 (1967), 741-42 and fig. 4; Charitonidis, 1968b, no. 135 (p. 92) and pl. 46β; Kontis, 1978, 332; Axiotis, 1992 II, 487 and pl. 108.

142. *Meladia* (Eresos); 329703; 40m; HL.; SP. At the place known as Meladia, ca. 3.5 kms nw. from Eresos in the Tsichliontas valley, a group of *mandria* beside a chapel of the Panagia incorporate the remains of a square tower of isodomic masonry, with sides 11.3 m in length and preserved up to 1.6 m in height. The w. and s. sides are in the best state of preservation, but the blocks which formed the other sides have largely been removed for building stone when the *mandria* were constructed. Neither of the brief reports concerning the site give details of any associated ceramics.[65]
Bibliography: Axiotis, 1992 II, 488 and pl. 109; Koumarelas, 1995, 44, fig. 1a-b (pp. 42-43) and map (p. 41).

143. *Skordalos* (Sigri); 303677; 25m; --; --. Beside a chapel of the Panagia, at the w. foot of the Skordalos hill (ca. 5 kms sse. from Sigri), Axiotis described the foundations of a structure which he stated to be a tower, but no measurements or associated finds are given to further define the remains.
Bibliography: Axiotis, 1992 II, 487 and pl. 110.

144. *Lesbados* (Sigri); 295684; 20m; A., HL./R(?); HAB, SP. Ca. 4.5 kms sse. from Sigri, the coast road from Sigri turns inland towards Eresos in the plain of the Tsichliontas River. The hill which forms the n. border of the plain is known as Lesbados, and low down on its s. slopes are a cluster of ancient building remains. A newly built chapel of the Panagia lies immediately s. of the road, and opposite (20 m above the road) a large worked stone stands upright representing one gatepost of a square enclosure, the foundations of which are visible to the n. and e. (constructed in polygonal masonry). Further uphill to the n. are the foundations of buildings, including one of the 'megaron-shape' structures reported by Charitonidis and Kontis. Around this group of remains is a concentration of ceramics including tiles, bases of amphorae and grey ware sherds. The nearby chapel has reused a number of ancient blocks including door jambs and a threshold slab. Axiotis also reported pieces of unfluted columns (of trachyte and marble), the base of a perirrhantirion and a block possibly from an ancient altar.
Bibliography: Charitonidis, 1964, 397 and fig. 3; Kontis, 1978, 332; Axiotis, 1992 II, 484-85 (and unnumbered photograph p. 486) and pls. 108, 110.

145. *Pharkobnar* (Sigri); 2970; --; A.(?); HAB/SP(?). On the hill named Pharkobnar, ca. 2 kms sse. from Sigri and immediately se. of the Tur. hani (#146), Axiotis reported the remains of a rectangular enclosure 15.6 m x 26 m, the walls of which were said to be constructed of Lesbian polygonal masonry (see Appendix 2). No associated

[65] A further tower in this area which it is impossible to place accurately on a map is reported by Koumarelas at a place known as 'Bali Alonia' or 'Taphios', 'ca. 1 km further north [from the tower at Meladia, #142]'. Koumarelas reported a tower measuring 10 x 6.1 m, the n. wall of which has pseudo-isodomic masonry preserved. Traces of house foundations and a group of five tombs are apparent nearby also. See B. Koumarelas, 'Ενας άγνωστος πύργος της αρχαίας Ερέσου', *Aiolika Nea* (19/6/94), 15; id., 1995, 44 and fig. 2 (p. 43). A number of the other remains noted by Koumarelas in the west of the island near Eresos (1995, 44-45 and figs. 3-10), comprising towers and enclosures of isodomic, coursed polygonal and Lesbian polygonal masonry are impossible to locate on the maps of either the British Army or Axiotis.

ceramics were described, and it is impossible to elucidate the precise location of the structure from Axiotis' brief report.

Bibliography: Axiotis, 1992 II, 483-84.

146. *Pharkonias* (Sigri); 288708; 20m; Tur.; HAB. On the coastal road which proceeds s. and then e. from Sigri to Eresos, ca. 2 kms sse. from Sigri, the road bridges the small ravine of the Pharkonias River, and immediately s. of the river the ruins of a Tur. hani (incorporating an old cheese-factory) stand on the e. side of the road. The building is a large square structure with a high wall around its courtyard, and inside a complex of buildings including storerooms and *mandria* face inwards towards the central building. A water supply is provided by a nearby spring. In the walls of the hani's courtyard are a number of ancient blocks, some with cuttings and dowel holes, and Axiotis described foundations of an older structure beside the hani, possibly the structure from which the ancient blocks had originated.

Bibliography: Axiotis, 1992 II, 483.

*147. *Megalonisi* (Sigri); 269722; 10m; BA.(?), EByz.; CEM, SP. On the rocky, s. point of the small islet 1.5 kms wsw. from Sigri, Koldewey was the first to report ruins at a spot known by the Turks as 'Eski-Kilissa' (or 'Old Church'). A subsequent excavation carried out in this same area in 1952 (beside a modern chapel of Agios Georgios) revealed the remains of an EByz. basilica. The basilica was a small structure, almost square (10.75 m x 10.20 m). A number of the architectural pieces of marble and trachyte found during the excavation have been gathered together inside the apse, including Doric and Ionic column capitals. At the e. side of the basilica a tomb was located, covered by thin marble slabs. On this s. end of the islet, near the basilica, Axiotis noted a scatter of sherds (including amphorae bases) and tiles.

Also on the islet near Agios Georgios, Roland reported two shallow pits (one on either side of the chapel) 'four feet long, two feet wide and three feet deep'. Inside each pit was a skeleton,

> seated in a crouching position, the knees drawn up, both arms crossed above them and the head bowed down to rest on these. One of them wore a bracelet and they assumed it was a woman but when they touched it, it crumbed to dust and there was nothing they could salvage out of the grave.

Despite their proximity to the chapel, typologically these crouched burials cannot be Christian[66] and would seem best-placed in the BA., but this can only be a working hypothesis since no ceramics or other grave goods were recovered.

Bibliography: Koldewey, 85; Charitonidis, 1960, 238; Daux, 1960, 808; B. Roland, *Lesbos: the pagan island* (Melbourne, 1963), 122; Charitonidis, 1968a, 39 and pl. 16α; Axiotis, 1992 II, 735 and pl. 105.

*148. *Paliokastro* (Sigri); 286740; 10m; R.(?), LR.-Byz., Ven., 'MAge', Tur.; HAB, SP. The medieval kastro at Sigri (probably originally of Ven. date, see below) stands on the n. end of the Bay of Sigri, ca. 1.5 kms n. from the modern settlement, and was originally equated with ancient Antissa by Conze (a mistake later corrected by Koldewey).

Foundations of another structure to the w. of the kastro were seen by Axiotis (perhaps an earlier fortification), and 0.2 km to the n. the remains of an EByz. basilica were excavated by villagers. Of the latter, the wall of the apse was preserved up to ca. 1 m in height and an associated group of rooms were found beside it. Column capitals and architectural pieces were recovered in the excavation, and Axiotis reported that a large pile of worked blocks, architectural *membra*, tiles and sherds are visible near the site of the basilica today. The column drums and base which Koldewey saw to the e. of the kastro in the 19C may also have originated from the basilica, although Koldewey thought the column base to be R..

The whole shore between the kastro and the basilica is covered in ceramics including sherds from pithoi, pointed-based amphorae and tiles (including some with a whitish glaze). In the 19C 'MAge' walls of mortared stone were also visible in the same area, and further ne., on the hill known as Adamania, Axiotis described more foundations of mortared small stones, LR.-Byz. 'combed' wares, pithoi fragments, 'MAge' glazed sherds and millstones. Ca. 50 m to the e. of the track which heads n. past the kastro are the parts of clay pipes together with a mortared tile and stone wall, suggested by Axiotis to be the remains of an aqueduct, and Koldewey found evidence of another water channel running along the shore s. of the kastro.

The post-antique kastro and associated settlement at Sigri has a *terminus ante quem* of the early 15C, since Buondelmonti refers to a kastro at 'Secri' in Lesbos which is probably to be equated with that at Sigri. Ottoman records attest to a settlement at Sigri in 1602,[67] but soon afterwards both the kastro and any associated settlement had been reduced almost to nothing, with Gabriel of Methymna stating (in 1636-41[68]) that the place 'was once a great town, but now only foundations remain in some places'.

Bibliography: Conze, 25-26 and pls. I-Ia; Koldewey, 37-38; Taxis, 139; Charitonidis, 1960, 238 and pl. 210γ; Daux, 1960, 809; Moutzouris, 1962, 55, 68; Charitonidis, 1968a, 39-40, fig. 21 and pls. 16β-17; Kontis, 1978, 338; Axiotis, 1992 II, 478-79, and pls. 104-05; id., 1994, fig. Δ.

149. *'Kusu-Mandrassi'* (Sigri); 3073; --; HL., SP. Koldewey reported the remains of a tower of isodomic masonry e. from Sigri on the hill of 'Kusu-Mandrassi' which was almost destroyed even by the time of his visit in 1885. The only details of the location which he gives in his main text are that the hill is part of the ridge to the w. of the Tsichliontas valley, and that the Bay of Sigri could be watched from the tower. The compass bearings from the tower which he provides in his travel diary (p. 85, journey #47) need to be corrected,[69] but when this is done they place the tower in approximately the same place as Kontis does, near the w. edge of the Tsichliontas valley and in a place where a view to the sea is possible. Even in the 19C many of the blocks had been removed from the site and

---

[66] Eric Ivison, pers. comm. (1995).

[67] M. Kiel, pers. comm. (1995). Concerning an earlier 16C Ottoman census of the island, see n. 4 above.

[68] For this dating of Gabriel's text, see n. 47.

[69] The bearings which are given suggest that the compass was held the wrong way up since the Palaiokastro of Sigri (#148) is said to be at 92° from the tower (ie. east) and the Hypsilo Monastery (#174) at 267° (ie. west) when the opposite must be true. If the bearings are altered so that they are the opposite of what Koldewey records, then the tower would be in the same area as that suggested by Kontis.

used to construct a *mandri* nearby, and these were probably the same isodomic blocks (some with cuttings for clamps) seen recently by Koumarelas built into two *mandria* on a hill named 'Chourmadia' just above (ie. to the e. of) Sigri (the precise location is unclear). Koldewey noted among the worked blocks one with a carving of a kantharos-style vessel in low relief, 0.42 m in length the top of which had been broken.
Bibliography: Koldewey, 62 (with unnumbered illustration), 85; Kontis, 1978, 330; Koumarelas, 1995, 45 and map (p. 41).

150. *Pigados* (Sigri); 3072; --; --; HAB. On the ridgetop known as Pigados, ca. 2 kms e. from Sigri,[70] Axiotis noted that some of the cluster of modern walls around a *mandri* and well were based upon ancient foundations. The nearby well from which the area takes its name is constructed of ancient blocks, and more foundations of rectangular rooms are visible to the e. and n. of the *mandri* (with walls ca. 0.7-0.8 m thick). Some of the walls are said to be constructed in a polygonal style of masonry, and all over the plateau Axiotis reported a dense scatter of ceramics (but gave no details).
Bibliography: Axiotis, 1992 II, 482.

151. *Oikia* (Sigri); 3273; 200m; HL.; SP. Ca. 4 kms ene. from Sigri, to the s. of the main road from Sigri to Antissa, Koldewey noted the remains of two towers of isodomic masonry at a place named Oikia (or 'Sta Oikia'). The towers stand in a narrow valley which runs n.-s., eventually joining that of the Tsichliontas River, and therefore are located on a significant route of communication in the w. of the island.

The first tower (visible today only as foundations), stands ca. 0.3 km s. of the main road on the w. slope of the valley, and only parts of the e. and s. walls survive together with the nw. corner (Koldewey gave the dimensions as 8.3 m x 8.26 m, Axiotis 9 m x 7 m). Inner dividing walls of small stones joined with clay were clearer at the time of the visits of Koldewey and Kontis than they are today. Axiotis saw a large block on the s. side of the structure which he suggested was the threshold for the doorway (Koldewey also placed the doorway on the s. side).

Ca. 0.4 km se. from the first tower, on the facing e. side of the valley, Axiotis gave a description and plan of the confusing cluster of walls and building foundations part of which Koldewey interpreted as the two sides of another tower (neither of which seemed complete). The walls of isodomic masonry which were visible in the 19C are still apparent, as is the large threshold block built into another structure slightly to the w. (which itself overlies a small rectangular building). More worked blocks have fallen down the slopes nearby into the valley floor, where a spring and a (now disused) trough for animals also incorporate a number of ancient blocks. Near the foundations on the e. side of the valley, and on the valley floor between the two towers, Axiotis reported scatters of ceramics and a disused *aloni* beside an old *mandri*.
Bibliography: Koldewey, 62 and pl. 27.1-2; Charitonidis, 1964, 397; Kontis, 1978, 330; Axiotis, 1992 II, 470-71, 474, and pls. 103-05.

152. *Paliochorion* (Sigri); 305752; 20m; 'MAge'; HAB. In a narrow valley to the e. of the large coastal plain n. from Sigri, at a place known as Paliochorion, a number of settlement remains are apparent near a chapel of Agia Paraskeui (which was in ruins when Koldewey visited the area but seems now to have been rebuilt). Koldewey reported antiquities (including a stone inscribed with a 14 cm high 'Ω') together with 'MAge' ceramics and worked blocks built into the ruined chapel. Axiotis also saw these blocks in the chapel and spoke of foundations of buildings, tiles and sherds (including pithoi).
Bibliography: Koldewey, 37; Charitonidis, 1960, 238 and pl. 211δ; Kontis, 1978, 316; Axiotis, 1992 I, 480 and II, pl. 105.

153. *Agios Nikolaos* (Sigri); 313762; 10m; LR.-Byz., LByz.-Tur.; HAB, CEM, SP. On the s. side of the valley through which the Tapsas River flows, 4 kms ne. from Sigri (and 1 km ne. from Paliochorion, #152), the apse and part of the n. wall of an EByz. basilica are visible beside the newly rebuilt chapel of Agios Nikolaos. The remainder of the basilica lies under the modern chapel. The basilica walls are constructed of mortared tile and stone, and at the site a number of marble architectural *membra* (including unfluted columns and column capitals) remain. A few metres to the e. of the chapel and basilica is an old springhead from where the water was once channelled using clay guttering (which is still apparent).

The basilica near the Agios Nikolaos chapel seems to mark the s. boundary of a settlement which extended across the river to the n. as far as the chapel of Agia Anna (into which more architectural pieces from the basilica are built). Onto this n. side of the river valley extends a dense scatter of tiles, sherds (including LR.-Byz. 'combed' wares, pithoi, and glazed, probably Byz.-Tur., sherds), more pieces of marble and worked blocks. Also, foundations of walls have been discovered here during cultivation work. Ca. 0.2 km sw. from the chapel of Agia Anna, near an old *spitaki*, a rock-cut tomb is visible, presumably to be associated with the nearby settlement.
Bibliography: Charitonidis, 1960, 238 and pl. 211γ; Daux, 1960, 809; Charitonidis, 1968a, 40 and pl. 18α-β; Axiotis, 1992 II, 480-81 and pls. 105-06.

154. *Tsouloumountas* (Sigri); 326785; 140m; R.; HAB. Ca 7.5 kms nne. from Sigri, the small hamlet of Tsouloumountas stands on the n. slopes of the Kophinida hill overlooking Cape Petinos at the nw. tip of the island.[71] At this location Koldewey reported an ancient press-stone together with sherd and tile scatters (including a large pithos rim). A R. marble column base (ca. 0.49 m in diameter) was built into the ruin of a small chapel (which was being used in the 19C as a *mandri*), but it is unclear whether it originally came from elsewhere.
Bibliography: Koldewey, 37; Kontis, 1978, 316; Axiotis, 1992 I, 481 and II, pl. 105.

155. *Tsiphos* (Gabathas); 354798; 20m; HL., R., LR.-Byz., 'MAge'; HAB, SP. On the e. arm of the Lapsarna Bay, 4 kms w. from Gabathas, the remains of a significant site were first noted by Koldewey on the w. slopes of the Tsiphos hill and subsequently visited by Charitonidis,

---

[70] The hill described by Axiotis may be that labelled as 'Khamandroula' on the 1943 British Army map (Grid Ref. 3071-3072)

[71] There are two promontories on the n. coast of the island known as Cape Petinos, this one at the far nw. tip of the island (Grid Ref. 3180), and another further e. between ancient Antissa and modern Petra (Grid Ref. 5083).

Kontis and Axiotis. On the lower w. slopes of the hill near the shore, an extremely dense scatter of sherds and tile associated with walls of houses (up to 5 m high in the 19C) indicated the remains of a large settlement. Axiotis noted R. *terra sigilata* and LR.-Byz. 'combed' wares, handles and bases of amphorae, pithoi fragments and yellowy-buff glazed sherds (of 'MAge' date) to add to the red glazed and polished sherds reported by Koldewey. Kontis gave a more general report of similar nature, namely that R. material abounded at the site but the periods represented also indicated activity up to the 'MAges'.

In the middle of this scatter the old chapel of Agios Antonios exhibits architectural blocks of EByz. date, and many other marble and trachyte elements were noted nearby by Koldewey and Charitonidis. These pieces probably originated from an EByz. basilica which once stood near the shore, a site now occupied by the chapel of Agios Panteleimonas. In recent years digging near this chapel revealed the conch of a basilica constructed with mortared tile and stone, a doorway, and large amounts of tiles and sherds.

Bibliography: Koldewey, 36-37; Charitonidis, 1968a, 41 and pl. 19β-γ; Kontis, 1978, 316; Axiotis, 1992 I, 445-46 and II, pl. 96-98α.

156. *Sal-taschi* (Gabathas); 378793; --; --; HAB. On the w. coast of the Gabathas promontory, ca. 1.7 kms sw. from the modern settlement, at a place known as Sal-taschi, Koldewey reported the remains of an 'ancient farm'. This report was repeated by Kontis with no additional detail.
Bibliography: Koldewey, 37, 85; Kontis, 1978, 316.

157. *Pyrgo* (Gabathas); 388792; 15m; EBA., R., LR.-Byz., 'MAge', Tur.; HAB, SP. At the se. foot of the Koukla hill (a spot known as Pyrgo) which borders the settlement of Gabathas to the w., Axiotis located a dense scatter of sherds including R. *terra sigilata*, LR.-Byz. 'combed' wares and 'MAge' glazed sherds. Trachyte and marble worked blocks of EByz. date were scattered nearby, and the digging of wells in the area located structural remains of mortared small stones. Sections of an aqueduct together with a number of cisterns are also preserved up on the hillslopes known as Lygeri further to the sw..[72] Kontis asserted that at Lygeri there was an ancient quarry, but no such remains have been noted by Axiotis or any other scholar.

On the Koukla hill itself Axiotis found coarse 'Prehistoric' (probably EBA.) black sherds, a lithic scatter, press-stones and a millstone.

The Panagia chapel in the hamlet of Liota which stands on the hill adjoining Koukla to the s. has wall-paintings of 17C AC date on the n. wall and EByz. architectural *membra* can be seen in the courtyard. Parts of an old kalderimi are preserved around the settlement.[73] To the w. of the settlement, a pair of low knolls on the hill show the remains of houses constructed with dry-stone walls. On the slopes to the s. of the e. knoll, Axiotis reported red, grey and black burnished EBA. sherds, lithics, grinding stones and sea-pebbles.

Bibliography: Kontis, 1978, 316; Axiotis, 1992 I, 437-40, 448 (and unnumbered photograph p. 440) and II, pls. 87, 95.

158. *Agioi Archangeloi* (Gabathas); 398798; 40m; EBA., R., EByz., Byz./Tur.; HAB(?), CEM, SP. On the e. arm of the Gabathas bay is a low rocky plateau with cliffs on its n. and w. sides. A small, newly-built chapel stands on this plateau, known as 'Agioi Archangeloi', and during the construction of the new chapel in 1964 the remains of an EByz. basilica were uncovered. Bedrock formed the w. wall of the chapel, and within the narthex were two rock-cut graves (noted first by Koldewey).[74] Charitonidis and Axiotis reported a number of architectural pieces from the basilica nearby made of grey marble and red trachyte (including an Ionic column capital), and Axiotis also stated that the whole coastal plateau was covered by a dense scatter of ceramics amongst which was R. *terra sigilata*.

Axiotis described the lower plateau (to the s. and e. of the chapel) as being covered with ceramic scatters of Byz./Tur. date. The same scholar noted also that crudely made black, red and buff 'Prehistoric' (probably EBA.) sherds, together with a scatter of lithics and a press-stone, were found in the same area.
Bibliography: Koldewey, 37 (with unnumbered sketch); Charitonidis, 1965, 494 and pl. 629β; id., 1968a, 42 and pl. 20; Axiotis, 1992 I, 436-37 and II, pl. 95.

159. *Agios Georgios* (Gabathas); 398787; 10m; LR.-Byz., LByz./Tur.; HAB. In the coastal plain ca. 1.4 km sse. from Gabathas, a chapel of Agios Georgios stands on the n. side of the main road which leads s. to modern Antissa (Telonia). A number of EByz. architectural elements are built into the chapel, mostly made of trachyte, but including also column capitals of grey marble and an inscribed marble stele (*CIG* 8900) visible at the nw. corner. Ancient architectural *membra* built into the chapel of the Panagia in the village of Tzithra are also said to come from this building. There is no evidence to suggest, however, that the elements at the Agios Georgios chapel are *in situ*, and they may have been brought from elsewhere (possibly from Agioi Archangeloi, #158). There are traces of habitation activity nearby, however, since the field adjoining the chapel is covered with an extremely dense scatter of sherds and tiles, including LR.-Byz. 'combed' wares, handles and bases of amphorae, and glazed sherds (probably of LByz./Tur. date).
Bibliography: Charitonidis, 1968a, 42 and pl. 19α; Axiotis, 1992 I, 434-35 and II, pls. 87, 95.

160. *Tsephos* (Gabathas); 418793; 167m; EBA.(?); HAB(?). On the peak of the Tsephos hill which divides the plains of Gabathas and ancient Antissa, 3 kms ese. from Gabathas, Axiotis noted the remains of an irregularly-shaped small structure 3.76 m (n.-s.) x 3.5 m (e.-w.). The foundations stand on the ne. side of the peak, and only the lowest course are now preserved. Associated with the structure were plain red and grey ware sherds. On the same hill Axiotis noted a press-stone, spindle-whorl and lithic scatter, suggested to be of 'Prehistoric' date (although none are particularly diagnostic).
Bibliography: Axiotis, 1992 I, 437 and II, pl. 98β.

---

[72] In the 19C the water of this area (near Liota) was known for its cathartic properties, see Axiotis, 1992 I, 438.
[73] A Tur. settlement at 'Gavathas' is attested in 1602, M. Kiel, pers. comm. (1995). Concerning an earlier 16C Ottoman census of the island, see n. 4 above.

---

[74] An inscribed EByz. funerary stele (*IG* XII.2.525) is also said to have come from Gabathas, see Charitonidis, 1968a, 42.

*161. *Obriokastro* (Gabathas); 430808; 10m; EBA.(?), MBA., LBA., EG.-LG., A., C., HL., R., Byz., Ven., Tur.; HAB, CEM, SP. The site of ancient Antissa, one of the six original Archaic *poleis* of Lesbos, was identified by Koldewey on the n. shore of the island 5.5 kms nw. from Skalochori at the promontory of Obriokastro, a promontory now crowned by the ruins of a Ven. kastro.[75] The earliest evidence for settlement activity at the site may date to the EBA. (Mellaart is said to have identified sherds from Antissa as being of Troy II period). There are significant LBA. strata on the promontory including substantial walls extending below sea level. Myc. sherds are also associated with a wall on the acropolis, and details of more (unpublished) LMyc. sherds exist in the archives of the BSA. Bayne dated the LBA. grey wares to the LH IIIB-C period (with LH IIIB predominating).

The first traces of an EIA. reoccupation date from the EG. period with successive MG., LG. and A. strata. The settlement traces of these periods are concentrated at the n. foot of the acropolis (where the digging of wells has located foundations with associated ceramics, inscriptions and worked blocks), and a large cemetery (LG.-C.) was excavated by Lamb to the se. of the acropolis with the tombs lying in three main groups. Åkerström reported architectural terracottas of A. date and Lamb also excavated a (probably 4C) stoa building overlying an A. street. Later HL. structural remains survive together with R. sherds (the latter within the walls of the ruined kastro). The traces of an ancient harbour mole lie submerged in the sea immediately to the e. of the acropolis (known as the 'Kokkino Limani'), an area where the shore is covered with a dense scatter of ceramics.

The ruined Ven. kastro (now overlying the promontory) had a Byz. predecessor, probably that known as 'Agioi Theodoroi' in early travellers accounts, which housed within its walls the Monastery of Odigitria (attested in 1331 and abandoned in 1462[76]). Axiotis reported a scatter of glazed (probably Byz.) pottery amongst the rubble within the kastro which would support this identification. The associated settlement of Agioi Theodoroi is attested in Ottoman records in 1602[77] but was abandoned later, certainly by the 17C, since in 1636-41 the Methymnaean Gabriel spoke of the area as deserted[78] and in 1690 the French traveller Dumont saw only ruins and no settlement at the spot.

Bibliography (main): Koldewey, 19-21, 84-85 and pls. 6-7; Rouse, 147; Taxis, 133; Lamb, 1930-31; Payne, 1931, 202-03; Lamb, 1931-32; Payne, 1932, 251; id., 1933, 284-86 and figs. 10-11; Moutzouris, 1962, 54, 65-66; Bayne, 118-22, 230-40 and figs. 4.XI, 14.A1-17, 17.3, 17.5, 17.15-16, 24-25A; Åkerström I, 31; Chatzi, 1972, 580 and pls. 531α-β, δ; ead., 1973, 517-19 and pls. 487-8, 489β-γ; Buchholz, 123-24, 133, 137; Kontis, 1973, 19 and fig. 14; id., 1978, 306-11; Axiotis, 1992 I, 401-06 (and unnumbered photograph p. 402) and II, pls. 88-89; BSA W. Lamb archive, unpublished.

162. *Kouphi* (Skalochori); 4379/4479; --; C./HL.; HAB(?), SP. On the n. slopes of the Kouphi hill, ca. 4 kms wnw. from Skalochori, Axiotis described the hollow chamber of an ancient trachyte quarry. Above the quarry, the remains of a 2 m thick wall formed of two outer faces of blocks and a rubble fill can be traced along the hilltop for ca. 0.1 km. To the s. of this wall a piece of bedrock has been flattened, creating a table (suggested by Axiotis to be an altar) and a scatter of sherds nearby included C./HL. black-glazed pieces.
Bibliography: Axiotis, 1992 I, 406-07.

163. *Salbaradis*[79] (Skalochori); 446805; 40m; EByz., LByz.-Tur.(?); SP. In the region known as Salbaradis, 1 km sw. from the Kalos Limenas harbour (see #164), a small LByz./post-Byz. chapel named Agios Theodoros stands on the s. side of the coast road which leads w. to Obriokastro. Beside the chapel, fragments of the walls and apse of an EByz. basilica are apparent. The mass of large stones nearby are the sole remnants of the other walls. A column capital and another EByz. architectural block were noted by Charitonidis, but neither remained when Axiotis revisited the site recently.
Bibliography: Charitonidis, 1963c, 272 and pl. 313β; id., 1966, 73 and pl. VIβ; id., 1968a, 43; Axiotis, 1992 I, 400-01.

164. *Panagia Kokkinou* (Skalochori); 453808; 10m; EByz., Tur.; HAB, SP. To the s. and w. sides of the small hamlet at the harbour of Kalos Limenas (also known by its Tur. name of 'Tsamour-limani'), 4 kms nw. from Skalochori, Charitonidis reported the remains of Byz. and Tur. habitation activity. A settlement at the 'Kalos Limin' ('Καλὸς Λιμήν') is attested in the description of Lesbos by Gabriel of Methymna dated to 1636-41,[80] and Axiotis noted a dense scatter of ceramics in the area of the harbour.

Beside the harbour, Charitonidis described a thick wall of mortared tile, and on the e. side of this wall has been erected a chapel to the Panagia. A large number of EByz. architectural *membra* are built into the modern chapel, suggesting that the mortared tile wall may well be the remaining part of an EByz. basilica. Nearby, to the sw. of the harbour, are the ruins of a chapel dedicated to Agios Nikolaos into which another worked EByz. block has been built, presumably also from the basilica beside the chapel of the Panagia.
Bibliography: Charitonidis, 1968a, 42-43 and pl. 21α; Axiotis, 1992 I, 400 and II, pl. 88.

165. *Kastri* (Skalochori); 451779; 400m; A.; SP. The hill of Kastri stands ca. 2.5 kms wnw. from Skalochori and is most easily approached from the e. along the track which bears right from the main road from Skalochori to Batousa (0.5 kms w. from Skalochori). The peak of the hill lies some 2 kms further w. from the main road, and on its n.

---

[75] Koldewey, 19-21, 84-85 and pls. 6-7. The site of ancient Antissa had been wrongly placed previously by Conze on the west coast of the island just north of the modern village of Sigri, Conze, 25-26 and pl 1a (see #148). It seems that both Pococke and Kiepert previously had visited the correct location of the site, however; the former in the mid-eighteenth century and the latter on 28th October 1841, making Conze's erroneous placing of the site all the more puzzling: Pococke, 18; Koldewey, 84-85 (for the visit of Kiepert).

[76] The inhabitants of Agioi Theodoroi fled to n. Evia with the arrival of the Turks in 1462 and on 10th June 1463 the Venetian admiral Orsatus Giustiniani helped to evacuate those who remained at the site on the pretext that their pro-Venetian sympathies would illicit severe penalties from the Turks.

[77] M. Kiel, pers. comm. (1995). Concerning an earlier 16C Ottoman census of the island, see n. 4 above.

[78] For this dating of Gabriel of Methymna's description of Lesbos, see n. 47.

[79] Charitonidis (1968a, 43) employs an alternative toponym for this spot, 'Kephalos'.

[80] See n. 47.

edge Kontis noted an irregular, approximately circular, construction of Lesbian polygonal masonry (see Appendix 2, section 2.2) with dimensions of 23 m (n.-s.) x 20 m (e.-w.). When Kontis saw the site the walls stood to 1.5 m, and were 2.25 m thick (a similar state of preservation is apparent today). Axiotis added that the walls were constructed of two large faces of outer blocks with a fill of rubble between and that the best preserved sections are on the n., w. and s. sides. Moreover, Axiotis noted traces of foundations within the outer enclosure wall amongst which were squared blocks and a scatter of tiles, suggesting an inner roofed structure. Both Kontis and Axiotis spoke of a sherd scatter in association with the structure, which included grey wares.

As with the other enclosures of Lesbian masonry near Skalochori, the views from Kastri are extensive. To the n. Antissa is visible; the two valleys on the n. and s. sides of the hill which lead down towards the Boulgaris plain and ancient Antissa (the Saitan Deres and Katopetra respectively) are also overlooked; further to the e., beyond Koutlougouni (#190), Koja Dag (#193), Prophitis Ilias (#194) and Phonias (#195), Methymna can be seen 16 kms to the ne..
Bibliography: Kontis, 1973, 58-60, 82 and fig. 34; id., 1978, 312; Koumarelas, 1989a, 4; id., 1989b, 3; id., 1989c, 3; Axiotis, 1992 I, 408 and II, pl. 87.

166. *Apastra* (Gabathas); 4277/4278; --; A./C.(?), EByz; SP. On the e. bank of the Boulgaris River, ca. 3.5 kms ese. from the settlement at Gabathas (and ca. 3 kms ssw. from Obriokastro), a tributary joins the main body of the river from the e. at Apastra. At this junction, Axiotis reported that Koumarelas had found a circular enclosure of Lesbian polygonal masonry (see Appendix 2) and the foundations of a rectangular structure within it. Nearby to the s., on the lower slopes of the Ypnia hill, the same scholar found another rectangular structure of polygonal masonry. Axiotis gives no further details of the structures, or any associated ceramics, but presumed both to be part of a defence system on the approaches towards ancient Antissa which lies to the n..

Axiotis also reported that slightly to the ne. of these structural remains, near a chapel of Agios Konstantinos, EByz. architectural *membra* were apparent.
Bibliography: Axiotis, 1992 I, 406 and II, pl. 110.

167. *Monastiri tis Peribolis* (Tzithra); 413760; 150m; Byz.(?), Tur.; SP. As the road from Batousa to Antissa descends to ford the Boulgaris River, a road leads n. to the small, deserted Periboli Monastery (ca. 1.8 kms nne. from Tzithra) which stands above the e. bank of the river. The main church is nearly square in plan and exhibits wall-paintings dating from the end of the 16C AC and the mid-17C (which are now crumbling). No earlier records attest the existence of the monastery, and whether it existed in the Byz. period is unclear. In 1590 the monastery (which was for nuns) is referred to in the records of the Leimonos Monastery (#119) as the coenobitic monastery of the nearby Kreokopos Monastery (#172) which housed monks. The flour mill of the Periboli Monastery was still in use in 1909 when 2-3 nuns still lived at the site.
Bibliography: Taxis, 136, 138-39; Charitonidis, 1963c, 271 and pl. 312; Axiotis, 1992 I, 427-28.

168. *Routhia* (Batousa); 448758; 280m; A.; SP. On the s. side of the Xirolimni hill, ca. 2 kms nnw. from Batousa, a small spur of the hill offers a narrow plateau on which

stand the remains of a two-roomed structure (possibly an irregularly-shaped tower). Only the e. wall of the small, narrow room is preserved (to ca. 0.5 m), but the outer wall adjoining this small building preserves (on the e. side) well-cut and fitted Lesbian masonry blocks (see Appendix 2). Axiotis does not give dimensions for the structure or details of any associated sherd material. The plateau is extremely steep on all sides and the location affords a wide vista to the s. and w. over the Krinelouda valley which joins the Boulgaris River valley, offering an easy approach to Antissa on the n. coast of the island.
Bibliography: Axiotis, 1992 I, 409 and II, pl. 100.

169. *Kabouros* (Skalochori); 466766; 400m; Byz./Tur.; HAB. Ca. 1 km sw. from Skalochori the main road to Batousa crosses a bridge across the Katopetra ravine. The area to the se. of the road at this point (known as Kabouros) is covered with foundations of buildings, tiles and sherds of Byz./Tur. date (including pieces of pithoi) and the nearby hillsides display the traces of disused terracing. Axiotis reported that the remains extend upslope and include a fountainhead (near ruins which Axiotis thought to be the remains of a Tur. konak). Two large alonia nearby (together with the terracing) suggest that the area was once under intense cultivation.
Bibliography: Axiotis, 1992 I, 409.

170. *Agia Kyriaki* (Batousa); 447738; 260m; LR.-Byz.; HAB. On the s. slopes of the Olympos hill (which borders the n. side of the main Batousa-Antissa road immediately to the nw. of Batousa), a chapel of Agia Kyriaki stands on a rocky plateau which drops steeply to the e. and s.. A kalderimi leads up from the modern road towards the chapel. Axiotis reported encountering a dense scatter of sherds immediately one starts to ascend, including LR.-Byz. 'combed' wares, Byz. sherds, and tiles. Foundations of old buildings are visible around the chapel and a number of cut blocks and architectural *membra* lie nearby.
Bibliography: Axiotis, 1992 I, 427.

171. *Agia Paraskeui* (Tzithra); 410743; 150m; Byz.(?), 'MAge', Tur.; HAB, SP. Immediately to the e. of the modern village of Tzithra stands the chapel of Agia Paraskeui amid the extensive remains of the Tur. (and possibly earlier Byz.) settlement of Tzithra which preceded the modern village.[81] All around the chapel Axiotis reported a mass of 'MAge' sherds, tiles, ruins of buildings and kalderimia, and the chapel itself is the remnant of a small monastery of the same name referred to in the early 18C AC, at that time a dependency of the larger Kreokopos Monastery nearby (#172). The chapel of Agios Nikolaos in the modern village exhibits wall-paintings of the 16C AC (dated by an inscription).
Bibliography: Axiotis, 1992 I, 429-31 and II, pl. 93.

172. *Monastiri tou Kreokopou* (Tzithra); 396739; --; LByz., Tur.; SP. On a lower n. peak of the Kourouklos mountain known as Chalakas, ca. 0.6 km se. from modern Antissa and between the toponyms 'Skamniouds' (to the w.) and 'Throupar' (to the e.), a chapel of Taxiarchis is the sole remnant of the Byz. monastery of Kreokopos dedicated to the Archangel Michael and first attested in 1331 AD. After the Tur. conquest of the island, the monastery

---

[81] A Tur. settlement at 'Tsitra' is attested in Ottoman records in 1602, M. Kiel, pers. comm. (1995). Concerning an earlier 16C Ottoman census of the island, see n. 4 above.

continued in existence but was forced to pay taxes in kind on its oil production. The monastery seems to have reached its peak in the 17C when it was the richest in the entire island and its estates stretched as far as the area around Sigri.[82] The Periboli Monastery (#167, visible from the site) was one of three other monasteries belonging to it,[83] and although the Kreokopos site was finally abandoned in the early 19C, the monastery's lands (now belonging to the Greek state) are still scattered through the plain of Antissa.

Bibliography: Taxis, 136, 138-39; P. Phrankellis, 'Τὸ μοναστήρι τοῦ Κρεωκόπου', *Lesbiaka* 3 (1959), 82-91; Axiotis, 1992 I, 431-32.

173. *Klimaki* (Antissa); 3773; 260m; Byz.; SP. Just to the s. of the fork in the road w. from Antissa, where one heads s. to Eresos or w. to Sigri, a group of four small chapels stands below the road to the e. and w. in the area known as Klimaki (ca. 1.7 kms wsw. from Antissa). A number of EByz. architectural pieces are associated with the chapels (some of grey marble), and beside the Agia Eirini and Agios Georgios chapels are the foundations of older buildings. Axiotis associated the remains with the site of a Byz. monastery referred to in Patriarchal records in 1331 AD at 'Klimation'.

Bibliography: Axiotis, 1992 I, 453-54 and II, pls. 101-02.

174. *Moni Hypsilou* (Antissa); 356746; 510m; Byz., Tur.; CEM, SP. Ca. 3.5 kms w. from Antissa, immediately s. of the road to Sigri, rises the conical hill on which the Hypsilo Monastery stands, first attested (by epigraphical records) in 1131 AD. The first recorded name of the site was the Korax Monastery (in 1331 AD), named after the toponym at a nearby spring (three springs exist on the hill), and the present-day name was known first in 1707.[84] After the Tur. conquest the monastery was dissolved, but later (in 1584) it was revived, and during the Tourkokratia the site was pillaged three times, lastly in 1821.

The central church is a building comprising a nave and two flanking aisles and is dedicated to Agios Giannis ('o Theologos'). The complex includes also a number of cells, some of which form a museum with books, manuscripts and ecclesiastical vestments of the 17C. In 1636-41 Gabriel of Methymna reported that 15 monks lived in the monastery[85] (and there were still 25-30 monks in 1909). Kalderimia lead down from the monastery to the modern road, and to the w. are a few crosses indicating the cemetery beside a small chapel of Agios Panton built in the late 17C (which exhibits wall-paintings of similar date inside).

Bibliography: Taxis, 137-38; Charitonidis, 1968a, 41 and pl. 18γ-δ; Axiotis, 1992 I, 457-59 (and unnumbered photograph p. 459).

175. *Megalos Lakkos* (Eresos); 368709; 330m; A.; SP. To the w. of the main road from Eresos n. to Antissa, at the junction with the Methalia valley (see #176), stand the remains of an irregular shaped enclosure of Lesbian polygonal masonry (see Appendix 2, section 2.2). Only the e. wall and part of the n. wall are preserved (up to 2 m in places), the former projecting out from the slopes upon an outcrop of bedrock. The e. wall of the enclosure follows the contours to form an irregular shape and on the platform inside the enclosure wall some of the ancient blocks have been used to create a small *mandri* and an aloni. Axiotis reported that all around the enclosure was a dense concentration of sherds (no diagnostic fabrics are mentioned).

The significance of the structure is that the location looks over the precise spot where the Methalia valley (running e.-w.) joins the narrow valley leading n.-s. towards Eresos, the two easiest low-level approaches to the Eresos valley from the n..

Bibliography: Charitonidis, 1964, 397 and pl. 464α; Kontis, 1978, 332; Axiotis, 1992 I, 455-56 and II, pl. 102.

176. *Agios Alexandros* (Eresos); 374703; 170m; R., LByz.; SP. Ca. 3.5 kms ne. from Eresos, the valley through which the modern road winds n. towards Antissa is joined from the e. by the valley of the Methalia River. At this junction of the two valleys, in the centre of the valley floor (where the seasonal streams of the two valleys meet), stand the walls of a Byz. chapel now worshipped as Agios Alexandros. The plan of the chapel is in the shape of a cross (suggesting a LByz. date, see #3, #9, #241), and its walls are constructed of mortared tile and stone (the n. and s. walls are preserved to a height of ca. 2 m). Worked blocks of an older structure are incorporated into its walls, one large rectangular slab at the sw. corner showing cuttings for clamps. A mass of tiles, sherds and building foundations all over the valley floor around the chapel indicate that there was once an associated settlement. Amongst the ceramic material Axiotis noted R. *terra sigilata*.

Bibliography: Charitonidis, 1963c, 272 and pl. 313α; id., 1966, 73, fig. 2 and pl. VIIα; id., 1968a, map 1; Kontis, 1978, 339 and figs. 29-30; Axiotis, 1992 I, 456 and II, pl. 102.

177. *Aetos* (Eresos); 3768/3769; --; C./HL.; HAB(?). On the w. slopes of the Aetos hill, ca. 2.5 kms ne. from Eresos, Axiotis reported the foundations of a rectangular structure 5.3 m x 4.3 m constructed with polygonal masonry. Amongst the sherds in association with the building were black-glaze pieces, and more (undefined) foundations were apparent nearby.

Bibliography: Axiotis, 1992 II, 515.

178. *Kourouklos* (Chydira); 3971/4071; --; A/C.(?); SP. (S.) Paraskeuaidis, Kontis and Axiotis have all reported the traces of a tower high up on the slopes of the Kourouklos mountain, ca. 3 kms w. from Chydira, to the e. of a chapel of Agios Kyrikos. Only the se. wall and part of the sw. wall are preserved. The former stands 2 m high, is 8 m long, and the masonry is a coursed polygonal style (standing up to ca. 5 courses in places). An entrance is visible in the part of the sw. side which is preserved with a long slab forming the threshold. None of the reports give details of any associated scatter of sherds or tiles.

Bibliography: Paraskeuaidis, 26/9/29; Kontis, 1978, 330-31; Axiotis, 1992 I, 450, 460.

---

[82] The westward extent of its lands led to disputes in 1723 with the Hypsilo Monastery (#174).

[83] The other two monasteries were one dedicated to Agia Kyriaki in the plain of Telonia (Antissa), and the small monastery of Agia Paraskeui at Tzithra (#171).

[84] Axiotis (I, 458) notes that between 1331 and 1707 the Monastery was known by a number of different names: 'Korakas' (1595), 'Zisyras' (1605, 1609 and 1661), 'Zisyrios' (1662), 'Zhsra' (1682), 'Zisiros' (1689), 'Sisyros' (1700).

[85] For Gabriel of Methymna, see n. 47.

179. *Agios Ilias* (Chydira); 408712; 490m; LR.-Byz.; HAB, SP(?). On the se. slopes of the Kourouklos mountain, ca. 2.5 kms w. from Chydira, stand the ruins of a chapel of Prophitis Ilias, around which are gathered a large number of EByz. architectural blocks (of coarse trachyte) including unfluted columns and column capitals. To the sw. of the chapel are foundations of houses, worked blocks and a dense scatter of sherds and tiles including LR.-Byz. 'combed' wares, suggesting that the EByz. *membra* may not have travelled very far. A spring exists further down this s. slope, on which the traces of old terracing are apparent also. On the plateau near the top is a large, disused aloni and on the hill Axiotis reported an old press-stone.
Bibliography: Axiotis, 1992 I, 453 and II, pls. 100, 102; id., 1994, fig. Δ.

180. *Tyrrani* (Chydira); 429710; 420m; N./EBA., A./C.(?); HAB, SP. On the oval-shaped, rocky peak of the hill named Tyrrani, 0.3 km sw. from Chydira, stand the foundations of a tower of coursed polygonal masonry. The site was first reported by (S.) Paraskeuaidis in 1929 and later revisited by Axiotis (Kontis erroneously places the site to the ne. of Chydira). Paraskeuaidis gave only approximate dimensions for the tower, and the precise measurements as given by Axiotis are 11.5 m x 9.5 m. The walls are 1.15 m thick and constructed with two outer faces of large blocks and an inner fill. Both Axiotis and Paraskeuaidis spoke of internal dividing walls and the former reported a scatter of sherds and tiles, indicating that the structure was at some point roofed. Worked blocks from the structure can be seen near the chapel of Taxiarchis below the summit to the w. The view from the site is extensive over the village of Chydira below and beyond the Boulgaris valley at the n. foot of the hill e. towards Reuma, Batousa and Pterounda.

At 'Leperna' (the name of the slope on the e. side of Tyrrani), a scatter of N./EBA. lithics and ceramics indicates a significant prehistoric settlement. Axiotis described the stone blades and tools (including a polished axehead) as being made of very hard green and black stone, one was 7 cm (length) x 3.5 cm (width), another 6 cm x 3.2 cm. More lithics and ceramic finds including spindle whorls and sherds of brown, black and red fabric (many burnished), were found further w. on the Tyrrani hill as far as the Taxiarchis chapel below the summit to the w.
Bibliography: Paraskeuaidis 29/9/29; Kontis, 1978, 315; Axiotis, 1992 I, 421-22, 425-27 (and unnumbered photograph p. 426) and II, pls. 75, 92.

181. *Pyrgi* (Chydira); 4069/4070; --; A./C.(?); HAB/SP(?). On a rocky spur at the far e. end of the Methalia valley, ca. 2.5 kms wsw. from Chydira, Koumarelas located the foundations of a rectangular structure. The walls were constructed of polygonal masonry and inside the outer wall were a number of internal divisions. Amongst the ceramics associated with the remains were pieces of black-glaze wares. No dimensions for the structure are given, and the assertion of Axiotis that it served as a fortification (possibly a tower) is difficult to judge since the precise location is unclear.
Bibliography: Axiotis, 1992 I, 451.

182. *Kladomantri* (Chydira); 4069/4169; --; A.; SP. Ca. 3 kms sw. from Chydira, on the n. slopes of the Leukorachtes mountain, a group of ancient structures stand beside an ikonostasis dedicated to Agia Paraskeui at a place known as Kladomantri. Around the ikonostasis are the remains of what seems to be a tower constructed of isodomic masonry (ca. 15 m x 10 m). The nw. and se. corners are preserved *in situ*, but the n. and s. walls have been largely destroyed. The preserved sections indicate that the walls were ca. 0.7 m in thickness and a large number of cut blocks lie around the site. Beside a well, 13 m to the n. of this rectangular tower, are the foundations of a substantial circular structure 8 m in diameter which spans the wall of a *mandri* (which has led to its w. side being largely destroyed). The walls of the structure (possibly a circular tower) are constructed of extremely well-fitted Lesbian masonry blocks (see Appendix 2), and two gate jambs are preserved upright on the s. side.
Bibliography: Axiotis, 1992 I, 424-25 (and unnumbered photograph p. 424) and II, pl. 93.

183. *Gigi* (Chydira); 401689; 586m; C./HL.(?); SP. On the peak of the Gigi mountain, ca. 3.8 kms sw. from Chydira near an unroofed chapel of Prophitis Ilias, Koumarelas described foundations of a rectangular structure said to be constructed of polygonal masonry. No pictures or dimensions of the walls are offered, and the associated sherd scatter was said by Axiotis to be much the same as that nearby at Pyrgi (#181), presumably therefore including black-glaze sherds.
Bibliography: Axiotis, 1992 I, 451.

184. *Batoudia* (Chydira) 4169; --; A./C.; SP. In the Potamia valley (the e. end of the Methalia valley), ca. 2.5 kms sw. from Chydira at a place known as Batoudia, Koumarelas discovered an enclosure of Lesbian polygonal masonry (see Appendix 2).[86] The walls of the enclosure (no dimensions of which are given by Axiotis) were preserved up to 2 m in height, with an associated sherd scatter including black-painted sherds and fragments of tiles.
Bibliography: Axiotis, 1992 I, 425 and II, pl. 92.

185. *Balana* (Chydira) 4167/4267; --; A; SP. On the w. side of the deep pass which leads s. to form the Maliontas River valley, ca. 3.8 kms ssw. from Chydira, Axiotis described an irregular-shaped enclosure of polygonal masonry at a place known as Balana. The enclosure stands 0.5 km sw. of the point where the road s. from Chydira along the valley ceases, immediately e. of a small ravine on the hillside. The enclosure (of which the w. and nw. walls are best-preserved) measures ca. 23 m (n.-s.) x 16 m (e.-w.). On the w. side the wall stands to a height of 2.2 m and is constructed of polygonal masonry blocks. Internal dividing walls are apparent on the w. and se. sides built up against the enclosure wall. An associated sherd scatter was reported by Axiotis inside the enclosure, but no detailed description is provided.
Bibliography: Axiotis, 1992 I, 423 and II, pl. 92.

186. *Skoteino* (Chydira); 4368; --; LR.-Byz.; HAB(?), SP. Ca. 3.5 kms s. from Chydira along the road which leads eventually to Mesotopos through the upper reaches of the Maliontas River valley, just as the road begins to turn sw., is an area known as Skoteino. On the w.-facing slopes below the road stands a chapel of Agios Giannis around

---

86 The precise location is unclear since no similar toponym is marked on the British Army maps and the map of Axiotis is not detailed. From Axiotis' maps, the site seems to lie on the n. side of the rema which runs e.-w. at the n. foot of the Leukorachtes mountain.

which are the foundations of an EByz. basilica. Foundations of the basilica walls are visible to the n. and s. of the chapel (including part of the apse), and architectural *membra* (of red trachyte) are incorporated in the modern building. Around the chapel are a mass of tiles and sherds (including LR.-Byz. 'combed' wares). Axiotis also reported that around the chapel on the small plateau, the enclosure of a *mandri* was built upon an 'ancient' wall similar to that of ancient Arisbe (#116). On the n. side of this enclosure three courses are preserved, but the lack of ceramics earlier than the LR. period suggest that this wall may date to the period when the *mandri* itself was built rather than to any phase of antiquity.

Bibliography: Axiotis, 1992 I, 422-23 and II, pls. 90, 92.

187. *Bigla* (Agra); 4366; --; A.; HAB, SP. A number of ancient enclosure walls and associated remains of habitation activity have been noted at 'Bigla' on the hill of Aetos (near the village of Agra). There has been confusion, however, over the location of the enclosure of Lesbian masonry first noted by Charitonidis in 1961-62 because of the existence of another toponym 'Aetos', where there are also ancient remains, further to the e. between Apothiki and Parakoila (#126). Axiotis specifically stated that the enclosure Charitonidis described is to be found on the hill 'Aetos' with the toponym 'Bigla' to the w. of Agra, not on the coast where Kontis places the site.

Charitonidis originally reported stretches of Lesbian polygonal masonry, forming the fragmented remains of an enclosure high up on the Aetos hill. The n.-s. wall measured 33.3 m, the e.-w. wall 14.9 m. The best-preserved sections were those towards the s. (including the s. part of the long n.-s. wall which formed the e. side) and inside the structure some internal dividing walls were visible, again preserved best in the s. part of the structure.

Axiotis added that on the e. slope of Bigla the chapel of Agia Parakseui is founded upon a platform created by a Lesbian masonry terrace wall 21 m in length and up to 3 m in height. A column capital is built into the floor of the chapel and the whole surrounding slope is full of old foundations and scatters of ceramics. Ca. 50 m nw. from this platform another structure (probably originally rectangular) with walls of large polygonal blocks was described by Axiotis, with the n. side and ne. corner in the best state of preservation.

Bibliography: Charitonidis, 1961-62, 265 and pl. 320α; Kontis, 1973, 82; id., 1978, 332; Axiotis, 1992 II, 523, 537 (and unnumbered photograph p. 524) and pl. 122.

188. *Paliokastro* (Agra); 4365/4465; 500m; 'MAge'; SP. On the Paliokastro hill, ca. 2 kms wsw. from Agra (the exact location is unclear), stand the remains of a 'MAge' kastro attested in historical sources and visited by Axiotis. The latter spoke of a chapel of Agios Georgios standing near the ruins on a plateau of the hill's rocky peak. The remains of walls and a cistern are still visible together with a concentration of sherds of 'MAge' date (the precise dating of the kastro is unclear[87]).

Bibliography: Moutzouris 1962, 68; Axiotis, 1992 II, 523.

189. *Pente Agioi* (Pterounda); 475716; 440m; Byz., Tur.; CEM, SP. Beside a spring on the w. slopes of the Prophitis Ilias mountain, ca. 1.5 kms ese. from Pterounda, stands the small chapel dedicated to the 'Pente Agioi' ('Five Saints'), the present-day remnant of a number of monasteries and hermitages on the mountain referred to from the 12C (the mountain was known in Byz. sources as 'Libanos').[88] In 1636-41 Gabriel of Methymna stated that until just before his time there had been fourteen monasteries on the mountain, but that only five were still occupied.[89]

In the 17C AC few monks lived at the monastery of the Pente Agioi, but the mountain served as the retreat of hermits whose bones were found in caves nearby. The remains of an older chapel are visible beside the present-day Pente Agioi building (more elements have been taken to Pterounda). In the late 19C a painting of the Mother of God ('Theotokos') was still just visible on the rock nearby (said to be one of a group of paintings now worn away). The traces of a cemetery beside the chapel have been reported also, and in 1988 villagers from Pterounda found remains of an older chapel 2 m below ground exhibiting more wall-paintings.

Nearby, another former monastery on the mountain was that of Agios Antonios, also of Byz. date (Axiotis does not specify its location apart from saying that a modern chapel of the same name stands on the spot[90]). Axiotis reported that foundations of the monastery's cells are apparent beside the modern chapel. In the neighbouring field, structural remains of the Kalami/Kalamiotissa Monastery (attested in 1480 AD) were uncovered in 1970, including the apse of one of its chapels together with a large number of tiles and sherds. Another four of the monasteries which existed in the area (attested largely through the island's ecclesiastical records) are named as Agios Blasios, Agios Georgios, Agios Nikolaos and Agios Dimitrios (the latter now standing near an old Tur. bridge), but little remains of any of them.

Bibliography: Moutzouris, 1962, 52-53; Axiotis, 1992 I, 415-18.

190. *Koutlougouni* (Skalochori); 484819; 120m; A.; SP. The high, narrow promontory of Koutlougouni stands 4.5 kms almost due n. from the village of Skalochori. The site is reached by taking the road which leaves Skalochori to the ne. (leading eventually to Skoutaros), and after 2.5 kms turning left along a track signposted 'Koutlougouni' which bears n. along the w. slopes of the Koja Dag mountain. Near the coast, as the track bends sharply e. and slightly downhill, is a farmstead and associated outbuildings beyond which on a narrow ridgetop are the remains of an irregular shaped enclosure. The published reports of Kontis, Koumarelas and Axiotis speak of the enclosure exhibiting walls of Lesbian polygonal masonry (see Appendix 2), which are only visible in short stretches of the e. side where a few *in situ* blocks remain. The remaining walls

---

[87] A Tur. settlement at Agra (possibly one which was associated with the kastro) is attested in Ottoman records in 1602, M. Kiel, pers. comm. (1995). Concerning an earlier 16C Ottoman census of the island, see n. 4 above.

[88] In the 12C Grigorios who had lived as a monk near the Gulf of Gera (and later had a monastery dedicated to his memory, see #60) visited the Libanos area and reported a 'large number of monasteries and hermitages'. In 1310 Gregory of Sinai also visited the 'Libanos Mountain'. See Axiotis, 1992 I, 417.

[89] For Gabriel of Methymna, see n. 47.

[90] This chapel of Agios Antonios is not marked on any of his maps or the British Army map. In the mid-17C Gabriel of Methymna stated that the mountain of Libanos was also known by the name of Agios Antonios and that the latter monastery was inhabited by 12 monks, see Axiotis, 1992 I, 416.

39

have been broken down to their lowest courses or rebuilt completely in much less careful fashion.

The shore line on all sides of the promontory culminates in steep cliffs for 0.9 km to the w. (before the narrow coastal plain of Belitsas) and for ca. 2 km to the e. as far as Cape Petinos. The view from the Koutlougouni promontory is very extensive both e. and w.. To the e., the coastline all the way to Methymna 13 kms away is clearly visible, and to the w. the Phournia promontory (15 kms distant) is seen jutting out into the sea beyond ancient Antissa.

Bibliography: Kontis, 1973, 82; id., 1978, 311; Koumarelas, 1989b, 3; Axiotis, 1992 I, 396.

191. *Xirolimni* (Skoutaros); 497824; 10m; R., EByz.(?), 'MAge'; HAB, SP(?). On the plateau and w. slope of the rocky promontory which forms Cape Petinos, ca. 3 kms ene. from Skoutaros, Axiotis reported the remains of an extensive settlement. On the plateau of the promontory itself are the remains of disused alonia, and extending down to the shore at its w. foot is a scatter of white-glazed 'MAge' sherds together with R. *terra sigilata*. A large number of EByz. architectural pieces of grey marble and trachyte are built into a ruined structure on the e. side of the promontory (which Axiotis took to be the site an EByz. basilica), and more are apparent at the ruined chapel of Agia Photia on the promontory's w. point.

Bibliography: Axiotis, 1992 I, 395-96 and II, pl. 86.

192. *Tsichrantas* (Skoutaros); 511824; 5m; C., R., EByz.; HAB, SP(?). In the coastal plain of the Tsichrantas River, near the shore, stand the remains of a small *skala* settlement which once exported raw materials for tanning. Two large storage houses used in this trade stand in ruins, and into the larger of these (above the arched door) has been built a triglyth and metope block from the frieze of an ancient building made of local red trachyte. More worked blocks with cuttings for clamps were incorporated into other parts of the building.

On the e. side of the same narrow coastal plain, near a chapel of Taxiarchis, Axiotis reported EByz. architectural pieces, a Doric capital and a large fluted column. Beside the Taxiarchis chapel to the sw., the remains of a circular structure ca. 18 m in diameter are visible as a mass of fallen stones which once formed its walls (which Kontis assumed to be a small defensive post). Amongst the sherds and tiles associated with this circular structure was R. *terra sigilata*.

Chatzi gave a general report of C. ceramics in the valley, and Axiotis reported traces of a kalderimi, but the precise location of both these features is unclear.

Bibliography: Chatzi, 1972, 579 and pl. 529δ-ε; Kontis, 1978, 311; Axiotis, 1992 I, 384-85.

193. *Koja Dag* (Skalochori); 506808; 376m; A.; SP. Ca. 3 kms nne. from Skalochori is the mountain still known today by its Turkish name of 'Koja Dag'. The mountain peak is easily approachable from the s. via the upland plateau to the ne. of Skalochori, by following the signposted road to Koutlougouni (#190) and then bearing ne. where an old bridge leads across to the e. side of the mountain. On a small plateau (on the lower e. side of the peak) above the spectacularly sheer drop to the Tsichrantas valley, Kontis, Koumarelas and Axiotis all reported the remains of two towers within an enclosure wall. The walls of both the towers and the enclosure wall, of which there is little preserved, are of Lesbian polygonal masonry ca. 1.5

m in thickness (for this masonry style, see Appendix 2). Both the towers are rectangular, one measuring 14 m x 10.5 m, the smaller one 9 m x 6 m, and around both structures Axiotis reported a dense scatter of tiles and sherds, suggesting that the towers were roofed at some point. Kontis noted that lower down the slopes were fragments of other polygonal masonry walls, but that their masonry was less finely worked than that immediately around the towers on the peak.

The location of the tower on the high spur of the Koja Dag mountain means that the view from the site is extensive. To the e. one looks over the Tsichrantas valley far below beyond the hill of Selles (#205) and the Petra plain all the way to Methymna 12 km away. To the w. Antissa is visible, and to the n. one looks down over the n. slopes of Koja Dag towards Cape Petinos.

Bibliography: Kontis, 1973, 82; id., 1978, 311 and fig. 52; Koumarelas, 1989a, 4; Axiotis, 1992 I, 383-84; Spencer, 1994, 208-10 and figs. 1-3.

194. *Prophitis Ilias* (Skalochori); 481787; 542m; A., HL.; SP. The hill of Prophitis Ilias stands immediately to the n. of the village of Skalochori, and on its peak (ca. 1 km n. from the village), beside a chapel of the same name, are traces of an ancient enclosure with two distinct phases. On the small rocky plateau to the e. of the chapel are the remains of polygonal masonry walls (ca. 1 m thick) which form a small, irregularly-shaped enclosure. The walling only exists on the ne., se. and sw. sides (the latter forming the base of the chapel's se. wall), because the natural rock outcrop and steep drop to the nw. create the other side of the enclosure. Some polygonal blocks have been reused in a badly constructed low terrace wall around the chapel. A second element to the enclosure is apparent immediately to the sw. where traces of (probably HL.) isodomic walls 2 m thick form an extension to the upper enclosure. Foundations of internal structures are visible within this outer walled area. A gate exists at the se. corner of the outer enclosure where a break in the rock outcrop allows an easy passage up onto the peak.

Koumarelas and Axiotis both spoke of dense scatters of pottery and tiles within the enclosures but offered no specific date for the material. Some of the tile fragments are closely associated with the chapel and probably relate to its recent rebuilding (the foundations of the old chapel lie on a lower terrace below the n. edge of the peak).

From the peak of the hill there are impressive, panoramic views: Petra and Methymna, the latter over 15 km away, stand out beyond the Koja Dag mountain (#193), and the view extends n. to Koutlougouni (#190), nw. down the Langada valley to ancient Antissa and Gabathas (#157-64), w. to Ordymnos and s. beyond Batousa to Chydira.

Bibliography: Koumarelas, 1989a, 4 (with unnumbered plan and photograph); id., 1989c, 3 (with unnumbered plan and photograph); Axiotis, 1992 I, 399 and II, pl. 96.

195. *Phonias* (Skalochori); 494775; 505m; A.; HAB, SP. The hill of Phonias rises immediately e. from the village of Skalochori and is terraced on its gently sloping s., w. and e. sides. On the terraces were once cultivated tobacco and vines, and Axiotis noted an old, stone-built drainage channel on the s. slopes of the hill and a circular cistern to the se.. On the rocky peak, the remains of an irregularly-shaped enclosure of Lesbian polygonal masonry are apparent with dimensions of ca. 18 m in an e.-w. direction and 16 m n.-s. (see Appendix 2, section 2.2). Stretches of the wall are visible on the se., s. and nw. sides (in places up to 1 m in height), indicating that the outer wall was 2

m in thickness and formed by two outer faces of large worked blocks with a fill of rubble in-between. Faint traces of less substantial internal dividing walls survive within the outer enclosure. A few plain, undiagnostic sherds and tiles are visible near these internal walls, suggesting that part of the structure was roofed at some point.

Further down the slope of the Phonias hill to the w. are foundations of substantial buildings, a small rock-cut niche with a triangular pediment-shaped cutting above, and a dense tile and pottery scatter (including sherds from pithoi and grey ware amphorae).
Bibliography: Kontis, 1978, 312; Koumarelas, 1989b, 3; Axiotis, 1992 I, 394-95 and II, pl. 84.

196. *Pedia* (Skalochori); 501772; 390m; R., EByz., 'MAge'; HAB, SP. Immediately to the n. of the main (asphalt) road from Philia to Skalochori, 2.2 kms e. from the latter village, the chapel of Agios Dimitrios stands at the e. foot of the Phonias hill. When Charitonidis visited the site, the chapel was an old unroofed structure which has since been rebuilt (in 1987), and before the rebuilding Charitonidis described seeing the apse and w. ends of walls belonging to an older structure beside the chapel together with the remnants of a floor of clay slabs and some architectural *membra*.

Axiotis reported that many of the architectural pieces seen by Charitonidis (nearly all of the local red trachyte, except for a marble column capital) have been built into the new (1987) chapel or placed within it, and foundations are visible at the se. corner of the new building.[91]

It was in this area between Skalochori and Philia (known as Pedia[92]) that Kontis reported a surface scatter of R. ceramics, and that in the 19C both Boutan and Koldewey noted remains (including a number of architectural blocks and 'traces of houses' which were dated to the 'later MAges' by Koldewey). Since the local traditions in Skalochori assert that at Pedia lay one of the 'MAge' villages from which the modern settlement formed, Koldewey's dating of these remains may well be correct.[93]
Bibliography: Koldewey, 37, 84; Charitonidis, 1968a, 43-44 and pl. 21β; Kontis, 1978, 317; Axiotis, 1992 I, 391, 394 and II, pl. 85.

197. *Mitropolis* (Anemotia); 508765; 350m; HL/R(?), EByz., Tur.; CEM, SP. To the e. of the village of Anemotia is the upland plain known as Kambos, traditionally an area where earlier settlements had existed which coalesced to form the modern village.[94] Nearby, ca.

1 km ne. from Anemotia on the slopes e. of the modern road which leads n. towards Philia and Skalochori, (S.) Paraskeuaidis discovered the paved floor and architectural *membra* of an EByz. basilica in October 1946. As well as EByz. columns and capital elements, an earlier Doric cornice with triglyths and metopes was also found. A number of tombs were scattered in close proximity to the basilica amongst which (on its w. side) was a monolithic sarcophagus with a ridge on its rim for the fitting of a lid.

On the visit of Axiotis more recently much less was preserved. A great amount of material (mostly squared blocks with cuttings for clamps but also EByz. architectural elements) had been built into a terrace wall. Above this terrace lay a pile of stones including other architectural fragments and around this whole area was a dense scatter of tiles and sherds. These remains are now worshipped as a shrine to Agios Georgios, and the chapel of Agia Anastasia a little further to the e. (beside a *mandri*) contains another block from the nearby basilica.

The squared blocks and Doric cornice reported by Charitonidis and Axiotis suggest that an earlier (possibly HL./R.) structure stood on the spot, but it is impossible to ascertain the precise date (or function) of this building.
Bibliography: Charitonidis, 1968a, 44; Axiotis, 1992 I, 388.

198. *Erimopyli* (Philia); 541761; 520m; C./HL.(?), Tur.; HAB, SP. On the high plateau named Erimopyli,[95] ca. 1 km sse. from Philia at the very edge of the uplands before the sheer drop e. to the Kalloni Plain, a whole cluster of remains have been noted by visitors since the 19C AC. Anagnostis and Taxis both reported a large number of wells and cisterns in the area and more recently Kontis mentioned a substantial wall (of undetermined date) running n.-s. along the side of a deep ravine.

Axiotis recorded the site (which seems to date chiefly to the Tur. period) in much more detail. In addition to a number of the wells seen by the early visitors, Axiotis reported the remains of old drainage channels, threshing floors, blocks from olive presses and the traces of extensive terracing on the n., e. and w. sides of the plateau. There were also the remains of a number of houses near the ravine to the s. together with three ruined chapels (all now existing merely as ikonostases, but with foundations and worked blocks nearby) of Agia Lemoni, Agios Georgios and Agios Dimitrios. The traces of an old street system were apparent in the form of a kalderimi near the centre of the remains, and a dense scatter of (undiagnostic) sherd and tile covered the whole area.

The wall which Kontis reported runs along the s. side of the settlement for ca. 0.2 km, is 2 m thick, and in places 2.5 m high. It is constructed of large, crudely-worked blocks (without mortar) and is formed with two faces of large outer blocks within which is a fill of rubble and earth. A gate and possible tower can be distinguished near the w. end of the wall and one large block (3 m x 0.3 m x 0.3 m) seems to be a lintel from the gate.

In sum, the remains seem to be mostly of Tur. and early modern date, but the large enclosure wall to the s. is curiously not mortared and may be ancient (Kontis does not mark the site as being of C. and HL. date on his site distribution maps, but there is nothing in his text to explain why). Anagnostis associated the toponym

---

[91] Axiotis (I, 391) was informed in Philia that the EByz. blocks built into the main church of that village (Taxiarchis) also came from the Agios Dimitrios site. For details of these blocks in Philia see Charitonidis, 1968a, 44, who speaks about more similar pieces built into the chapel of Agia Photeini near the nw. edge of the village (ibid.).

[92] Incorrectly (and amusingly) named 'Apesia' by Koldewey, 37, 84.

[93] By the early 17C a large Tur. settlement is attested in Ottoman records at 'Çömlek' (Skalochori), M. Kiel, pers. comm. (1995). Concerning an earlier 16C Ottoman census of the island, see n. 4 above.

[94] The existence of a kalderimi leading down into the plain ('Kambos') from the modern village supports this tradition, see Axiotis, 1992 I, 388. A Tur. village at 'Anemotia' is attested in the 1602 Ottoman archives, M. Kiel, pers. comm. (1995). Concerning an earlier 16C Ottoman census of the island, see n. 4 above.

[95] 'Ερημοπύλη'. The location is known also as Erimopylaia ('Ερημοπύλαια') or Ermotilia ('Ερμοτίλια'), see Kontis, 1978, 291, 312, and Axiotis, 1992 I, 374.

Erimopyli (literally 'Ερημο - πυλα' 'Deserted Gateway') with the ancient 'Mount Pylaion' said to be in Lesbos by Strabo (Str. 13.3.3), but this etymology and the association is hardly secure. Lastly, it may also be worthy of note that no settlement with a similar name is mentioned by Gabriel of Methymna in his description of Lesbos dated 1636-41[96] which suggests that if there was a settlement here during the Tur. period (and if Gabriel was thorough in his gazetteer), it was not in existence during the mid-17C AC.
Bibliography: Taxis, 132 and n. 1; Kontis, 1978, 291, 312 and figs. 21-26; Axiotis, 1992 I, 374-78 and II, pls. 81-82.

199. *Paliochora* (Philia); 5477/5577; --; HL./R.(?), 'MAge', Tur.; HAB, SP(?). On the n. side of the main Philia - Kalloni road, ca. 1.5 kms e. from Philia, the remains of a deserted settlement (probably dating from the Tur. period[97]) were noted by Axiotis at the place known as Paliochora. A (possibly defensive) upper enclosure stands above an area exhibiting building foundations of unworked, mortared stones which include a number of worked blocks. Wells and cisterns are scattered over the area, stretches of a kalderimi are apparent, and Axiotis also reported a press-stone together with 'MAge' tiles and sherds (including a number of large pithos fragments). Kontis marked the site as dating from the HL. and R. periods on his site distribution maps but did not refer to the site in his text and Axiotis found nothing ancient at the site.
Bibliography: Kontis, 1978, figs. 23-28; Axiotis, 1992 I, 373-74 and II, pl. 81; id., 1994, fig. Δ.

200. *Katopetro* (Laphionas); 5478; --; --; HAB, CEM. Kontis gives an extremely vague report that 'sw. from Ametelli [#202]' (no distance is given) are a large number of rock-cut graves and traces of settlement activity. Kontis continues that

> a little further [it is not clear exactly from where] are the traces of a large building in a narrow valley, where there are preserved some large, carved rectangular blocks with grooves similar to those which Koldewey found in other places and interpreted as press-stones for grapes and olives.

Whether this site is to be associated with the tombs found by Axiotis at Ametelli (#202), and whether the remains of the building (possibly a farmstead) and presses are ancient, or only of early modern date, is unclear.
Bibliography: Kontis, 1978, 283; Axiotis, 1992 I, 286.

201. *Ambelia Skoteinou* (Philia); 544789; 600m; A.; SP. Kontis and Axiotis both reported an irregular shaped enclosure of Lesbian polygonal masonry (see Appendix 2) high up on the Skoteino mountain, 2.5 kms se. from Skoutaros (a more easy approach can be made from Philia which is 2 kms ssw. from the enclosure). The dimensions given for the enclosure by Kontis are 45 m x 40 m, although on his fig. 45 the scale rather suggests measurements of ca. 25 m x 15 m. The thickness of the walls (where preserved) is ca. 2 m. Axiotis agreed with the larger of the two sets of figures for the structure's

dimensions and added that a scatter of sherds is visible near the structure.
Bibliography: Kontis, 1978, 282 and fig. 45; Axiotis, 1992 I, 286 and II, pl. 61; Spencer, 1994, 209-10 and figs. 1, 4.

202. *Ametelli Skoteinou* (Laphionas); 572797; 520m; A., Tur.; HAB, CEM, SP. Ne. from the enclosure at Ambelia (#201), at an elevation of 520m above sea-level, Kontis reported that an extensive area ca. 1.1 kms x 0.5 km contained remains of Lesbian masonry walls (see Appendix 2) and dense tile and sherd scatters of different periods.
It seems that this large area of remains was approached by Axiotis from the abandoned village of Klapados to the e.. In a very similar area to that mapped by Kontis (but one which he named 'Sentoukia'), Axiotis described a large number of wall foundations, monolithic door jambs (still standing), stone basins and bedrock cuttings. Around the structural remains were traces of a large-scale enclosure wall (of two outer faces and a rubble fill) creating a small walled settlement. Axiotis also reported two monolithic sarcophagi nearby and a scatter of undiagnostic tile and sherds over the whole area of the remains. Disused threshing floors and drinking troughs for animals attest to more use of the area in the early modern era.
Bibliography: Kontis, 1978, 283; Axiotis, 1992 I, 285-86 and II, pls. 60-61.

*203. *Agios Alexandros* (Laphionas); 5481; --; EByz., Tur.; HAB, CEM, SP. The path which leaves the village of Laphionas heading w. to the chapel of Agios Giannis on the e. side of the Roudi hill continues along the n. slopes to the site of the EByz. basilica of Agios Alexandros (half an hour from Laphionas). The latter was uncovered near a deserted chapel of the same name (built in 1954) on a small plateau ca. 2 kms w. from Laphionas on the w. slopes overlooking the Anaxios river and the village of Skoutaros (which lies wsw. from the site). Into the walls of the modern chapel are built many architectural elements from the original EByz. structure.
Excavations were carried out by Aliprantis in 1972-73, revealing the EByz. basilica with a paved central nave and two flanking aisles, a number of EByz. architectural pieces (including Ionic column capitals), and also two (probably EByz.) burials. Over the whole site a number of other architectural *membra* were reported recently by Axiotis, together with some remaining stretches of mortared tile and stone walling and a dense scatter of glazed Tur. sherds.
The Turks were said to have intruded upon the place by the 17C AC and disturbed the monolithic sarcophagus which exhibits an EByz. epitaph (probably coffin of the saint himself). The sarcophagus was found subsequently lying beside the basilica.[98] In the Tur. period a mosque and a group of small houses were constructed at the site (Axiotis found a number of Tur. pipes near the basilica) and in Spring 1962 floors of older buildings and more architectural remains came to light. These ruins of the Tourkokratia are still visible today ca. 30 m sw. from the modern chapel.
Bibliography: Charitonidis, 1968a, 53-56, figs. 27-29 and pl. 27; Aliprantis, 1972, 616-17 and pls. 576-77; id., 1973, 556 and pls. 525-26; Touchais, 1977, 624; Kontis, 1978, 282; Axiotis, 1992 I, 282-83 and II, pls. 57, 59.

---

[96] See n. 47.
[97] A settlement is attested in Ottoman records at 'Filia' in 1602, M. Kiel, pers. comm. (1995). Concerning an earlier 16C Ottoman census of the island, see n. 4 above.

---

[98] It was no doubt from this sarcophagus that one of the Turkish names for the spot, 'Tekesh' or 'Tomb' originated.

204. *Chlios* (Skoutaros); 529826; 5m; Tur.; HAB. At the ne. edge of the coastal plain of the Mikri Tsichranta, 1.6 kms n. from Skoutaros, are the remains of a settlement of the Tur. period referred to by Gabriel of Methymna in 1636-41.[99] Foundations of buildings and a dense scatter of ceramics show the extent of the former village (one of those from which modern Skoutaros was formed). The ruined apse and walls of the former parish chapel of the Panagiouda stand 50 m from the shore (constructed of mortared tile and unworked stone).
Bibliography: Axiotis, 1992 I, 280-81 and II, pl. 57.

205. *Selles* (Skoutaros); 532829; 109m; A.; SP. Ca. 2 kms nne. from Skoutaros rises the three-peaked hill of Selles, forming the sw. limit of the plain of Petra. On the neck of this hill which joins the n. and central peaks stands an irregular-shaped ancient enclosure within which are the remains of a tower. Much of the enclosure wall and the tower are broken down to ground level and can be seen only as foundations, but on the nw. side the wall is in a better state of preservation and exhibits intricate Lesbian polygonal masonry (see Appendix 2 and fig. 16). The w. side of the inner tower also is preserved to above ground level and exhibits similar style masonry.

The slopes of the hill around the enclosure, sheer to the w. but more gentle to the e. (and all now terraced with olives), are covered with a dense scatter of black-painted and grey ware sherds, and around the tower itself are a number of tiles, suggesting that this inner structure was once roofed.

The importance of the location of this tower and enclosure (defined as a defensive watchtower by all previous visitors) is that is stands above the only easy low-level pass into the Plain of Petra from the w. (where the modern road now runs). It also possesses a wide vista from the coastal bays to the w. of Methymna back to the town of Methymna itself (#217, the kastro is clearly visible).
Bibliography: Charitonidis, 1961-62, 265; Kontis, 1978, 282 and fig. 44; Axiotis, 1992 I, 276-77 (and unnumbered photograph p. 277) and II, pl. 58; Spencer, 1994, 208-10 and figs. 1-2.

206. *Kalejik* (Skoutaros) 536835; 40m; LR.-Byz., 'MAge'; HAB, CEM, SP. On the w. side of the Anaxios River, ca. 2.7 kms nne. from Skoutaros, a number of ancient remains stand on the low coastal hill named 'Kalejik' ('Small Kastro'). On the sw. lip of the plateau a stretch of mortared stone and tile walling is preserved for 15 m (up to 3 m in height). The ridge is densely covered in sherds including grey wares, LR.-Byz. 'combed' wares, and glazed 'MAge' sherds. A tomb (now empty) is cut into the hilltop (together with a well), and Axiotis reported another similar grave slightly to the w. together with other stone sarcophagus burials. The traces of habitation activity extend also immediately s. of the low ridge where Axiotis reported ceramics (including handles of amphorae) on the w. bank of the Anaxios River.

Just offshore, in the Bay of Petra, Touchais also described a large cache of broken R. amphorae were located, probably from the remains of a shipwreck.
Bibliography: Taxis, 132; Touchais, 1985, 831; Axiotis, 1992 I, 275-76.

207. *Agios Georgios* (Petra); 564842; 5m; LR.-Byz., 'MAge'; CEM, SP. Ca. 0.7 km w. from the modern village of Petra (following the main road w.), in the middle of a field which borders the road to the s., are three large oak trees below which is an open-air shrine of Agios Georgios. The modern-day worship is carried out in the apse of an older chapel, of which part of the n. and s. walls are also preserved. A section of the floor of the older building laid with clay floor slabs is also visible (at a lower level than the present field). The group of EByz. worked marble and trachyte blocks lying inside and around these walls suggests that the structural remains at the shrine are the site of an EByz. basilica. In the same field are significant scatters of tiles, LR.-Byz. 'combed' wares and glazed sherds of 'MAge' date.

Slightly further w. (ca. 0.2 - 0.5 km), Byz. tombs were reported by Axiotis near the small chapel of Agios Kyrikos and at another shrine of Agios Georgios, with locals claiming that at the latter site the tomb was that of the saint himself.
Bibliography: Charitonidis, 1968a, 56 and pl. 28β; Axiotis, 1992 I, 263-64 and II, pl. 54.

208. *Agios Dimitrios* (Petra); 5783; --; R., EByz.; HAB, SP. On the w. side of the main road which leads n. from Kalloni to Petra, ca. 1 km s. of Petra, a dirt road leaves the asphalted road to the left. Following this track, and turning left again before crossing the small river which flows parallel with the main road, one comes to the remains of an EByz. basilica now dedicated to the worship of Agios Dimitrios and Agios Nestor.[100] The remaining parts of the structure include sections of the apse, the foundations of the s. wall, part of a s. conch, significant parts of the w. wall, and the nw. corner. Incorporated in the walls of tile and mortar are large worked blocks. Some blocks show signs of holes for dowels and clamps and obviously have come from a structure older than the EByz. shrine. EByz. architectural *membra*, including columns and column capitals, lie inside the ruins and a coin of Commodus (180-92 AD) was found at the site. In the context of these R./EByz. finds it is worth noting that the village of Petra was one of those attested on the LR. census inscriptions (see Appendix 1). Axiotis also reported dense scatters of pottery in the surrounding area.
Bibliography: Charitonidis, 1968a, 56-57; Axiotis, 1992 I, 255 and II, pls. 54-55.

209. *Paliokastro Korphiou* (Laphionas); 584816; 370m; LR.-Byz.; SP. Immediately s. of the road which descends from Stypsi to the main Kalloni - Petra highway, 1.4 kms e. from Laphionas, is the conical hill of Korphi on which stand the ruins of a small kastro.[101] The kastro occupies the narrow hilltop and its walls (of mortared small stones) extend between two rock outcrops on the e. and w. ends of the hill which form natural defences. The ruins of a semi-circular tower (2 m high) are preserved in the centre of the n. wall, and in the walls are channels for water drainage. A large rectangular cistern faced with mortar is dug into the hilltop inside the s. wall (10 m long and 2 m deep), and the whole plateau is covered with a dense scatter of sherds and tiles, some of which Kontis dated (along with the kastro itself) to late antiquity (Axiotis noted LR.-Byz. 'combed'

---

[99] For this dating of Gabriel of Methymna, see n. 47.

[100] The basilica is dedicated mainly to the worship of Agios Dimitrios but the south conch is set aside for Agios Nestor.
[101] The kastro is named after the present-day owner of the area, see Kontis, 1978, 284.

wares).[102] Axiotis thought that the kastro was Byz. (specifically 9C-11C) on the basis of its similarity to the kastra of Gera (#51) and 'Metia' (#61) which he claimed to have dated from numismatic finds.[103]
Bibliography: Charitonidis, 1965, 495 and n. 20; Kontis, 1978, 284; Axiotis, 1992 I, 252-53 and II, pl. 54.

*210. *Agios Dimitrios* (Hypsilometopo); 623819; 260m; EByz.; SP. Ca. 1.2 kms to the s. of Hypsilometopo stands the chapel of Agios Dimitrios (built in 1954) on the site of an EByz. basilica. The basilica (comprising a nave and two flanking aisles) dates from the 6C AC. Villagers had first uncovered and excavated the structure during the Tourkokratia, but the building was still in good condition when Orlandos carried out systematic excavations in 1928.
Today a series of column bases and sections of the paved floor of the basilica are preserved along with large numbers of architectural fragments either built into the modern chapel or placed within it. Small fragments of the mosaic floor are also still visible within the modern chapel but were much better preserved 70 years ago when Orlandos was able to make a detailed drawing. Foundations of accompanying structures were noted by Axiotis, mostly on the n. side of the basilica, which presumably would have formed other parts of the building complex which usually surrounded such centres of worship.
Bibliography: Orlandos, 1928, 323-25 and figs. 1-3; id., 1929, 4-28, figs. 1-29 and pl. I; Sotiriou, 190-91, 216, 230 and figs. 22, 43, 57; Iakobos, 32-33; Daux, 1960, 808 and fig. 1; Charitonidis, 1968a, 52-53 and pl. 26; Buchholz, 237 and fig. 41; Kontis, 1978, 285; Axiotis, 1992 I, 245-47 (and unnumbered photograph p. 247) and II, pl. 53.

211. *Rousos* (Hypsilometopo); 6184; 620m; HL.; HAB, CEM. On the upper w. slopes of the Prophitis Ilias mountain, ca. 1 km nw. from the enclosure of site #221, Euangelidis, Kontis and Axiotis all reported extensive ancient remains in the property of the Rousos family. The reports of all three scholars are almost identical, stating that at the site are significant numbers of house foundations, grey ware pottery and tiles of HL. date. In the report of Euangelidis a fluted column is also mentioned. A short distance nw. from the settlement debris were disturbed cist graves. The area covered by the ancient remains was said to be 3-4 stremmata (0.3-0.4 hectares).
Bibliography: Euangelidis, 1925-26, 154; Kontis, 1978, 285-86; Axiotis, 1992 I, 247.

212. *Monastirellia*[104] (Bapheios); 6084; 350m; A., C./HL., R., 'MAge', Tur.; HAB, CEM, SP. There have been a number of reports of ancient remains on the n. side of the Lepetymnos range in the area ca. 2 kms n. from Stypsi called 'Monastirellia' (or 'Small Monasteries'). It is extremely difficult to correlate the location of the finds with each other, however, since toponyms have become confused and precise locations (or maps) are not provided.
Axiotis, who gave the most detailed analysis of the area, stated that the toponym Monastirellia is associated by local villagers with the area around the chapel of Agios Dimitrios, ca. 1.5 kms n. from Stypsi on the e. side of the deep ravine through which the Ligonas River flows down towards the Plain of Petra. At this place the only pre-modern material he noted was a scatter of sherds and tile of 'MAge' and early modern date around foundations, wall sections and worked blocks of an older chapel. It was these remains of older structures which he suggested may have been the original 'Small Monastery' from which the area took its name.
Chatzi, however, reported that an enclosure of Lesbian polygonal masonry stood at the place named 'Monastirellia' (for this masonry style, see Appendix 2), the n. wall standing 5-6 courses high, a structure to which Axiotis made no reference. Axiotis did report a fortified enclosure of such masonry slightly further n. (further down the valley) at 'Agia Katerini' where a circular structure now used as an open-air shrine is founded upon polygonal masonry walls.
In association with the polygonal masonry enclosure at Monastirellia, Kontis spoke of pithos sherds and fragments of terracotta figurines being found, but Axiotis placed these finds to the e. of his 'Agia Katerini' location (in the property of Baliontis). At this spot, Axiotis described a number of old terrace walls, foundations of buildings, sherds from pithoi, grey wares, black-painted and red-figure vessels, tiles, clay figurine fragments and Tur. pipes, a group of finds which must be that referred to by Kontis.
Axiotis also noted a cist tomb in association with the dense scatter of ceramics to the e. of Agia Katerini, a tomb which may be one of those Kontis describes in his vague reference to R. graves and 'later tiles' having been found in the vicinity of the polygonal masonry enclosure and the scatter of pithos sherds and figurine fragments.
Bibliography: Kontis, 1978, 284-85. Chatzi, 1972, 579 and pl. 529α-γ; Axiotis, 1992 I, 268-71 and II, pl. 50.

213. Petri (village); 587835; 260m; Tur.; HAB, SP. The present village of Petri stands on the site of a mixed Tur. and Christian settlement of the same name attested from 1602 onwards.[105] In 1909 Taxis reported that there were 60 households in total, of which 10 were Ottoman. The mosque of the Tur. village is still preserved along with cisterns which collect the water from the strong springs on the terraced hillside. The traces of Tur. habitation extend immediately e. from Petri to a place named Liontari, where there are foundations of buildings, dense scatters of ceramics, cisterns, wells and two unroofed chapels of Taxiarchis and Agios Giannis. The traces of old terracing which once surrounded the village on the slopes to the e. are clearly visible.
Bibliography: Taxis, 131; Axiotis, 1992 I, 267-68.

214. *Achilopigada* (Petri); 586841; 170m; C./HL., Tur.; HAB, SP. The ruins of an abandoned village of the Tur. period lie ca. 0.6 km n. from the small village of Petri at a place known as Achilopigada. A kalderimi leads up to the ruins from the w., and a large cistern near the spring from

---

[102] Kontis (ibid.) proposed that the type of mortar in the wall, which he stated to be a strongly adhesive cement ('πορσελάνη'), suggested a late-antique rather than a 'MAge' date.

[103] The dating evidence of Axiotis is unclear since he reported a single coin from the Paliokastro Geras site (#51) (of which he gave no details), and in his report of the Kastri site near Plagia (#61) he makes no mention of any numismatic finds, see Axiotis, 1992 II, 678, 691.

[104] This is the site named 'Monastirakia' by Chatzi, see the explanation of toponyms in Section 2.1 (b) at the beginning of the catalogue.

[105] The earliest mention is in Ottoman records, M. Kiel, pers. comm. (1995). Concerning an earlier 16C Ottoman census of the island, see n. 4 above.

which the village took its name is still full of water. The first record of the village is in the 17C AC when it was named 'Chiliopigas' ('Χιλιοπηγάς'). By the 19C the population was small and only 20 Tur. households remained in 1909.

To the se. of the village ruins an ikonostasis of Agios Konstantinos stands on a rocky plateau, along the e. side of which is a wall of crudely-worked isodomic blocks. The plateau is approachable solely from this e. side (a narrow gateway exits at the se. corner) with outcrops of rock bounding the plateau to the n., s. and w.. On the plateau, the C./HL. black-glazed and grey ware sherds found by Axiotis suggest that the structure is ancient, possibly a watchtower built in order to protect the approach to the Plain of Petra from the passes over the Lepetymnos mountains to the se..
Bibliography: Taxis, 131; Kontis, 1978, figs. 23-26; Axiotis, 1992 I, 265-67 and II, pl. 56.

215. *Agia Kyriaki* (Petra); 572847; 5m; Byz.(?); SP(?). Immediately to the e. of the village of Petra (ca. 0.1 km), on the w. side of the main road from Kalloni to Methymna, Axiotis reported the ruins of a chapel (worshipped now as Agia Kyriaki) which he proposed were the remains of an EByz. basilica. Amongst the rubble a large number of worked blocks, architectural pieces, sherds and tiles were apparent, together with the foundations of the entrance and the conch. The precise dating of the chapel as early as the EByz. period is not proven (the architectural elements could have come from elsewhere), but the remains could well be of Byz. date.
Bibliography: Axiotis, 1992 I, 256.

216. *Rachonas* (Methymna); 572868; 140m; --; SP(?). To the e. of the road which leads from Methymna to Petra (near the shore) rises the hill named Rachonas, ca. 2 kms from both Petra and Methymna and 0.6 km ese. from the Agia Lemoni chapel. When digging was carried out on the flat ridgetop of the hill, large worked blocks of andesite were found from a structure of undetermined purpose. One block had a curved line on its upper surface. Kontis suggested that the material present at the site was not of the kind found at defensive structures in the area of Methymna and that the structure was possibly an altar.

Nearby, to the ne. of the Agia Lemoni chapel, Axiotis reported a scatter of grey ware sherds (including some of very dark colour) and architectural blocks including the fluted base of a perirrhantirion.
Bibliography: Kontis, 1978, 278; Axiotis, 1992 I, 233-34 and II, pl. 50.

*217. Methymna (town); 5688, 5689, 5788, 5789 (finds spread over all 4 squares); --; EBA., MBA., LBA., PG., G., A., C., HL., R., EByz., LByz., Ven., Tur.; HAB, CEM, SP. At the w. tip of the most n. part of the island is Cape Molybos,[106] where a modern tourist town overlies the site of ancient Methymna, traditionally considered the second most important city in the island for much of antiquity.

The town is dominated by the (originally Byz.[107]) kastro on a high rocky acropolis (0.114 km high), and the small modern harbour near the w. tip of the promontory is also the site of the ancient harbour. EBA. and MBA. sherds were found by Buchholz in the small plain named 'Palaia-Methymna', ne. from the modern town area. LBA. settlement activity is attested in the Dabia quarter of the town site, from where Buchholz also picked up a MG. sherd. Lamb found LG. grey wares near bedrock in trenches w. of the Agia Marina chapel and cemetery, and another trench included A. pottery associated with structural remains. BA. material, circular structures of PG.-G. date and G. pottery were found underlying A. houses and an A. street s. of the modern kastro. A., C., and HL. tomb finds are scattered all around (and within) the area of ancient habitation.

There is a dense scatter of HL. and R. pottery all over the town site, C. and HL. coins have been found, but curiously structural remains for the C., HL. and R. periods are almost completely lacking. Remains of only three buildings are reported; an isodomic (possibly HL.) stretch of walling ne. from the Kastro; a HL. triglyth block sketched by Koldewey which was reused in the Agia Marina cemetery; and lastly, blocks from the 4C BC aqueduct survive which brought water from the slopes of Lepetymnos ca. 7 kms to the se.. Elements from EByz. basilicas have been found built into many structures within the modern town itself, but their place of origin is unclear.

Basiakos also reported that to the ne. of the town at the coastal spot known as Pharos there were the remains of pottery works including an ancient kiln.
Bibliography (main); Koldewey, 16-19, 35-36 and pls. 4-5; Rouse, 147-48; Lamb, 1932, 5-11 and figs. 1-3; Charitonidis, 1960, pl. 211β; Charitonidis, 1961-62, 264 and pl. 319ε-ζ; Moutzouris, 1962, 52, 54-55; Bayne, 242-45 and fig. 25C; Petrakos, 1967c, 459; Chatzi, 1972, 595-96 and pls. 546ζ-η, 547β-γ; ead., 1973, 520 and pl. 490α-β; Kontis, 1973, 19 and fig. 13; Buchholz; Kontis, 1978, 274-76; Acheilara and Archontidou-Argyri, 1986, 202-03 and pl. 142γ; Archontidou-Argyri, 1986-87, 58-59, 71-72; Acheilara and Archontidou-Argyri, 1987, 481-82, fig. 6 and pl. 289β-γ; Basiakos, 210; Archontidou-Argyri, 1988, 463-65, figs. 12-13 and pls. 280-81α; Axiotis, 1992 I, 220-230 and II, pls. 47-49; BSA W. Lamb archive Methymna 1 and plans 2-3, unpublished.

218. *Temenos* (Bapheios); 5886, 609859, 6087;[108] --; C.; SP. Four 'oros' inscriptions of C. date recording the limit of an unlocated temenos have been reported.

(a) On the e. side of the Rachonas hill, 1 km from its s. lip 'on an irregular plateau' (Kontis), part of an outcrop of bedrock is inscribed

ΟΡΟΣ
ΤΕ

(ὅρος τε[μένεος).

The inscription faces w. (possibly implying the temenos lies behind it to the e.), and the height of the letters ranges from between 0.065 m - 0.075 m.

[106] Molybos was also the Turkish name for the town of Methymna.

[107] It is not clear when the kastro of Methymna was first built, but it is possible to construct a *terminus ante quem* of the early 14C AC (ie. LByz.) with the knowledge that it is named amongst those which the Phocaean commander Dominikos

Katanis failed to take in 1334, see Moutzouris, 1962, 52. The kastro is also one of those handed over to the Gattelusi in 1355 AD, and in 1373 AD the castle was 'renewed'.

[108] The three grid references given relate to the separate locations of the first three inscriptions catalogued here.

(b) The second is built into the e. wall of the Agia Parakseui chapel in the village of Bapheios

ΟΡΟΣ
ΤΕΜΕ

(ὅρος τεμέ[νεος]).

The stele is of local grey trachyte (0.62 m x 0.81 m), and the letters (0.05 m in height) are cut at the bottom. Axiotis suggested that this inscription had not been moved very far and had marked the e. boundary of the 'temenos'.

(c) The third oros inscription was found 1.1 kms n. from Bapheios near the road to Methymna, built into the *mandri* of a villager of Bapheios. On a broken stele of local grey-red stone 0.275 m x 0.24 m (only the lower part remains) there is the inscription

ΟΡΟΣ
ΤΕΜ
ΕΝ . ΟΣ

(ὅρος τεμέν[ε]ος).

The height of the letters ranges from 0.05 m - 0.09 m.

(d) A fourth inscription (which it is impossible to place accurately on a map) was found by Koumarelas 'near Bapheios' and published recently by Axiotis.

ΟΡΟΣ
ΤΕΜΕ
ΝΟΣ

(ὅρος τέμενος).

The height of the letters ranges from 0.07 m - 0.09 m.

The lettering of all four inscriptions is very similar (Kontis proposed that [a], [b], and [c], had been cut by the same hand), and suggests a date in the second half of the 5C or the first half of the 4C.[109]
Bibliography: A. Wilhelm, 'Inschriften aus Lesbos', *AM* 16 (1891), no. 3 (p. 132); *IG* XII.2 no. 521; Kontis, 1978, 278-79; Axiotis, 1992 I, 215, 218, 234 and II, 568 and pl. 46.

219. *Ekklise Bagir* (Bapheios); 617872; 460m; C./HL., LR.-Byz.; HAB/SP(?). Immediately to the e. of the road from Argenos to Bapheios, 1.5 kms ne. from the latter village, is the hill known as 'Ekklise Bagir' in Turkish ('Chatzologou' in Greek). On the small plateau immediately above the road are foundations (more clearly visible on the n. edge) together with a threshold block. Digging at the spot brought to light a mass of sherds and tiles. Surface material on the s. slope included grey wares and black-glazed sherds (probably of C./HL. date) and pieces of LR.-Byz. 'combed' wares. The threshold block (which in this case is not associated with any EByz. architectural *membra*) is similar to those found by Koldewey in the w. of the island at the sites of watchtowers (eg. Koldewey, pl. 27.2). The similar stone and foundations in a comparably prominent position at this location may be the remains of a similar structure.

Bibliography: Axiotis, 1992 I, 212-13 and II, pl. 45.

220. *Agios Thomas* (Argenos); 626878; 410m; --; CEM. Ca. 1.6 kms w. from Argenos, on the n. side of the road towards Methymna (just before the turning to Bapheios), stands a ruined shrine dedicated to Agios Thomas (which incorporates a number of EByz. architectural pieces). Between the shrine and the main road (ca. 20 m from the shrine) Axiotis reported that tombs had been uncovered, the clay cover slabs of which lay broken nearby. No more details of the finds are provided, but in the area near the tombs a number of tiles and sherds were found, possibly the disturbed contents of the graves.
Bibliography: Axiotis, 1992 I, 212 and II, pl. 45.

221. *Prophitis Ilias* (Hypsilometopo); 626841; 620m; A.; HAB(?), SP. Ca. 1.1 kms n. from the village of Hypsilometopo, on the slopes immediately below the summit of the Prophitis Ilias mountain, Kontis noted the remains of an enclosure of Lesbian polygonal masonry (see Appendix 2). Some of the walls were supporting terraces, others were part of a defensive enclosure. Foundations within the enclosure were suggested to be parts of an inner roofed stronghold. No dimensions are given for the enclosure. On the British Army map a spring is marked very close to this spot on the s. slopes of the mountain which may help to explain the feasibility of establishing a garrison point at this location. The view from the site is spectacular, extending over the Kalloni plain to the mouth of the Gulf of Kalloni near Makara and Niphida more than 30 kms to the s..
Bibliography: Kontis, 1978, 285; Axiotis, 1992 I, 247.

222. *Viran Köy* (Hypsilometopo); 638833; 460m; 'MAge'; HAB. Beside the newly rebuilt chapel of Agios Nikolaos, 1 km ene. from Hypsilometopo on the n. side of the road to Kapi, are the remains of a deserted settlement. The surrounding area is known by its Tur. name of 'Viran Köy' ('Ruined Village'), a name which is used often in Turkish to imply that there are antiquities nearby. On the slopes above the chapel Axiotis reported that the foundations of houses, rubble and sherds of 'MAge' date are apparent.[110]
Bibliography: Axiotis, 1992 I, 241.

223. *Thermokastro* (Argenos); 643886; 310m; 'MAge'; HAB, SP. On the n. end of the ridge on which the village of Argenos stands (ca. 0.6 km n. from the village), before the steep drop down to the coast, the remains of a small 'MAge' kastro are preserved at a place known as Thermokastro. The 2 m thick walls are constructed of small mortared stones and the overall dimensions of the structure are ca. 50 m (e.-w.) x 30 m (n.-s.). A circular tower is preserved at the nw. corner, and the other corners of the kastro also seem to have once possessed similar towers. Inside the walls and on the saddle of the hill to the s. are the foundations of other buildings, and Axiotis reported that the whole area is covered with pottery of 'MAge' date. A more precise chronology for the site is difficult but Axiotis' description recalls many similar

---

[109] The sigma especially suggests such a date, since it is an example of the more early, angular four-barred variety.

[110] There was an earlier Tur. village of 'Ypsilometopo' attested in the Ottoman records in 1602 (M. Kiel, pers. comm. [1995]), and these remains could conceivably be of that settlement. Concerning an earlier 16C Ottoman census of the island, see n. 4 above.

fortified centres of Ven. and Tur. date in the island, of which Thermokastro is another example.
Bibliography: Axiotis, 1992 I, 211-12 and II, pl. 42.

224. *Prophitis Ilias* (Sykamia); 665884; 270m; EByz.; SP. On the main road w. from Sykamia towards Chalikas and Argenos, ca. 0.5 km nw. from Sykamia and 0.1 km below the road to the n., is a small rocky plateau known as Prophitis Ilias. On the s. side of the plateau is a *mandri*, and on the ridge itself are the foundations of an EByz. basilica with associated architectural *membra* and dense scatters of sherd and tile. An ikonostasis has been formed to the w. of the foundations on the plateau using blocks from the basilica. It is probably from this site that the large number of EByz. architectural blocks (without associated foundations) reported by Daux, Charitonidis, Chatzi and Axiotis in Sykamia and Skala Sykamias originate.[111]
Bibliography: Charitonidis, 1961-62, 263-64 and pl. 319α-δ; Daux, 1962, 876 figs. 5-6; Charitonidis, 1968a, 58-59, fig. 30 and pls. 31, 32α-β and 33; Chatzi, 1973, 519 and pl. 489α; Axiotis, 1992 I, 204-06 and II, pls. 41-42.

*225. *Agia Anastasia* (Kleio); 714888; 50m; EByz.; SP. At the w. edge of the bay and small coastal plain known as Tsionia, 3.3 kms ne. from Kleio, Orlandos discovered (but never published fully) the remains of a basilica comprising a nave and two flanking aisles dated to the second half of the 6C AC. The basilica stands on the low plateau to the n. of a small seasonal flow which enters the plain of Tsionia from the w.. Today much of the building is buried under the olive grove in which it lies and the remaining architectural pieces have been gathered together in the apse of the n. aisle. More worked blocks from the chapel can be found near the chapel of Agios Athanasios (ca. 1 km to the se.). The whole s.-facing slope on which the monument stands, as far as the river-bed, is densely scattered with ceramics.
Bibliography: Orlandos, 1937, 115 n. 1; id., 1952-54, 212-13 and fig. 168.5; Charitonidis, 1968a, 59-60 and pl. 32γ; Kontis, 1978, 287-88; Axiotis, 1992 I, 200-01 and II, pl. 40.

226. *Agia Sotira* (Kleio); 728889; 5m; Byz.(?); CEM, SP(?). On the n. arm of the Tsionia Bay, ca. 4 kms ne. from Kleio, stands a chapel of Agia Sotira (Christos Sotir) underneath which foundations of an older structure were found when renovations were carried out to the chapel. Other rock-cut features are visible nearby and over the whole area is a dense scatter of ceramics. The remains of four or five cist graves with cover slabs are visible near the shore which Axiotis suggested to be of Byz. date. The chapel here is associated with the tradition that a monastery (dedicated to Christos) once stood in the parish of Korakas (a toponym attested nearby, see #227 and #229). A block was dredged from the sea in the bay with the word ']ΩΘΗΚΕΝ' inscribed on it, and the toponym of 'Tsionia' is explained locally as deriving from the 'columns' ('kionia') that were also reportedly found in the bay by fishermen.
Bibliography: Axiotis, 1992 I, 199-200; Mason, 1993, 247.

227. *Korakas* (Kleio); 715882; 100m; Ven., Tur.; HAB(?), SP. Near the ne. point of the island, 3 kms ne. from Kleio, the ruins of a kastro stand on the end of the ridge before the steep drop to the shore. The approach is easiest from the sw. where on the terraced slopes Axiotis reported a dense scatter of glazed sherds, suggesting that there may have been an associated settlement outside the walls. A lower, outer wall constructed of mortared, unworked stones (and including a well-preserved circular tower) stands up to 1.5 m along the w. and n. sides of the ridge with foundations visible inside the wall. Also inside the wall a chapel of Agia Kyriaki (with EByz. architectural pieces nearby) stands near a spring which the wall encloses. An inner enclosure wall with another circular tower stands around the upper slopes, ca. 2 m thick and 5 m high on the ne. side. On the n. and e. sides of the hilltop is a mass of fallen rocks, tiles and sherds from the other collapsed walls. Less debris is apparent to the w. where the blocks have been employed to construct numerous terrace walls. A square tower of similar construction was also reported by Axiotis, standing slightly to the s. of the main fortification apparently serving as an outlying watchtower. At the n. foot of the hill are the traces of a kalderimi which leads e. to the bay of Tsionia (see #225-226).

The kastro at Korakas is almost certainly that referred to by Gonzalez de Clavijo as the kastro of 'Cuaraca' seen on his voyage between Methymna and Mytilene in 1404 AD, thereby dating the site's construction to the Ven. period at the latest (Mason dated the site specifically to the 14C AC). Axiotis noted, however, that on later maps from 1420 onwards the site is referred to as 'Palaiokastro', taking this name to mean that the kastro had been abandoned by this time.[112]
Bibliography: Moutzouris, 1962, 54, 67; Axiotis, 1992 I, 198-99, 201 and II, pls. 36, 39; Mason, 1993, 240.

228. *Pegia* (Kleio); 720880; 15m; LR.-Byz., 'MAge'; HAB. At the e. foot of the Palaiokastro hill, 3 kms ne. from Kleio, stands a (now unroofed) chapel of Agios Athanasios, near which (in the area known as Pegia) are reused blocks from the EByz. basilica of Agia Anastasia (#225) and traces of habitation activity. A dense scatter of tiles and glazed sherds of 'MAge' date are apparent near the chapel, and on the shore immediately to the se. are foundations of buildings and more sherds (including LR.-Byz. 'combed' wares).
Bibliography: Axiotis, 1992 I, 200-01 and II, pl. 40.

229. *Agios Blasis* (Kleio) 693868; 200m; 'MAge'; HAB, CEM, SP(?). Beside the late 19C chapel of Agios Blasis, ca. 0.7 km n. from Kleio, Axiotis reported that a bulldozer cutting near the chapel revealed four cist graves with stone cover slabs. The associated funeral goods were poor, comprising only some glazed 'MAge' sherds. A short distance to the e., near a chapel of Agios Ioannis, three or four more tombs were uncovered when the chapel was

---

[111] The only possibly *in situ* antiquities ever reported in Skala Sykamias are the 'squared ashlar blocks and other dressed stones' underlying the modern harbour mole described by Green, 214, suggested to date back at least to the HL. period (ibid.).

[112] Axiotis, 1992 I, 199, refers to the maps of Buondelmonti (ca. 1420), Porcacchi (1576) and Coronelli (1688) which label the site as a 'Palaiokastro'. The hypothesis that the kastro had already been abandoned by 1420 does not necessarily conflict with the report of de Clavijo, however, since the latter does not describe the condition of the kastro when he sailed past in 1404. For two other topographical discussions of voyages around this ne. tip of the island see Mason, 1979, 157-62; Green, 213-14 (with the map, p. 211).

renewed in 1934, and on the hillside a dense scatter of tile and sherds of 'MAge' date is reported.

In a patriarchal edict of 1331 AD reference is made to a monastery of 'Agios Ioannis Theologou' in the parish of 'Korakas' (see #227) which may relate to the remains beside these two chapels.[113]
Bibliography: Axiotis, 1992 I, 196-97.

230. *Prophitis Ilias* (Kleio); 704858; 320m; C.(?); SP. On the peak of the Prophitis Ilias hill, ca. 1.3 kms ese. from Kleio, the small chapel of the same name is built partly over a rectangular tower of coursed polygonal masonry 11.5 m (n.-s.) x 6.5 m (e.-w.). Up to three courses are preserved on the w. and s. sides, and a natural rock outcrop forms the s. half of the e. wall. Immediately to the s., a lower plateau has a passageway cut into its sw. side to allow an approach to be made to the upper area where the tower stands. Axiotis noted very few sherds on the plateau around the tower, none of which were diagnostic as to its possible date.
Bibliography: Axiotis, 1992 I, 189-91 (and unnumbered photograph p. 190) and II, pl. 38.

231. *Koukmidos* (Kleio); 705854; 200m; Tur.; HAB, CEM, SP. In a sheltered location on the sides of a well-watered valley between the hills of Prophitis Ilias (#230) and Agia Sotira (#237) are the remains of the Tur. village of Koukmidos, attested in Ottoman records from 1602,[114] abandoned in 1912 after the island gained independence from Turkey, and razed by neighbouring Greek villagers soon afterwards (on 8th December 1912). A neighbouring village of Tzoukaloton lay a few hundred metres to the n. (at the place now known as Skalota). Gabriel of Methymna recorded that in the mid-17C[115] Koukmidos possessed 43 Christian households, whilst Tzoukaloton had only 40 poor families. The latter village had been abandoned by 1850 (with the people dispersing to other nearby villages) and in 1909 Koukmidos was itself only a small village of 30 Tur. households.

At the site of Koukmidos, amongst the mass of ruined buildings are preserved a wall of the village mosque, part of the bath building and an olive press. Nearby are springs with ruined, arched fountainheads. A neighbouring field is known to be the location of the village cemetery.

The ruins of the neighbouring Tzoukaloton lie above Koukmidos on the valley slopes to the n., where a mass of foundations, tiles, pithoi and fine wares with green, yellow and white glaze are apparent in large quantities. Slightly to the w. of the site lie stretches of a kalderimi which linked the area with the e. coast at the Geni Limani (#237).
Bibliography: Taxis, 127; Axiotis, 1992 I, 191-92.

232. *Kastri* (Kapi); 694834; 400m; A./C.(?); SP(?). At Kastri on the e. edge of the peak of the Mauria hill, 1 km nw. from Mandamados, Axiotis reported a substantial ancient enclosure. The outer face of the wall is built of polygonal masonry with two well-formed outer faces and a rubble fill, 1 m in thickness and in places up to 1 m high.

An external tower is built against the w. wall, and on the s. side is a small gate. Foundations are apparent inside the enclosure but Axiotis found few sherds anywhere on the hill.
Bibliography: Axiotis, 1992 I, 193-94 and II, pl. 39.

233. *Karanik Çay* (Kapi); 677824; 250m; Tur.; HAB, CEM. A well-preserved kalderimi leads steeply downhill (s.) from Kapi, following the e. bank of the Tsiknias River, eventually reaching Napi over 7 kms away. Ca. 2.3 kms ssw. from Kapi (after crossing an arched Tur. bridge), the paved road passes beside the remains of an abandoned settlement of the Tourkokratia which are apparent on either side of a tributary of the river (known as the Karanik Çay) on the sw. slopes of the Mauria hill.[116] The surrounding slopes (which have a steady water supply from two nearby springs) are covered in old, stone-built terraces and a dense scatter of sherds and tiles. An old water mill, threshing floors, cisterns and press-stones, together with the ruin of a chapel and a rock-cut tomb (still with its crudely-worked cover slab intact), all indicate that a significant settlement once existed at the spot.
Bibliography: Axiotis, 1992 I, 237; id., 1994, fig. Δ.

234. *Agia Photia* (Napi) 6579; --; 'MAge'; HAB, CEM. Below the s. slopes of the Katimaltis hill, ca. 2.5 kms nnw. from Napi, a cluster of remains of 'MAge' (probably Tur.) date are apparent on a small plateau known as Agia Photia. The plateau is sited on the w. bank of the Tsiknias River with a spring at its n. foot, around which Axiotis reported a dense scatter of 'MAge' tiles and sherds. A kalderimi passes below the plateau to the w. (which leads sw. to the Kremasti bridge, #110), and at the n. foot of the rise are two rock-cut tombs. On top of the plateau are foundations of buildings, an old chapel (presumably that of Agia Photia) and a disused aloni.
Bibliography: Axiotis, 1992 I, 353-54 and II, pls. 73-74.

235. *Drakou Pidima* (Napi); 666787; 250m; A., C./HL.; SP. To the ne. of the village of Napi (ca. 1.3 kms), the dirt road heading ne. to Mandamados winds over the saddle of a ridge running n.-s.. As the road turns sharply e. in the saddle, before descending to head n. along the w. side of the narrow valley below (the 'Daimonolangas'), it passes a rocky outcrop and small plateau to the right of the road known as the 'Drakou Pidima' or 'Dragon's Leap'.[117]

The outcrop has sheer cliffs on its n., e. and se. sides, and in the only direction from which it is approachable (the w.) are stretches of Lesbian polygonal masonry (see Appendix 2 and fig. 20) which wall off the small plateau of the outcrop and make the area in effect a small fortified acropolis.[118] Traces of other Lesbian masonry walls, together with a number of isodomic blocks, lie on the plateau above the outer enclosure, the latter possibly the

---

[113] The monastery referred to in the edict could also be in the west of the island since some scholars have associated it with the Hypsilo Monastery (#174), also near a toponym 'Korakas', see Axiotis, 1992 I, 196.

[114] M. Kiel, pers. comm. (1995). Concerning an earlier 16C Ottoman census of the island, see n. 4 above.

[115] Gabriel's description of Lesbos probably dates from between 1636-41, see n. 47.

[116] The Tur. toponym 'Karanik' is the equivalent of the Greek 'Mauria', and other Tur. placenames are preserved in the area including Haji Bey ('Mr. Pilgrim', namely 'one who has been to Mecca') and Güzel Tepe ('Beautiful Mound').

[117] The toponym is explained in local legend by the unprecedented leap of an athlete from Methymna, a coppersmith by trade, between the two widely-spaced, prominent rocks of the outcrop. So unbelievable was the leap made by the smith that everafter the spot was known as the 'Dragon's Leap'.

[118] This impression explains an alternative Turkish toponym for the place, 'Kale' ('Kastro').

remains of a later tower at the site. Many of the polygonal walls are now in danger of collapse and were in much better condition when Euangelidis visited the site and published a photograph of the polygonal walls some 70 years ago.

In 1971 Chatzi noted a few C./HL. black-glazed sherds on the peak to the s. beside the possible inner tower of isodomic masonry, and Axiotis reported a dense scatter of tile in this area as if this structure was once roofed. The latter also reported amphora sherds at the site. In a field nearby (the exact location of which was not given), Euangelidis found an inscribed weight of 5 minas ('MMMMM'), which Axiotis dated to the 3C BC.

The main feature of the site's location is its strong defensive position on a natural route from the ne. edge of the Arisbe plain, ne. towards the e. coast of the island where modern Mandamados is situated. Kontis suggested, however, that the outpost could watch the e. seaboard and a large area of the lands of Arisbe (to the s.), but these are two directions in which the topography blocks a wide vista.[119]

Bibliography: Taxis, 125; Euangelidis, 1924-25, 51-52 and fig. 19; Chatzi, 1971, 456-57 and pl. 459; Kontis, 1978, 291-92; Axiotis, 1992 I, 354-55 and II, pls. 74-75; Mason, 1993, 239-40 and pls. I-II.

236. *Taxiarchis* (Mandamados); 706829; 130m; Tur.; SP. The earliest records of a church on the site of the Taxiarchis Monastery (1 km nne. from Mandamados) are in the mid-17C AC when ecclesiastical records, and an inscription on a well near the site, attest its existence in 1661 and 1662 respectively. Traces of a kalderimi lead from Mandamados to the monastery. The first description of the site as a 'monastery' is in a patriarchal document of 1728. In the later 18C a tower was built at the nw. side of the enclosure along with cells for the monks. In 1838 the whole region around the monastery was declared a holy area by the Tur. governor Abdul Mejit. Pilgrims came from far around for the festival of Taxiarchis, with records stating that in 1897 people travelled from as far away as Adramyttium as well as the area of Ayvalik opposite the island (see #239).
Bibliography: Newton I, 108-09; Rouse, 150-51; Taxis, 126; Mason, 1979, 163; Axiotis, 1992 I, 181-84.

237. *Agia Sotira* (Kleio); 721854; 170m; A., C./HL., Byz./Tur.; HAB, SP. The hill and chapel named Agia Sotira stand ca. 3 kms ese. from Kleio, overlooking the small hamlet of Neo (Geni) Limani on the e. shore of the island. The location is of significance since it dominates the only easy approach inland (w.) from this part of the coastline towards modern Kleio and thereby a route around to the n. side of the Lepetymnos mountain range.

Around the peak of the hill (on top of which stands the chapel of Agia Sotira) are the traces of an enclosure wall of Lesbian polygonal masonry, ca. 1 m thick (see Appendix 2). The wall follows the ridge of the hilltop except where rock outcrops offer a natural barrier at the sw. corner. The cruder courses of walling on top of the Lesbian masonry gives clear signs that the wall has been rebuilt in places since antiquity, and the date of this rebuilding may be related to the kalderimi which approaches the hill from the sw.. Foundations of buildings inside the enclosure are associated with a dense scatter of tiles, sherds and cut blocks (with cuttings for clamps). The latter group of blocks may be the remains of a C./HL. tower constructed subsequently inside the outer enclosure wall. A scatter of grey ware and black-painted sherds extends over the top of the hill and also on the sw. slope. At the nw. point, beside the chapel, the foundations of an ancient structure of isodomic blocks are visible, quite possibly the foundations of a tower.
Bibliography: Axiotis, 1991a; Axiotis, 1992 I, 188-89 and II, pl. 37.

238. *Angourelia Sarakinas* (Mandamados); 739845; 232m; EBA.; HAB. Following the road past the Taxiarchis Monastery (#236), one reaches an area known as Sarakinas ca. 4 kms ne. from Mandamados. A chapel of Agios Giannis stands at the sw. foot of a hill, steep from the w. approach, named Angourelia. A path leads up onto the hilltop from the w., and at this w. end Axiotis reported a scatter of EBA. material including black and grey Troy I sherds, pieces of pithoi, a spindle whorl and a scatter of lithics and millstones. The location dominates the immediate area, and the view from the site is panoramic especially to the n. and e. where the coastline of Anatolia is clearly visible. Two springs on the hill also ensure that a water supply is available in this generally more barren region of the island.
Bibliography: Axiotis, 1991b; Axiotis, 1992 I, 185 (and unnumbered photograph p. 186) and II, pl. 35; French, 1993, 65.

239. *Palios* (Mandamados); 773835; 15m; HL., R., EByz., Tur.; HAB, CEM. Ca. 7 kms ene. from Mandamados are the remains of an extensive coastal settlement near the small hamlet and harbour of Palios. The low hill on the shore at Palios (ca. 0.2 km across) is densely covered in ancient remains: R. and Byz. pottery (including Syrian amphorae) is present in large amounts; ancient walls, monolithic EByz. columns and 4 ancient wells are apparent on the plateau of the hilltop; HL. cist graves together with rock-cut EByz. tombs (sometimes containing more than one body) lie beyond the n. limit of the hill on which the settlement was sited.

The ancient harbour lay below the settlement site to the sw., an area from where the sea has since regressed. This spot is 0.5 km sw. along the coast from the early modern harbour at Anoiktos, a location of great importance in the 18C, 19C and early 20C as the harbour where pilgrims from Asia Minor landed when visiting the Taxiarchis Monastery near Mandamados (#236). However, after the Treaty of Lausanne in July 1923 which initiated the return of Greeks from Asia Minor, the harbour ceased to function since one of its main sources of sea traffic was ended.
Bibliography: Newton I, 109-10; Conze, 20; Koldewey, 36; Taxis, 126 and n. 2; Charitonidis, 1968a, 60; Kontis, 1978, 287-88.; Mason, 1979, 162 and fig. 2; D. E. Psarrou, 'Ο Παληός καί η σημασία του στον Αιολικό χώρο', *Mytilini* 2 (1982), 81-103; Basiakos, 210; Paraskeuaidis, 1987, 71-85; Axiotis, 1992 I, 170-73 and II, pls. 33-34; Mason, 1993, 235, 245 and n. 89.

240. *Nisos Panagias* (Mandamados) 800822; 5m; BA.; HAB(?). On the islet of the Panagia, the northernmost of the small group known as the 'Leukai Nisoi' (9.5 kms e. from Mandamados), Axiotis reported that sherds of BA. date were once found, but gave no more details.

---

[119] To the s. the view is blocked by the brow of the hill behind the site, and to the e. the higher slopes across the narrow valley 1 km away form an impediment to a wide panorama, so the comments of Kontis (1978, 292) are difficult to understand.

Bibliography: Axiotis, 1992 I, 173.

241. *Agios Stephanos* (Mandamados); 753808; 20m; LByz.; SP. Near the e. shore of the island, 5 kms ese. from Mandamados, where a number of clay sources are still used by the local potters,[120] stands the Byz. church of Agios Stephanos constructed of blocks of red trachyte. The church is cross-shaped in plan (suggesting a LByz. date, see #3, #9, #176), exhibits three apses (one on the end of each aisle as well as on the end of the nave), and once possessed a domed roof. The original roof had already collapsed when Newton visited the site in the mid-19C, but has since been rebuilt (quite 'unskilfully', according to Charitonidis). Architectural blocks of an older chapel (and a R. inscription) are built into the walls, and in the 19C a decree on a marble statue base was visible, forming part of the paved floor inside the church (*IG* XII.2.516).[121]

Bibliography: Newton I, 109; Conze, 20; Taxis, 127; Charitonidis, 1966, 72 and pl. V; Green, 211, n. 14 and map (p. 211); Axiotis, 1992 I, 166-67 and II, pl. 34; Mason, 1993, 245-47.

242. *Taxiarchis tou Stenaka* (Mandamados); 7380; --; LR., 'MAge', Tur.(?); HAB, SP. Ca. 3.5 kms ese. from Mandamados, on a plateau above the w. bank of the Libadi rema, are the traces of a deserted settlement associated with which Axiotis reported pottery of LR. and 'MAge' date. The n. and s. walls of a small chapel known as 'Taxiarchis tou Stenaka' (constructed of mortared tile and stone) are also preserved amongst the other structural remains and ceramic scatter. The ruins have been associated with one of the villages which Gabriel of Methymna reported as lying close to Mandamados in his description of Lesbos dated 1636-41.[122]

Bibliography: Axiotis, 1992 I, 165.

243. *Kabakli* (Mandamados); 729770; 160m; Tur.; HAB, CEM. To the s. of the Makri Gialos bay, 5.5 kms sse. from Mandamados, a chapel of Agia Marina stands on the edge of the upland ridge which overlooks the coastline and the main road to Mytilene. The area is known as Kabakli (Turkish for 'poplar grove') a name which has led some scholars to equate the remains at the site with those of ancient Aigeiros (the ancient Greek word for 'black poplar') mentioned by Strabo (13.2.2).[123] At present, however, the only find in the area possibly of antique date is a sarcophagus burial unearthed at the settlement of the Makri Gialos which contained two skeletons together with bronze, glass and gold offerings. All of the other remains at Kabakli seem to date to the Medieval period. These include millstones and cist graves described by Anagnostis in 1850, and a number of finds published recently by Axiotis: the remains of a Tur. chiftlik to the se. of the Agia Marina chapel; an enclosure of undiagnostic date slightly further to the s. with two external towers; a millstone; part of an olive press; a rock-cut tomb; a scatter of undiagnostic tiles and sherds. Also, (S.) Paraskeuaidis apparently found the remains of a rural shrine or basilica near an unroofed chapel of Agios Georgios at Kabakli, but gave no further details regarding its location or possible date.

In sum, the finds at Kabakli seem to be the remains of a Medieval village (possibly that of 'Geiros' which is listed among a group of villages on the east coast of the island in the Mitropolitan codex of 1567[124]), but as yet there is no significant ancient component to the site which might help clarify the location of Aigeiros.

Bibliography: Taxis, 127; Petrakos, 1967c, 459; Charitonidis, 1968a, 60; Kontis, 1978, 234, 262, 287; Mason, 1979, 156-60; Green, 212 and n. 21; Axiotis, 1992 I, 162-65 and II, pl. 32; Mason, 1993, 238-43.

244. *Prasologos* (Nees Kydonies); 767778; 3m; BA.; HAB. On the islet of Prasologos, ca. 5.5 kms nne. from Nees Kydonies in the bay of Makri Gialos, Axiotis gave a very brief report that sherds of BA date had been found (no further details were offered).

Bibliography: Axiotis, 1992 I, 162.

---

[120] Basiakos, 209, noted that a large numbers of clay beds and ca. 20 modern kilns can be found in the immediate surrounding area.

[121] In 1850 Anagnostis reported that the inscription had been visible twenty-five years before but was no longer apparent. A broken part of it was later seen at the Taxiarchis Monastery near Mandamados, and it is now reported to be at Methymna (see *IG* XII.2.516 [p. 109] and Mason, 1993, 245 n. 91).

[122] For this dating of Gabriel's description, see n. 47.

[123] As a warning to this attractive association of these two placenames, Mason, 1993, 243 (and n. 77), noted that the Turkish toponym 'Kabakli' is not particularly rare, frequently appearing in the European provinces of Turkey.

---

[124] The relevant section of the 16C AC codex (which catalogued all the communities administered by the Mitropolitan of Mytilene) listed (in order): Kydona [see sites #2-3], Pigi, Geiros ('Γεῖρος'), Mystegna [see site #4], Thermi, Afalonas [see sites #13-15] and Moria. See Mason, 1993, 238.

EPIGRAPHICALLY-ATTESTED SITES IN LESBOS

1.1 Introduction

An important addition to the pattern of settlement established through archaeological sources presented in the gazetteer is that which can be pieced together from a small corpus of Hellenistic and late Roman inscriptions.[1] Only two inscriptions date from the former period,[2] and the larger latter group relate to censuses carried out during the late third and early fourth centuries AC by Diokletian as the basis for a new system of taxation (censuses which were carried out in many parts of the province of Asia). The importance of these inscriptions in the context of settlement distribution is that they list a number of 'villages' ('χωρία'), many of which can be placed with confidence on the map of Lesbos (fig. 15).[3]

The inscriptions catalogue estates of landowners spread amongst the lands of different villages, detailing the way in which each estate was divided up between land for sown crops, vines, olives and pasture. One of the Lesbos inscriptions[4] has the added refinement of the land assessed being divided into two rates depending on its varying quality, a complication in the assessment which was abandoned later.[5] Where the names of the villages can be mapped they are found largely in the southeast of the island, a situation which has led to suggestions that the preserved records concern solely the lands of Mytilene.[6] A significant number of placenames are still unlocated, however, and given the common pattern of fragmented agricultural landholding there is no *a priori* reason to deny that certain other toponyms on the inscriptions which match places in the centre and north of the island are indeed referring to these known sites.[7]

There is no explicit statement elucidating to whom the estates belonged, but similar lists cataloguing rural estates (such as those from Thera and Astypalaia) are arranged under the names of individual landowners, 'δεσποταί' or 'δεσποτίαι', who possessed lands in many of the islands' villages.[8] In an inscription from Tralles, southeast from modern Izmir,[9] the estates are listed by 'field' ('ἀγρός') with the toponym following, and are again probably those of individuals, although this is not made explicitly clear on the surviving portion of the inscription.

1.2 Site Gazetteer

In Lesbos, the villages listed whose names can be read with confidence are as follows (an asterisk signifies a village the location of which is known, see fig. 15):

IG XII.2.74.

Col. (b)   * ἐν τῶ χωρίω ἐπάνω τᾶς Κιλλάω[[10]

IG XII.2.76.

Col. (b)	Χω.[ρίον] Μάγδια σὺν σπαρτ.
Col. (c)	Χω.[ρίον] Τείχεα
Col. (d)	Χω.[ρίον] Ὑποχόρια
	Χω.[ρίον] Τείχεα
Col. (e)	Χω.[ρίον] Ἀκτάων
Col. (g)	Χω.[ρίον] Πύργου μερ. <
	* Χω.[ρίον] Συκοῦντος μερ. δ'
Col. (h)	* Χω.[ρίον] Πυῤῥίου
	* Χω.[ρίον] Πέτρ(α)
Col. (i)	Χω.[ρίον] Τριοδότο[υ]
Col. (k)	* Χω.[ρίον] Ἡρακλεους μερ. --
	Χω.[ρίον] Σεμπρωνίου[11]

IG XII.2.77.

Col. (b)   Χ[ωρίον] Κενχρέω[ν[12]

---

[1] **Hellenistic:** *IG* XII.2 74-75; **late Roman:** *IG* XII.2.76-80, Charitonidis, 1968b, no. 17 (pp. 13-17); Williams and Parker.

[2] For this dating see Charitonidis, 1968b, 13-14 (citing H. Pistorius, *Beiträge zur Geschichte von Lesbos im vierten Jahrhundert v. Chr.* [Bonn, 1913], 153-54); Kontis, 1978, 29-30.

[3] In the Hellenistic inscriptions a number of other estates are attested at certain toponyms (some of which can be located), but there is no evidence to suggest that actual 'villages' (or other settlements) existed at these places in the same way as the late Roman inscriptions specifically state. For a discussion of some of these Hellenistic toponyms see Mantzuranes, 411.

[4] *IG* XII.2.79.

[5] A. H. M. Jones, 'Census records of the later Roman Empire', *JRS* 43 (1953), 49 and n. 1.

[6] Mantzuranes, 412.

[7] There are late Roman villages mentioned on the inscriptions at Pyrrha (Πυῤῥίου), Petra (Πέτρ[α]), Nape (Νάπ[α]) and Gerissi (Γερισσι[, possibly ancient Aigeiros) which could certainly be equated with the sites bearing these names on the east shore of the Gulf of Kalloni, the northern coast, the centre, and eastern coast of the island respectively; *pace* Déléage, 178.

[8] F. H. de Gaertringen (ed.) *IG* XII.3 (Berlin, 1898), nos. 343-49 (Thera); *CIG* vol. IV, no. 8656 (Thera), 8657 (Astypalaia).

[9] M. A. Fontrier, 'Inscription de Tralles', *BCH* 4 (1880), 336-38.

[10] Equated by Mantzuranes, 411, with the toponyms 'Τσίλια' and ' Ὄρος' near modern Plomari.

[11] Déléage, 177-78, noted that this name, along with 'Μακρινιανῶν' and '<Ο>ὐιτελλίου', also could have been the names of estates rather than village names.

[12] Mantzuranes, 412, and Déléage, 177, placed Kenchreai near to Thermi on the evidence of *IG* XII.2.103 which spoke of a fountain and aqueduct running from Kenchreai to the sanctuary of Artemis at Thermi. The length of the aqueduct is unclear, however, and says little about the spatial relationship of the villages at its beginning and end.

Col. (d)   *   Χω.[ρίον] Μακρινιανῶν[13]
Col. (e)   *   Χω.[ρίον] Νάπ[α[14]

IG XII.2.78.

Col. (b)   *   Χω.[ρίον] Ἡρακλῆς
                *   Χω.[ρίον] Μέσου ἀγροῦ
Col. (c)   Χω.[ρίον Ο]ὐιτελλίου τοῦ αὐτοῦ
                    μερ. δ'[15]

IG XII.2.79.

Col. (a)   *   Χω.[ρίον] Τύδαι Ελπι[δήφορος
                *   Χω.[ρίον] Λευκὴ ἀκ[τ]ὴ σὺν
                    τεμένει
Col. (b)   Χω.[ρίον] Μαρμαρίνη ληνὸς ὑπὸ
                    Διονύσιον γεωργ.
                    Χω.[ρίον] Πυργίου ὑπὸ τὸν αὐτόν

Charitonidis, 1968b, no. 17.

Col. B   *   Χω.[ρίον] Κώμης
                    Χω.[ρίον] Τενιάς
                *   Χω.[ρίον] Κέντρον
                    Χω.[ρίον] Εὐγρενική
Col. Γ   *   Χω.[ρίον] Ἡρακλῆς
                *   Χω.[ρίον] Σκόπελος
Col. Δ   Χω.[ρίον] Γορύτριον
                *   Χω.[ρίον] Πατρικοῦ

Williams and Parker 1995.

line 1,   (?*)   Γερισσι[.

---

[13] See n. 11.
[14] The reading of this village name was proposed by Déléage, 177, but other commentators have considered the remains of letters on the stone too incomplete for a secure reading.
[15] See n. 11.

THE LESBIAN STYLE OF POLYGONAL MASONRY

2.1 Introduction

A number of the sites listed in the gazetteer (largely in the centre and west of the island) are a group of ancient towers and enclosures where sections of walling are preserved, described above as being constructed in a style of masonry termed 'Lesbian polygonal'.[1] These remains have been classified as dating to the Archaic period (ie. ca. 700-480 BC), and in order to support this assertion (and clarify the precise definition of the Lesbian style) it is necessary to devote a few pages to a discussion of the masonry. The analysis focuses upon those sites for which there are available detailed published reports (and illustrations), including not only the towers and enclosures, but also a number of other walls built in the Lesbian style which are found at the *polis* centres (Mytilene [#27], Pyrrha [#99], Arisbe [ie. Palaiokastro, #116], Eresos [#135], Antissa [#161] and Methymna [#217]), together with those at Klopedi (#111) where a small structure within the large archaic temple exhibits similar style masonry.[2] Illustrations of the walls have been provided here where the quality of the illustration in the original publication is sufficient to permit reproduction (figs. 16-32).

The discussion will be structured as follows. First, two sections shall examine the definition and possible origins of the style. There shall then be a detailed discussion of the walls of the enclosures and towers, together with the other Lesbian masonry walls in the island. A short section will then present the evidence for the dating of the walls in Lesbos, the conclusions from which will briefly be compared to those reached from studies of Lesbian masonry in the Aegean area as a whole. Many of the sites presented in the gazetteer where this masonry style is apparent have been discovered since the publication of Scranton's detailed study of Lesbian masonry.[3] Since Scranton's work, authors have given only cursory treatment to Lesbian masonry, their brief accounts usually being derivative from Scranton's with no new insight or testing of the latter's theories.[4] This lack of further research makes a review of the new evidence (published since Scranton's original work over 50 years ago) important to test some of the hypotheses and conclusions reached by Scranton with the new data now available, especially concerning the probable dating of Lesbian polygonal masonry.

2.1.2 *The definition of Lesbian masonry*

The basic feature which distinguishes the Lesbian style of masonry from other polygonal walling is the curved edges which the blocks possess.[5] The association of this trait with the term 'Lesbian masonry' comes from an allusion by Aristotle. When speaking of the irregularities of some situations which cannot be covered adequately by a specific law, Aristotle says the following:

> For something which has no constant, the rule [which covers it] also has no constant, like the leaden rule of Lesbian masonry which is fitted to the shape of the stone and is not fixed.[6]

Scranton devoted a whole chapter to the Lesbian style of masonry,[7] but was working with examples of the style drawn mainly from outside Lesbos. The only Lesbian masonry walls *in* the island discussed in his study were those at Antissa, Eresos, Mytilene, Xirokastrini and Apothiki.[8] Scranton's conclusion from the Lesbian masonry walls he examined in the rest of Greece and the Aegean was that 'characteristically the surface [of the wall-face] is tooled'.[9] All of the walls known to Scranton in Lesbos exhibited merely a quarry-face, occasionally slightly modified with crude chisel work, and it was therefore concluded by the scholar that no fine examples of the style

---

[1] These sites, for which detailed reports are available, comprise: Xirokastrini (#122), Apothiki (#130), Makara (#131), Kastri (#165), Megalos Lakkos (#175), Kladomantri (#182), Bigla (#187), Koutlougouni (#190), Koja Dag (#193), Phonias (#195), Ambelia Skoteinou (#201), Selles (#205), Monastirellia (#212), Hypsilometopo (#221), Drakou Pidima (#235) and Agia Sotira (#237). As is made clear in the discussion of the style's definition (section 2.1.2), the 'Lesbian' style of polygonal masonry is to be distinguished from other polygonal masonry styles.

[2] There are a number of sites in the gazetteer described as exhibiting either 'Lesbian' or 'polygonal' masonry for which so few published details are available (and rarely any illustrations) that it is impossible as yet to ascertain the precise nature of the remains or to consider the sites in any detail: Prophitis Ilias (#112), Agia Photia (#113), Prophitis Ilias (#121), Palaiokastro Issas (#123), Spilios (#141), Lesbados (#144), Pharkobnar (#145), Pigados (#150), Apastra (#166), Routhia (#168), Aetos (#177), Kourouklos (#178), Tyrrani (#180), Pyrgi (#181), Gigi (#183), Batoudia (#184), Balana (#185), Bigla (#187), Prophitis Ilias (#194), Ametelli Skoteinou (#202), Prophitis Ilias (#230) and Kastri (#232).

[3] Scranton, Chapter 2 (pp. 25-44).

[4] Winter, 79-81, 85-88 gave a more adequate discussion. More usual is the single paragraph of Lawrence, 236-37, (which cited Scranton's findings at the site of Eresos [below at section 2.1.3]), and the three generalised paragraphs of Adam, 27. Neither of Kontis' books specifically about Lesbos (Kontis, 1973; id., 1978) discussed the masonry style in detail; pictures were merely provided of the different walls.

[5] The term Lesbian masonry was first applied in 1847 by Forchhammer to all polygonal and some Cyclopean masonry. See Scranton, 27 n. 3.

[6] Arist. *EN*. 1137b29-32.

[7] See n. 3 above.

[8] Scranton, Appendix III, cat. A1.1 (Antissa), A1.8 (Eresos), A1.11 (Mytilene), A1.13 (Xirokastrini) (all p. 159), and A4.2 (Apothiki) (p. 161).

[9] Ibid., 25.

are to be found in Lesbos itself.[10] However, there are indeed three examples of fine Lesbian masonry in the island, at Selles (fig. 16), Methymna (fig. 17) and Pyrrha.[11] The latter was drawn first by Koldewey[12] and overlooked by Scranton whilst the first two walls have been discovered since the publication of Scranton's book in 1941.[13] At all three sites the large blocks have been well-tooled to an extremely smooth finish, but these are the only true examples of tooled work despite the large number of Lesbian masonry walls amongst the enclosures and towers which have been discovered since Scranton's study. Therefore, one cannot support Scranton's hypothesis that part of the definition of Lesbian masonry (in addition to the feature of curved joints) should be the presence of tooled work on the faces of the blocks.[14] In Lesbos, tooled work seems to be the exception; it appears in these three examples, but the other Lesbian masonry walls in the island do not even come close to rivalling the quality of the wall faces at Selles, Methymna and Pyrrha. In fact, the rougher 'quarry-face' is not infrequent at all in Lesbos, a claim which Scranton makes for the style generally.[15] Many walls show crude chiselling on the wall face with large pieces hacked off in an attempt to form a flatter outer side (for example, the wall on the south slope of the acropolis at Antissa shown in fig. 18 [mistakenly said to be on the north side by Lamb], together with some of the blocks at Apothiki, fig. 19).

Another main feature of the Lesbian masonry walls in Lesbos are small gaps between blocks, especially in corners, where it was considered too difficult to fit each block exactly with its neighbours. This characteristic occurs at nearly all of the sites in Lesbos, with gaps between some blocks, the other edges of which seem to have been worked to fit more precisely into the wall. The walls at the sites of Apothiki (fig. 19), the Drakou Pidima (fig. 20)[16] and Eresos (fig. 22) all exhibit such gaps, clearly showing that these gaps are the results of the original construction.

The habit of adding small 'chinking' stones between blocks to fill these gaps is another problem. This practice is exhibited most clearly at Arisbe (fig. 21) but is also apparent at Eresos (fig. 22) where the small stone to the left of the main block also seems to be part of the original construction. Such stones are often employed in the casual construction of modern walls in Greece, with the emphasis on speed of construction and a concentration on small, easily manipulated building material rather than aesthetic principles. However, this was an ancient practice as well as a modern one. One has only to look at the Archaic Lesbian masonry terrace wall of the temple of Athena at Old Smyrna to see small 'chinking' stones added which are

not specially shaped to fit into the gaps they fill.[17] They are merely an expediency, like their counterparts in modern, dry-rubble walls. Further reference to both these problems will be made below when discussing particular walls in detail.

It is difficult to generalise about other characteristics of the Lesbian masonry walls in the island which one could add to the definition of the style. Both large and small blocks are employed in different walls (sometimes even in the same one), so there can be no sub-categories determined by the size of the stones used. With regard to the method of construction of the walls, it is difficult to be dogmatic because many are now in a very poor condition. Many of the terrace sections of the walls are formed by an outer face of large worked blocks with a fill of rubble behind (as one would expect). Where sections above ground level are preserved, the wall is formed sometimes by two outer faces of large blocks laid back to back, or in the 'emplektos' manner;[18] a good example of the latter technique is the enclosure wall at Methymna (fig. 17) where the width approaches 1.7 m.[19] Both these methods of construction are hardly unique to Lesbian masonry edifices, however, and cannot be added as specific qualities of this style of walling.

2.1.3 *The origins of the style*

There is also the problem of the possible origins of the style. What would be the reason for starting to build polygonal-style walls with blocks that had *curved* edges? And how did the technique of fitting the blocks thus begin?

As was concluded by Scranton, from the comment of Aristotle (cited above) presumably we are to understand workmen using strips of lead as templates whilst cutting the Lesbian masonry blocks to ensure good joins in the wall.[20] Using the lead strip, blocks could be fashioned with almost exactly the same curvature and near-perfect joins were ensured. It still remains to ask whether this method of construction could possibly have been the *origin* of the style. Was the technique, possibly seen by Aristotle himself in Lesbos in the fourth century, the one which had always been used?[21]

The hypothesis put forward for the origin of the style by Scranton concerned the site of Eresos. His line of thinking ran as follows. At Eresos walls had been built of unworked, free-lying boulders which had broken from the bedrock of the acropolis; these boulders naturally possessed curved edges, and this inherent feature led to the formation of Lesbian style polygonal walls on the acropolis. Later,

[10] Ibid., 28.

[11] The only two published illustrations of this wall do not clearly show the face of the blocks; Koldewey, pl. 12.4 and Schiering, fig. 3b (p. 341).

[12] Koldewey, ibid..

[13] Chatzi, 1972, fig. 13 (p. 596); Buchholz, pl. 5c.

[14] See n. 9.

[15] Ibid., 'Infrequently, when the rock is such that it splits readily and evenly, the quarry surface is left'.

[16] The gaps are also apparent in the earlier photograph of Euangelidis, 1924-25, fig. 19 (p. 51).

[17] Akurgal, figs. 40-42 and pls. 55, 66.

[18] The form of ancient wall construction commonly labelled 'emplektos' ('ἐμπλεκτος') in modern Greek is that of a wall with two outer faces of large, worked blocks, between which there is a gap filled with rubble and earth. I have employed the Greek word because this is the term used in many site reports and articles to describe the construction technique of Lesbian masonry walls in the island.

[19] Chatzi, 1972, 595

[20] Scranton, 27.

[21] It is clear from the archaizing use of the style cited in section 2.5 below that there is no foundation in the comment of Lawrence, 237, that the style had 'long gone out of fashion' by Aristotle's day.

this 'natural' Lesbian style was imitated by others elsewhere more artificially, preserving the style for its decorative possibilities by actually cutting the edges of the blocks so that their edges were curved.[22] This idea found favour with Winter who was in 'little doubt' that the origins of Lesbian and polygonal masonry styles were to be sought in the irregular shapes of unhewn or roughly hewn stone walls.[23] Furthermore, he agreed that an aesthetic emphasis led to the sophistication of these types of walling and the development of finely cut and joined Lesbian masonry walls.[24]

However, the evidence Scranton cited in support of his 'natural' origin of the style is not without problems. He examined a block from a Lesbian masonry wall at Eresos (fig. 22), claiming (a) that only the face, and not the edges, exhibited signs of working, (b) that the edges of the block were naturally curved, and (c) that the reason the block's edges were naturally curved was due to the geology of the area.

> The native rock of the hillside [the Eresos acropolis] ... [is] ... a metamorphosed igneous material, apparently a slightly schistose diabase or gabbro. A small amount of iron in the rock has formed in concretionary bands throughout the mother rock, in such a way as to produce lines of division on which irregularly curved weaknesses have developed. On these lines the boulders have split naturally out of the hillside, irregularly but smoothly rounded.[25]

My own observations at the site, however, were as follows. Of the blocks which appear to have broken away from the hill recently (where the edges show fresh breaks) the majority of the edges are jagged, straight lines. Regarding the iron in the rock of which Scranton spoke, this is indeed often visible in rocks that have recently broken. No rock had actually broken along the line of the iron, however, nor were there any blocks in which 'irregular curved weaknesses' had developed near the iron. These observations made on my own visit are consistent with the geological and petrological data for this type of rock, because the rock strata of metamorphosed lavas would be expected to produce linear breaks.[26] On one occasion a block was visible, freshly broken, which had fallen from the south lip of the acropolis and smashed to leave one curved edge (fig. 23). This example is sufficient to show that such shapes can be produced 'naturally', even if they are the exception. An alternative explanation for the 'natural' curves in rocks, however, (not related to the iron in the rock) may come from the formation of the acropolis itself. The pillow lava cliffs which are apparent all along the coast where the acropolis of ancient Eresos stands could certainly produce small curved blocks because of the irregular shapes created during their formation.[27]

The above paragraphs indicate that the geological evidence of Scranton is clearly not as absolute and clear-cut as he would suggest, and alternative explanations are possible (even if one can continue to explore the theory of the 'natural' origin of the style, as shall be done below). For example, an additional problem which must also be considered is the effect of weathering on the ancient blocks used in the walls. Scranton observed that for the blocks at Eresos which he discussed and illustrated (fig. 22) the edges had 'no signs of working whatsoever'.[28] Yet on the majority of the blocks used in walls at Eresos it is impossible to detect traces of ancient working on the edges after over 2000 years of exposure to the elements. It is simply not possible to say with certainty that the edges have not been worked. The important question for this theory of the origin of the style is therefore whether the curves were actually formed by careful working rather than the utilising of curved pieces of natural rock.

To try and answer this question more conclusively than Scranton, other parts of the island were visited in order to examine rock formations in different regions.[29] Unworked rocks (the result of fragmentation from the bedrock), roughly quarried blocks, and also the stone used in the construction of modern walls, were all examined to investigate whether any notable curves could be detected either before blocks were worked, or at different stages during their working.

Near Daphia and Anemotia (two villages a little west from Kalloni) there are some very large blocks split from the volcanic bedrock lying in the fields which definitely possess natural curves. Nearby at Xirokastrini (an area with a similar geological constitution) some of the large outcrops of rock weather in such a way that their surface starts to break up into sections. Often these sections are extravagantly curved, and from a distance these natural weathered outcrops can even take on the appearance of curved, joined blocks.

In the north of the island on the road from Petra to Methymna a valuable opportunity was afforded to examine rock that had been roughly quarried for the construction of a retaining wall by the side of the road. The stone used was a pink andesite, brought all the way from Mystegna on the east coast of the island, and the blocks had not yet received any fine tooling for fitting into the wall. Some pieces, however, which had clearly been hit only once to make them smaller, exhibited clear curves (some quite exaggerated) along their single, fresh break lines. This example was sufficient to show that the andesite rock (like the metamorphosed schist at Eresos) has the *ability* to show significant curves merely by being roughly worked

---

22 Scranton, 28-30.

23 Winter, 84.

24 Ibid., 84-85.

25 Scranton, 30.

26 Sarah Vaughan, pers. comm. (1990).

27 Grant Head, pers. comm. (1991). The formation of pillow lava is explained by A. L. Bloom, *Geomorphology: a systematic analysis of late Cenozoic landforms* (Cornell, 1978), 61.

An extreme variant of pahoehoe or ropy lava occurs when hot, fluid lava flows into, or erupts under water. Blobs or lobes of lava up to a meter in diameter form steam-jacketed, tough, flexible skins and pile up like pillows or sandbags [ie. in irregular curved shapes] while still molten in their interiors. The result is pillow lava, a diagnostic feature of subaqueous eruption and perhaps the most abundant rock type on earth.

28 Scranton, 29.

29 I note here that except for the southeast segment of the island the whole of Lesbos is composed of various volcanic and pyroclastic rock formations, see Schaus and Spencer, 411 n. 1 for the collected references to the island's geology.

(or simply smashed), even if this does not happen every time.

Finally there are the modern walls to be considered. Do any of the blocks in the modern walls show any curved edges? Some certainly do, although the workmen at Methymna informed me that these edges were sometimes the product of fine chisel and hammer work. In other places, however, there are obvious curves in some blocks in modern walls which cannot have been the result of deliberate working. At the village of Mesagros near Papados on the Gulf of Gera there was a recently built andesite wall; a curve in one block had resulted in a 'chinking' stone being needed to fill the gap created between the curved edge and the adjacent block. In this case the rock must have broken in a curve, and to fill the awkward gap a stone was used. This provides further proof that on occasions the volcanic rock of the island can exhibit this 'curved' property.

To sum up, the hypothesis for a 'natural' origin of Lesbian masonry can be seen to have points to recommend it, even if such evidence can never be conclusive. It is not possible to state categorically that the edges of some stones in Lesbian masonry walls have not been worked to form curves, but it is clear in some cases (for example fig. 19) that the curves have not been cut to fit exactly with a neighbouring block. This alone suggests an accidental occurrence of the curve because more difficulties are created by having the curved edge. It is far more difficult to fit the neighbouring stones, and makes it virtually impossible not to leave a small gap in the corners between blocks (a phenomenon apparent in many of the Lesbian masonry walls in Lesbos).

A further reason to support a 'natural' origin of the style is quite simply the lack of any logical reason for consciously developing polygonal walls with curved edges to their blocks. It has no structural advantage over normal polygonal walling and, as has just been mentioned, it is an unnecessary impracticality and complication during construction. Winter and Scranton both saw the origins of the style as an aesthetic sophistication of dry rubble masonry walls which possessed blocks with naturally curved edges (see section 2.1.3 above), and this still seems to be the most plausible hypothesis, seeing the employment of the 'leaden rule' as a method used to enhance a natural (and potentially decorative) curved trait inherent in the masonry of other walls. The use of a rule to measure the blocks may not have meant that all the walls would suddenly have exhibited perfect joints, and the gaps visible between stones at many of the enclosures and *polis* centres in Lesbos (for examples see figs. 19-21) need not indicate that no measuring or cutting of the stones was carried out. The origin of the style could very possibly have lain in cruder dry rubble constructions. Parallels drawn from modern rock formations and wall construction have shown little working of the stone available in Lesbos is necessary to produce walls with curved-edged blocks.

2.2 The Lesbian masonry walls of the towers and enclosures[30]

2.2.1 *Introduction*

There now follows an examination of all the published examples of Lesbian masonry walling in the island. First, there shall be consideration of the tower and enclosure walls by examining the common features of the walls. In addition, any characteristics which are either unique or which apply only to a particular group of the sites shall be distinguished. The walls of Lesbian masonry at the *polis* centres and the example at Klopedi shall then be examined under the same categories.

The role and location of the structures exhibiting Lesbian masonry walls are two other factors to consider when one examines the style employed, especially the amount of care taken to join the blocks which could be (at least partly) a reflection of the site's function and importance. Since these questions have been given detailed attention elsewhere, however, in discussions concerning the role played by the enclosures in the *chora* of the *poleis*, they will not be re-examined here.[31]

2.2.2 *The scale of the walls*[32]

The first comment to be made concerns the overall scale of the walls, especially the size of the blocks used and the thickness of the walls (where detectable). The majority of the tower and enclosure walls are very similar in the former respect, although the size of individual stones in a single wall can vary (the irregular shape of the blocks makes a meaningful diameter measurement difficult). The walls usually employ stones ca. 0.5 - 0.7 m across, although at the Drakou Pidima (fig. 20) blocks of a consistently smaller size are used. At the Megalos Lakkos enclosure,[33] the size of the stones which form the walls vary considerably in size; some measure ca. 0.6 - 0.7 m across, whilst other very large rocks are utilised, some even approaching ca. 2 m in exceptional cases. Another feature of this particular enclosure wall (unlike some modern walls nearby where the largest blocks are employed in the lowest courses, possibly suggesting that large rocks were merely rolled into place and roughly worked to fit into the scheme of the wall), is that the longer blocks appear in the upper as well as the lower courses of the best-preserved east wall. A usual Lesbian masonry effect is apparent in the sections of the wall where shorter blocks predominate, whilst there is almost a 'herring-bone' look about some of the sections constructed of longer stones.[34] However, three points must be emphasised about the Megalos Lakkos wall. Firstly, both long and short blocks appear throughout the wall. Secondly, even where the longer stones have been

---

30 The following discussion includes only those sites where there are detailed published reports and the nature of the remains is clear, see section 2.1 and n. 1.

31 Spencer, 1994; Schaus and Spencer, 414-20; Spencer, 1995.

32 All dimensions of individual blocks and walls given in the text are necessarily approximate, since it was not possible to measure the walls and carry out detailed surveying of the sites.

33 See the illustrations cited in the gazetteer entry for the site at #175.

34 Ibid.

laid, the joints above and below them are well-fitted. Thirdly, there is an integration of the two styles throughout the wallface, and close-fitting joints exist even in the upper courses.

There is one Lesbian masonry wall, however, which dwarfs the others in the predominantly grand scale of the blocks used. This is the Lesbian masonry terrace wall at Apothiki (figs. 19, 24, 28). Large blocks are used throughout the wall even in the upper courses and the overall impression, no doubt heightened because the wall is preserved in places up to 5 m in height, is immense. The wall is without doubt one of the most impressive ancient remains on the island.

Regarding the thickness of the enclosure walls, these vary between ca. 1 m and 2.5 m.[35] There does not seem to be a clear-cut relationship between the size of the enclosure and the thickness of the walls except for Xirokastrini where the long Lesbian masonry wall closing off the hilltop (75 m long) is the most substantial of all the enclosure walls. Many of the other enclosure walls differ vastly in length, yet are of similar thickness. The construction technique (where visible) is nearly always the 'emplektos' method (see n. 18). Where traces of internal walls are described as being (or having been) visible inside the enclosures and towers at Apothiki (#130), Kastri (#165), Bigla (#187), Phonias (#195), Hypsilometopo (#221), Drakou Pidima (#235) and Agia Sotira (#237), all are less substantial (where dimensions are given).

2.2.3 *The faces of the blocks*

The treatment of the faces of the blocks in all of the enclosure walls (with one exception) is what Scranton termed 'quarry face',[36] where the blocks received little additional working since their removal from the quarry. This definition used by Scranton has been employed here merely to avoid confusion, and it has been applied to all the tower and enclosure walls following Scranton's description of the wall at Xirokastrini (fig. 25).[37] There are unquestionable signs of crude attempts to flatten the faces at this site, but if this wall is to be termed 'quarry face' (along with the blocks Scranton discussed at Eresos, fig. 22) then the other walls must undoubtedly be placed in the same category. Sometimes the faces of blocks have clearly been hacked into shape with a few strokes of a chisel, for example at Antissa, fig. 18 (a close-up of the wall also shown in fig. 29). However, even where many tool marks are visible (as at Apothiki, see fig. 19) there has been no attempt to work the blocks to a smooth finish.

The one exception of all the walls are those of the enclosure at Selles where some of the (very few) remaining blocks have been carefully worked to a fairly smooth finish. The Lesbian masonry enclosure around the tower is now broken down to its lowest courses, but Axiotis published a photograph where some of the 'fine' Lesbian masonry reported by Kontis is preserved in one short section (fig. 16).[38]

2.2.4 *The joints of the blocks*

The joining of the blocks is another feature of the walls to be considered, and in this aspect there is also general uniformity between sites. All of the walls (except the especially fine wall at Selles) exhibit gaps between some blocks, but this is caused largely by the curved edges which make it nearly impossible to fit each stone perfectly with its neighbours. It is only when some straighter edges are included in the walls that there are fewer gaps, such as the walls at Makara (see fig. 26, where the large number of straighter-edged blocks led to few gaps being left). Usually the gaps are small and left unfilled, for example in this wall at Makara, Apothiki (figs. 19, 28), and the Drakou Pidima (fig. 20), but occasionally some small stones are placed in them. Since the antiquity of some walls has recently been questioned (Lauter's enclosure wall at the late Geometric and Archaic site of Lathuresa in Attica is now seen as a modern construction[39]), it is important to consider whether these features of the joints between blocks suggest any post-antique construction work.

The use of small stones in gaps, and certainly the gaps between the blocks themselves, is not necessarily a result of modern construction (or reconstruction) work. What their existence does indicate is a lack of precision on the part of the builders, noted above in the use of 'chinking' stones in the ancient terrace wall at Old Smyrna (see section 2.1.2)

It *is* clear that some of the walls have been 'topped up' since antiquity. For example, the terrace section of the Drakou Pidima wall has been augmented to support the bank behind it (presumably because at some point a secure terrace section was required for modern cultivation purposes), but the lower sections of the wall are clearly the original ancient construction.[40] Some later building work (of small mortared stones) has been added above the original Lesbian masonry wall at Xirokastrini which clearly postdates the Lesbian masonry work (see section 2.5.3 [d] below),[41] and at Makara the wall has been heightened more recently (its north wall has been completely reconstructed to serve as a *mandri*).[42] All the other enclosure and tower walls remain broken down, however, (mostly to ground level) and the preserved walls (incorporating sections with small 'chinking' stones) are undoubtedly part of the original ancient construction.

2.2.5 *Squared corner blocks*

Three of the Lesbian masonry enclosure walls incorporate an interesting feature of roughly squared corner blocks. This characteristic is visible at Apothiki (fig. 24) and Xirokastrini (fig. 27), whilst at Makara similar corner blocks were also visible in 1841 (fig. 26), but this section of the enclosure/tower no longer survives.

---

[35] See the gazetteer entry for each site cited in n. 1.
[36] Scranton, 21.
[37] Ibid., 25.
[38] For a full bibliography of the site see the gazetteer entry at #205.

[39] H. Lauter, *Lathuresa* (Mainz, 1985), fig. 1 (between pp. 8-9).
[40] This recent rebuilding above the *in situ* ancient sections is most obvious in the photographs of Euangelidis (cited in n. 16) and that of Chatzi, 1971, pl. 459β.
[41] Axiotis I, unnumbered photograph (p. 302).
[42] Schaus and Spencer, 416 n. 27.

At these three sites the more regular blocks are clearly completely integrated with the Lesbian masonry sections of the wall, and both types of blocks must therefore be part of the original construction. This is especially clear because the squared corner blocks are abutted by Lesbian masonry blocks in the same course in which they lie.

The Archaic temple terrace wall at Old Smyrna again offers a good parallel in support of the contemporary use of more regular corner blocks in Lesbian masonry walls.[43] It should be noted, however, that the blocks are not really 'isodomic' as such, merely a more regular shape than the rest of the wallface (and with similar, rough working of the stone faces, exactly the same as the Lesbian masonry elements themselves). This technique may have been employed to make the corner structurally stronger, or simply to make a change of direction less difficult to manage.

2.2.6 *Coursing in Lesbian masonry*

At two of the enclosures, Bigla[44] and Apothiki (fig. 28), a clear feature of the Lesbian masonry is its tendency to be constructed in approximate courses.[45] At both sites the whole wall is not structured in courses, but there are some sections where blocks of a similar size placed side by side form an approximate 'course' in the wall. Whether this was an accident of construction, or a conscious methodological approach to make the wall more easy to build up in sections, cannot be known.

2.2.7 *The height of the enclosures and towers*

The majority of the enclosure and tower walls are now reduced nearly to ground level (see section 2.2.4 above), and how high the walls once stood is difficult to say. At all the sites it is clear from the trace of an inner face of blocks behind the terrace section of walling that the walls once stood to a greater height (ie. above the terrace section, except at Apothiki where the whole wall does indeed seem to be merely a terrace). That the walls are all a metre or more in thickness also means that (in theory) the walls could have been very much higher. At most of the sites however, the blocks which formed the further courses have completely disappeared and it is impossible to try and gauge the original height from any nearby debris.[46] At Makara (#131) and the Drakou Pidima (#235), ancient worked blocks are visible nearby, re-used in modern terrace/field walls and farmyard walls, but it is impossible to know the extent of the destruction of the ancient structures and the proportion of stone lost from their walls.

Even since Paraskeuaidis, Charitonidis and Kontis saw many of the towers and enclosures (over the past 60 years), there has been further dismantling and destruction at some sites.[47]

Of course it is possible that the walls were not built entirely of stone and that above a certain height a mud-brick superstructure was added. The Archaic Lesbian masonry walls at Eleusis were constructed in this way[48] and the practice continued in later periods for large-scale walls, a good example being the well preserved Hellenistic city wall at Eretria.[49] No indication of mud-brick has survived at any of the sites in Lesbos but, even if such a superstructure had once existed, it would have been destroyed even more easily than the stone walls which are severely damaged themselves.

It is thus impossible to gauge the height of the towers and enclosures with certainty. One should be wary of applying Young's formula for determining the height of the towers in Attica to the tower and enclosure walls in Lesbos. Young proposed that the height of a tower was 2-2.5 times as great as its diameter.[50] It can only be said that the diameter of the enclosure and tower walls means that theoretically a wall of considerable height could have been supported,[51] but the material which formed the upper courses (whatever their exact height) has either been removed or destroyed.

2.3 The Lesbian masonry walls at the *polis* centres and at Klopedi

2.3.1 *Introduction*

The Lesbian masonry walls built at the *polis* centres and the Archaic temple of Klopedi will now be considered under the same headings as the Lesbian masonry enclosure and tower walls. This is done as a comparative exercise to detect any similarities and differences between the two groups of sites.

2.3.2 *The scale of the walls*

The size of the blocks used in the various Lesbian masonry walls at the *polis* centres and at Klopedi vary considerably, even within a single wall (as at some of the towers and enclosures, see section 2.2.2 above). Examples of this feature are the Lesbian masonry walls at Arisbe (fig. 21) and Antissa (figs. 18, 29) where some blocks measure ca.

[43] Akurgal, figs. 41-42.

[44] See the illustrations of the Bigla wall cited in the gazetteer entry for the site at #187.

[45] Five other towers (and one rectangular enclosure) are said to exhibit this quality in their polygonal masonry (rather than specifically 'Lesbian' masonry) walls, but detailed reports are still awaited: Agia Photia (#113), Spilios (#141), Kourouklos (#178), Tyrrani (#180) and Prophitis Ilias (#230).

[46] The amount of stone visible nearby an ancient wall is (unconvincingly) used by Valmin to reconstruct the height of the outer curtain wall at Tzokaleïka in Messenia. M. Valmin, *Etudes topographiques sur la Messénie Ancienne* (Lund, 1930), 72.

[47] This destruction, and the changing nature of the preserved ancient remains at some sites, is especially noticeable at Makara (#131), see n. 42.

[48] Wrede, pl. 11.

[49] Dr. G. Sanders, pers. comm. (1990).

[50] J. H. Young, 'Studies in south Attica: country estates at Sounion', *Hesperia* 25 (1956), 135 (cited in Cherry et al., 286-87).

[51] I note that in the Bari house in Attica the more substantial walls of room VII in the southwest corner of the courtyard, thought to be the base of a 2-3 storey tower, were no more than 1 m thick (ie. thinner than all the enclosure and tower walls in Lesbos). See Jones et al., 'An Attic country house below the cave of Pan at Vari', *BSA* 68 (1973), figs. 2-3 (pp. 362-63), 366, 436-43.

0.5-0.6 m across while other pieces ca. 0.2-0.3 m in diameter are also employed.

Walls of consistently small or large blocks also exist. The former shall be considered first. At Methymna a short section of Lesbian masonry walling near the harbour employs consistently small blocks (fig. 30). Such small-scale work is also evident in the second apsidal building at Antissa (fig. 31) and the square structure inside the temple at Klopedi.[52] Larger scale work is preserved at Methymna (fig. 17), Mytilene (fig. 32) and Pyrrha.[53] At all three sites very large blocks are used, over 1 m across, sometimes as large as ca. 1.3-1.5 m. The walls at Methymna and Pyrrha are very poorly preserved however (only the lowest course and part of the second course of both survive), so it is not certain that such work was employed throughout the wall.

For the majority of the walls at the *polis* centres it is not possible to determine the width of the wall. Many are clearly terrace walls only, to which the question of thickness is not applicable. Also, the walls at Antissa (fig. 29) and Pyrrha[54] may have been only terrace walls. At Methymna (fig. 17), Arisbe (figs. 21) and Mytilene (fig. 32), however, it is clear that the Lesbian masonry walls were constructed above ground level. The inner face of the Methymna wall revealed the thickness to be 1.7 m, and the 'emplektos' system was again used, with two outer faces of large blocks and a rubble fill.[55] This method of construction is apparent at Arisbe and Mytilene where the walls are ca. 2 m and 3 m thick respectively.[56]

The Lesbian masonry wall inside the temple at Klopedi[57] seems to be a wall of special function since it is obviously neither a terrace nor an enclosure wall.[58] It may have been the foundations of a base for a cult statue or the remains of an earlier shrine, but Euangelidis' site report is not detailed enough to determine its purpose with certainty.[59]

2.3.3 *The faces of the blocks*

Following the definition of 'quarry-face' blocks used above for the enclosure and tower walls (section 2.2.3 above), the Lesbian masonry walls at the *polis* centres and at Klopedi must also be classified under the same heading. Even

within this broad category, however, there are three noteworthy points to be made concerning the different degrees of care taken to fashion the faces of the blocks:

(a) Very little attention seems to have been paid to working the wallface at Antissa (fig. 18) or Arisbe (fig. 21), with large slices of the blocks apparently having been taken off with one blow of a broad chisel.

(b) More care is evident in the large-scale walls at Mytilene (fig. 32) and Pyrrha,[60] although a completely smooth finish is never achieved and the tool strokes are still obvious.

(c) Also significant is the fact that despite the smaller stones which are used in the Lesbian masonry wall near the harbour at Methymna (fig. 30) and those of the second apsidal building at Antissa (fig. 31), the treatment of the faces is not significantly better. It may appear so at times simply because the blocks are smaller, but on close inspection the same crude fracturing of the faces is very similar.

2.3.4 *The joints of the blocks*

The joints between the blocks in the Lesbian masonry walls at the *polis* centres and at Klopedi show three different levels of workmanship:

(a) The first level is represented by the wall at Arisbe (fig. 21), where some gaping holes are apparent between the blocks, sometimes filled with small stones.

(b) The next level is visible at the apsidal building at Antissa (fig. 31), Mytilene (fig. 32) and at Klopedi.[61] All these walls leave some small gaps in the corners, which at Antissa and Klopedi are filled with small stones.

(c) The Lesbian masonry walls exhibiting the best-joined blocks include the large-scale wall at Methymna (fig. 17), the acropolis wall at Antissa (figs. 18, 29), the harbour wall at Methymna (fig. 30) and the wall on top of the acropolis at Pyrrha.[62] All of these are so well-fitted that no gaps whatsoever exist between each block. The overall impression is especially great with the walls which employ very large blocks of stone (at Pyrrha and Methymna). Moreover, it is interesting to note that despite the great care taken to *join* the stones, the faces (especially at Antissa) have been treated comparatively crudely (fig. 18).

With regard to the joints of the blocks at the *polis* centres (as for those of the enclosure and tower walls examined above), the different quality of the joints between blocks (and the 'chinking' stones in the walls) cannot definitely be used for determining some walls to be post-antique reconstructions. At Arisbe (fig. 21), the only wall where the apparent crudeness of construction might appear to indicate recent reconstruction of the original (ancient) wall, there are a number of small 'chinking' stones added between blocks. However, the comparison made above with the Archaic temple terrace at Old Smyrna (section 2.1.2) is sufficient to show that such unworked stones were used in

[52] The only photograph published of the structure at Klopedi (Euangelidis, 1928, fig. 10 [p. 133]) is of insufficient quality to be reproduced. I also note that the Archaic oval building of fine polygonal masonry in the Epano Skala quarter of Mytilene has not been included in this discussion. Chatzi, 1973, 515-17 describes the walls of this building (which are indeed of small-sized blocks) as being constructed 'in the Lesbian style', but the edges of the blocks are very straight, regular polygonal stones (ibid., pl. 483β). A string course is also employed, another difference from the Lesbian masonry walls at the other sites.

[53] See n. 11.
[54] Ibid..
[55] Chatzi, 1972, 595-96 and fig. 13.
[56] Acheilara and Archontidou-Argyri, 1986, 198 and fig. 2 (p. 199).
[57] See n. 52.
[58] For its location within the temple see Euangelidis, 1928, pl. 1β.
[59] Ibid., 132-33.

[60] See n. 11.
[61] See n. 52.
[62] See n. 11.

antiquity to fill gaps in polygonal walls. Furthermore, at Arisbe a close examination of Chatzi's 1972 photograph[63] reveals that, in fact, the majority of small stones drawn by Koldewey a century before (fig. 21) do actually survive. They are not recent additions.[64] Such unshaped 'chinking' stones are even visible in some of the tiny gaps in the walls of the second apsidal building at Antissa (fig. 31), further evidence of the technique's antiquity. Indeed, the only change undergone by the wall at Arisbe seems to have been its gradual destruction since it can be no coincidence that the wall is most badly broken down at the south end of the acropolis plateau where a modern farmyard complex exists with associated outbuildings. No doubt a close examination of the walls would detect a large number of the ancient blocks being re-used.

2.3.5 *Squared corner blocks*

Very few of the walls at the *polis* centres have any corners preserved from which to judge whether squared corner blocks were once employed. The Lesbian masonry edifice inside the temple at Klopedi *may* have had squared corner blocks, but it is impossible to be certain either from the report of Euangelidis or his poor photograph,[65] and the structure is now buried. The situation is further confused because two sides of the structure, the east and south, included 'isodomic' blocks according to Euangelidis (neither side is illustrated[66]). Euangelidis considered that in the south side both styles of masonry had been employed together ('συγχρόνως'), but no illustration is provided.[67] It is therefore impossible to tell from the photograph whether the 'isodomic' blocks were only employed at the corners of the structure (as at Xirokastrini, Apothiki and Makara see section 2.2.5 above), or indeed whether they are true isodomic blocks rather than the roughly squared stones visible at the four other sites in Lesbos.

2.3.6 *Coursing in Lesbian masonry*

None of the Lesbian masonry walls at the *polis* centres, nor the structure at Klopedi, show clear signs of being constructed in approximate courses. The only occasion where this feature may once have existed is in the large-scale wall at Methymna (fig. 17). Here the first course of large blocks (the only course fully preserved) are all of approximately the same height and therefore could once have been the base of further courses of similar height. It is pointless to speculate further, however, because all the blocks from the other courses have now disappeared.

2.3.7 *The height of the walls*

With the exception of the walls at Methymna (fig. 17) and Mytilene (fig. 32), which have been excavated to reveal

both wallfaces, and the wall at Arisbe (fig. 21) which still stands above ground level, all the other Lesbian masonry walls are preserved only as terraces. Unlike the enclosure and tower walls discussed above (section 2.2.7), it is not possible to detect an inner face for many of the other walls at the *polis* centres. It is clear from where sites have been excavated, however, that sometimes walls which appear now to be only terraces can be revealed to have two faces once excavated (for example the wall at Mytilene, see fig. 32) and may therefore have stood once to a much greater height. The Lesbian masonry wall on the acropolis of Antissa (figs. 18, 29) could be such an example. Further indications that the Lesbian masonry walls of the *polis* centres stood higher come from Eresos where monolithic gate jambs on the east side of the acropolis indicate that the acropolis was walled in antiquity.[68] The walls around the acropolis now survive only in their terrace sections, but once they must have stood higher to complete the walling around the gate.[69]

Even for the walls which have been excavated, it is difficult to know whether the upper sections were also made of stone or alternatively (as suggested above for the towers and enclosures, section 2.2.7) whether a cheaper mud-brick superstructure was applied. Fagerström concluded that the stone walls in the first apsidal building at Antissa (the building preceding the Lesbian masonry edifice) were of such height (up to 1.85 m) that the whole building would have been of stone, a feature unique in Iron Age Greece.[70] The walls of the second (Lesbian masonry) building and the fragment of the apse of another Lesbian masonry structure at Antissa[71] are not so well-preserved, so no conclusive evidence exists for restoring these other buildings as completely stone edifices. Some of the walls on the east slopes of the acropolis at Eresos do seem to have been intended to create terraces (probably for housing), but at other sites the very thick walls composed of large blocks (figs. 17, 32), may have stood much higher, especially if they were intended to establish a physical limit for the city and repel attackers.

2.4 Problems of sequence in the Lesbian masonry walls

It is relatively easy to note the common or distinguishing features amongst the Lesbian masonry walls in the island, thus grouping them and establishing typologies for the different forms of wall. What is more difficult is to shape these different characteristics into a sequence of development. The problem of discussing the development of a certain phenomenon when one must rely largely on the styles employed within it is particularly knotty. This difficulty exists whether the subject of study be painted pottery, architectural styles or styles of masonry. As Scranton pointed out, there are instances where identical Lesbian masonry walls have been proven to date from different periods.[72] Even if the 'features' can be placed in a credible sequence of 'progression' (which is doubtful in

---

[63] Chatzi, 1972, pl. 547a.

[64] The ca. 2 - 3 m thick 'emplektos' manner of construction of the wall at Arisbe (not clear from the published illustrations but obvious after even casual observation at the site) clearly indicates the wall to be ancient.

[65] See nn. 52, 59.

[66] Ibid., 133.

[67] Ibid., 'ἡ ν.[ότια πλευρὴ] κατὰ πολυγωνικὸν καὶ ἰσοδομικὸν συγχρόνως'.

[68] Koldewey, pl. 9.3.

[69] As restored by Koldewey, ibid..

[70] For Fagerström's discussion of this feature see Fagerström, 88-90.

[71] Chatzi, 1973, 519 and fig. 13.

[72] Scranton, 43-44.

itself), the time lapse which one should assign between walls displaying different features degenerates into pure guesswork. There may be many different factors (besides the ability of the workmen to construct walls in a certain period) which have influenced the style and quality of the wall, such as its location or function. For example, the Lesbian masonry walls at Athens, Eleusis, Rhamnous and Delphi are obviously by position and function designed to impress.[73] Such factors could have influenced the walls in Lesbos also (especially those at the *polis* centres and at centres of cult activity such as Klopedi).[74]

Therefore there can be no great value in constructing a (subjective) 'development' of the Lesbian masonry walls in Lesbos itself, or in looking elsewhere to Lesbian masonry walls in other areas of Greece as an indicator of the 'development' of the masonry style in Lesbos. The only true indicator of wall dating, both in Lesbos and in the rest of Greece, can be that gained from excavation, and it is to this (admittedly incomplete) source that attention must now be turned.

2.5 The dating of Lesbian masonry walls in Lesbos

2.5.1 *Introduction*

The Lesbian style of masonry has been considered hitherto a phenomenon of the Archaic period[75] (excluding one clearly archaizing example in the Kerameikos which betrays its real date by the very *un*-Archaic feature of bevelled edges, a feature apparent at none of the walls in Lesbos[76]). Scranton and Winter both saw the acme of the style in the Archaic period as a further (sophisticated) manifestation of eastern influence in art styles generally in the same era.[77] For Scranton the decline of the style was linked to the reaction against the east associated with the Persian wars,[78] whilst by Winter the parallel with art was again drawn, suggesting the 'sober' post-Persian period led to the more simple polygonal style of the Classical period.[79] However, these generalisations should not be applied freely to the walls in Lesbos without close examination of the archaeological evidence. The previous assertions of scholars stated here can then be tested from the data provided.

2.5.2 *Archaeologically dated Lesbian masonry walls in Lesbos*

There are three sites in the island with securely dated Lesbian masonry walls:[80]

(a) Methymna

In a recent excavation to the south of the Medieval kastro in Methymna, a group of ancient houses were located with a street running between them, and all the houses displayed Lesbian masonry walls on their outer faces (very similar in style to the walls of the second apsidal building at Antissa, see [c] below).[81] The construction of the complex is dated archaeologically to the Archaic period (specifically the early Archaic period).[82] The houses and street lie above other structural remains of the Protogeometric and Geometric periods which are based, in turn, on prehistoric strata.[83]

(b) Klopedi

The square Lesbian masonry edifice at Klopedi is built inside the sixth century BC temple, at the far (west) end of the cella.[84] However, although the temple may well represent the date of the wall's construction, it could also be a *terminus ante quem* for the Lesbian masonry wall. Despite the poor quality of Euangelidis' photograph,[85] it is clear that the illustrated west wall of the Lesbian masonry structure extends below the upper stylobate level on the west side of the temple. Euangelidis himself suggested that the structure may have pre-dated the temple, with the latter subsequently built around the small square structure[86] (which may have served as a previous open air focus of worship, a relic of earlier cult practice at the site[87]). It seems strange, for instance, that the decorative Lesbian masonry walls here fit tightly inside the temple (making them almost invisible), when at the majority of other sites the decorative style is obviously intended to be viewed, since only outer walls tend to be well-fitted in the Lesbian style. The published reports for Klopedi are clearly inconclusive, however, and a *terminus ante quem* of the late

---

[73] **Athens**: Wrede, pls. 15, 20; **Eleusis**: ibid., pls. 4, 5, 7, 9-11; **Rhamnous**: ibid., pl. 18; **Delphi**: M. F. Courby, *Fouilles de Delphes: la terrasse du temple* (Paris, 1927) II, 156-201, 231-36 and figs. 115-24, 185.

[74] See the articles cited in n. 31 for discussions of these factors.

[75] Scranton, 43-44; Winter, 81, 85-86; Adam, 27; Lawrence, 237.

[76] For this archaizing wall see Scranton, 34 (dated to the last third of the fourth century on p. 161 [cat. A3.1]).

[77] Scranton, 27, 44 (who noted that the style was largely to be found in areas of 'Ionic influence', especially Asia Minor and the Aegean islands); Winter, 85.

[78] Scranton, 44.

[79] Winter, 85.

[80] A fourth would be the oval apsidal building at Mytilene, which is of Archaic date (ca. 600). However, as noted above (n. 52), I have excluded it from the discussions here because its masonry is strictly polygonal rather than Lesbian.

[81] For the reports of the excavations in the plot (known as 'Mygia') see Acheilara and Archontidou-Argyri, 1987, 481, fig. 6 (p. 485) and pl. 289β; Archontidou-Argyri, 1986-87, 71-72 (and unnumbered photograph p. 64); Archontidou-Argyri, 1988, 463-65, fig. 12 (p. 466) and pl. 280α-ε; Axiotis, 1992 I, 228-29.

[82] Archontidou-Argyri 1988, 465; Eleni Bomboulaki, pers. comm. (1990).

[83] Archontidou-Argyri, 1986-87, 72; Acheilara and Archontidou-Argyri, 1987, 481; Axiotis, 1992 I, 229.

[84] See n. 58.

[85] Cited in n. 52.

[86] Euangelidis, 1928, 133.

[87] The high-quality finds of Geometric date recovered both by Euangelidis and much later by Chatzi (see the description of finds in the gazetteer entry at #111) suggests that there may well have been earlier cult activity at the location preceding the construction of the Archaic temple.

sixth century is all that can be granted with certainty for the square Lesbian masonry structure.

(c) Antissa (1)

The second apsidal (or oval) building at Antissa with walls of Lesbian masonry (fig. 31) was excavated over 60 years ago.[88] The construction of this building was placed in the eighth century by Lamb.[89] It continued in use until the seventh century at which point two large walls were built over it, which were both dated 'well before 600BC'.[90] Fagerström followed Coldstream in dating the construction of the second apsidal building of Lesbian masonry more specifically to the very end of the eighth century, ca. 700BC.[91]

(d) Antissa (2)

Overlying the two superimposed apsidal buildings was a paved area, apparently a street, flanked by two Lesbian masonry walls.[92] The whole complex of the street and associated buildings (including a threshold in the south wall of the street) was dated by stratified pottery finds to the end of the sixth century or the start of the fifth century.[93]

As an addendum to these securely dated Lesbian masonry walls, it should be added that many large 'polygonal' and 'quasi-polygonal' walls of Archaic date (some specifically early Archaic) have been found recently underlying structures of the Classical, Hellenistic and Roman periods on the lower town site in the Epano Skala quarter of Mytilene during the Canadian School excavations.[94] Whether these 'polygonal' blocks possess curved edges is not explicitly stated. Many of the walls are extremely fragmentary but all date to the Archaic period (mainly the sixth century BC).[95]

The above four examples from Methymna, Klopedi, and the two from Antissa, are the only securely dated Lesbian masonry walls in Lesbos. There are, however, two other hints towards the dating of Lesbian masonry in the island (and it is to be stressed that these are only *hints*, not criteria for establishing close absolute dates): the sequences of different styles in large-scale/fortification walls, and also the forms of two Lesbian masonry towers within outer enclosures built in a similar style.

2.5.3 *Sequences of masonry in large-scale/fortification walls exhibiting Lesbian masonry with a different style*

There are four large-scale/fortification walls in Lesbos exhibiting Lesbian masonry in which another style of masonry is employed also:

(a) Agia Kyriaki (Mytilene)

A short section of Lesbian masonry walling behind the churchyard of Agia Kyriaki on the edge of Mytilene town was examined in a brief excavation in 1986, revealing both inner and outer faces of the wall.[96] The wall was constructed in the 'emplektos' system, and parts of both faces comprised Lesbian polygonal masonry. On the outer face of the wall, a number of quarry-faced isodomic blocks of andesite had been added as a repair to the existing construction.[97] Where the isodomic blocks met the original wall of Lesbian masonry blocks, the latter had been cut into, in order to accommodate the new isodomic blocks,[98] which they must therefore pre-date.

(b) Odos Kydonion (Mytilene)

In the town of Mytilene a rescue excavation in Odos Kydonion investigated a large ancient wall which had been discovered during building work.[99] The sections of Lesbian masonry lie at the bottom of the preserved wall whilst on top are more regular courses of polygonal masonry, and an isodomic 'string' course forms the uppermost preserved layer. The building of the upper more regular part of the wall was dated to the first half of the fourth century by ceramic and numismatic finds, but the construction of the lowest elements could not be dated with accuracy.[100] Once again, the sequence from Lesbian masonry to more regular isodomic blocks above is clear, however, not least in the treatment of the faces of the stones. The lower Lesbian masonry pieces have only received minimal working whilst the coursed polygonal and isodomic courses have the outer faces of each block finely tooled.[101]

(c) Antissa

At Antissa, the Lesbian masonry wall on the south slope of the acropolis was drawn and photographed by Lamb during her excavations and mapping of the remains at the site (figs. 18, 29).[102] The west section of the wall is composed of well-fitted Lesbian masonry blocks (see especially 2.3.4 above), with a later buttress and tower

[88] Lamb, 1931-32, 41-63.

[89] Ibid., 47.

[90] Ibid., 47-48 and pl. 18 (walls V and VI).

[91] Fagerström, 89 (citing J. N. Coldstream, *Geometric Greece* [London, 1977], 262-64).

[92] Lamb, 1931-32, 48-49, fig. 4 (p. 49) and pls. 18, 19. 5.

[93] Ibid., 49. For the general view of the south wall of the street and the paving, ibid., pl. 19. 5.

[94] Millar; Williams and Williams, 1991, 181 and pl. 5; E. B. French, 'Archaeology in Greece 1990-91', *AR* 37 (1991) 63.

[95] Millar.

[96] Acheilara and Archontidou-Argyri, 1986, 198 and fig. 2 (p. 199); Archontidou-Argyri, 1986-87, 56.

[97] These isodomic additions are clear on Acheilara and Archontidou-Argyri, 1986, fig. 2 (p. 199).

[98] Ibid.

[99] Chatzi, 1971, 454-56, figs. 4-5 and pls. 455-57.

[100] Ibid., 456.

[101] The differentiation is especially clear on Chatzi (ibid.) pl. 455a.

[102] Lamb, 1930-31, 172-74. Lamb (ibid., fig. 4 [p. 173]) incorrectly labelled the wall as being on the *north* side of the acropolis.

added on the far west end.[103] To the east a repair and extension to the wall was fashioned of isodomic blocks, now preserved only in its first one or two courses. Where the two sections meet, some of the irregular shaped blocks continue under the west end of the isodomic wall and the Lesbian style stones clearly have been cut (sometimes quite severely) to receive the regular courses.[104] This is another clear example of a wall originally constructed of Lesbian masonry, later having an addition made with isodomic blocks.

(d) Xirokastrini

The large Lesbian masonry wall at Xirokastrini is founded on bedrock. Where the sections of Lesbian masonry are visible along the length of the wall they always form the lowest courses (figs. 25, 27). Above these courses there are preserved, in parts, traces of a second stage of building activity, this time consisting of generally smaller blocks, mostly unworked, which are mortared together.[105] This appears most unlike an ancient building technique and probably represents either Byzantine, Venetian or Turkish rebuilding work. The pattern remains the same however: the Lesbian masonry wall is the earliest at the site, pre-dating the later additions/rebuilding.

All four examples cited here suggest that in large-scale/fortification walls Lesbian masonry was employed before regular isodomic (or in the case of Xirokastrini, mortared) masonry became common. Unfortunately, only one of the sites (Odos Kydonion at Mytilene) offers a *terminus ante quem* for the Lesbian masonry section by providing a date for the later, more regular rebuilding work (the early fourth century BC). It is thus impossible to use the sequences to determine detailed absolute chronologies for the masonry, but it *is* useful to know that where two styles of masonry are employed in Lesbos, the Lesbian masonry is always the earliest at the site, and also that a different masonry style was chosen later. This observation in Lesbos is a good test of the 'law' proposed by Scranton, which ran as following:

> In general it may be said that wherever Lesbian masonry occurs in fortifications which include other styles as repairs or rebuildings, the Lesbian is always at the beginning of the series, when the series can be established.[106]

Although Scranton already knew of the walls at Xirokastrini and on the acropolis at Antissa,[107] neither of the isodomic repairs and rebuildings in the Lesbian masonry walls at Mytilene had been uncovered by 1941, yet the theory still holds good for those two walls as well.

The substantial (Archaic) 'polygonal' walls found during the Canadian excavations in Mytilene (see section 2.5.2 above) are also an important indicator for the sequence of masonry styles, even though they do not display two different styles in the same wall. Their importance is that the large polygonal walls represent the first attempt at large-scale building on the sterile beach layer which underlies the whole site (where the earliest activity is of Archaic date[108]), and they are significantly lower than the isodomic masonry employed in other buildings of later date.[109] Once again, it seems to be a clear statement of the sequence of architectural styles employed in Lesbos.

2.5.4 *The forms of the different structures exhibiting Lesbian masonry*

There is one further indication for the dating of Lesbian masonry walls at two sites where the enclosures incorporate an inner tower (also constructed in Lesbian masonry), at Koja Dag (#193) and Selles (#205). The towers at these sites measure 14 x 10.45 m and 11 x 6.5 m respectively and these dimensions (together with the style of masonry) immediately distinguish both from the large group of smaller, square Classical/Hellenistic towers of isodomic masonry measuring ca. 8-9 m found in Lesbos (once again, in the centre and west of the island[110]), elsewhere in the Aegean and also in mainland Greece.[111]

Given the fundamental differences between these Lesbian masonry towers and the smaller isodomic ones, including their size, shape, wall thickness, and the choice of a completely different style of masonry, it would seem to indicate that typologically the two Lesbian masonry towers are not to be grouped with those Classical/Hellenistic towers constructed with isodomic masonry, and that, almost definitely, they date from a different period. Indeed, the existence of isodomic towers at three sites where there are also Lesbian masonry enclosures[112] suggests that the two different forms were part of defensive systems which were created at different times, probably one augmenting (or replacing) the other.

2.5.5 *Conclusions to the dating of Lesbian masonry walls in Lesbos*

With finds only from surface survey rather than stratified data from excavation, one can only speak about the dating of sites in terms of probabilities. This caveat must be applied to any claims made concerning the dating of the Lesbian masonry walls in Lesbos. Nevertheless, the walls dated by stratified finds from excavation, the sequence of masonry at the sites in the island, and typology of the structures, give the following information:

(a) All of the securely dated Lesbian masonry walls in the island of Lesbos are of Archaic date (specifically the eighth to the sixth centuries).

---

[103] Ibid., 172.

[104] This was Lamb's opinion also, ibid..

[105] Axiotis, 1995 I, unnumbered photograph (p. 302).

[106] Scranton, 34.

[107] Ibid., fig. 4 (p. 26), 28, 31 and cat. A1.13 (Xirokastrini, p. 159); cat. A1.1 (Antissa, p. 159).

[108] Williams and Williams 1991, 181, and H. Williams, pers. comm. (1995).

[109] Millar, fig. 2.

[110] Spencer, 1994, fig. 1 (p. 212).

[111] This point concerning the typological difference between the Lesbian masonry structures and those of isodomic masonry is also made in Spencer, 1994, 207-08; id., 1995, 33.

[112] At Xirokastrini (#122), Apothiki (#130) and Makara (#131). There may also have been isodomic towers constructed inside the Drakou Pidima (#235) and Agia Sotira (#237) enclosures, see the entries for each site in the gazetteer.

(b) At all sites exhibiting large-scale/fortification walls in which there are *sequences* of masonry, be it Lesbian and coursed polygonal, Lesbian and isodomic, or Lesbian and mortared rubble, the Lesbian style is always the first masonry at the site. The other walls are later rebuildings or extensions of the existing walls.

(c) Where there are towers of Lesbian masonry constructed inside enclosures built in a similar style, the dimensions and shape of the towers are very different from the square towers of isodomic masonry which are of Classical/Hellenistic date. This suggests that typologically the Lesbian masonry towers are not to be grouped with the latter class of structure from which they are almost certainly chronologically distinct.

Given the chronology of the securely dated Lesbian masonry walls in the island, the clear sequence of masonry styles, the overall similarity both in the scale of all the Lesbian masonry walls and also the treatment of their faces and joints discussed above (see especially sections 2.2.2-2.2.4 and 2.3.2-2.3.4 above), it seems only logical to conclude from the evidence currently available that Lesbian masonry walls in Lesbos are of 'Archaic' date. The nature of the evidence means that any proposed dating can only be a working hypothesis until excavation data is available for more of the enclosures. However, the usual scatter of plain wares visible at the sites may mean that excavation does not help a great deal in establishing secure dates.[113]

It was suggested above (section 2.5.1) that a methodology which involves applying to the Lesbian masonry walls in Lesbos dating sequences established for Lesbian masonry walls elsewhere in Greece is not necessarily valid. Nevertheless, it has already been noted that the walls in Lesbos do seem to reinforce one of Scranton's general 'laws', namely that Lesbian masonry appears at the beginning of the 'style sequences' in walls at sites where it is employed. It is therefore interesting to note briefly the dating of the Lesbian masonry walls known to Scranton from all over the Aegean and western Turkey with the dates just established by independent means in Lesbos.[114]

Of the twenty-one securely dated examples of Lesbian masonry in Greece and the Aegean in his book, only one is certainly not Archaic (the fourth-century archaizing example in the Kerameikos, see section 2.5.1 above). The latest other Lesbian masonry wall is at Thermopylae, and even this is dated to 'before 470 BC'.[115] Once again, if one were dealing in 'probabilities' for the dating of a newly-discovered Lesbian masonry wall in Greece (based on

Scranton's data), an Archaic date would be the inevitable conclusion reached.[116]

The point shall be laboured no further. For the purposes of the sites presented in the gazetteer, the Lesbian masonry walls will be considered to represent structures of 'Archaic' date. No attempt will be made to be more specific either by attempting to create internal sequences in the masonry or a relative chronology. Such hypotheses are difficult to support given the evidence currently available.

---

[113] The difficulties in dating towers in many islands because of a lack of excavation, and the ambiguity of surface finds, is emphasised by Cherry et al., 1991, 291. Even at a *polis* centre (Arisbe), where fine wares are found more readily, Chatzi found it impossible to gain a clear indication of the dating of the large Lesbian masonry enclosure wall through excavation; Chatzi, 1972, 593-95. In Lesbos the only painted sherds found at two of the enclosures (apart from the number of fine wares at the cult place of Apothiki, #130) were black-glazed pieces at the Drakou Pidima (#235) and Agia Sotira (#237), and at both sites these sherds may be associated with the number of later isodomic blocks present (possibly the remains of later Classical/Hellenistic towers, see n. 112).

[114] In Scranton's cat. A; Scranton, 159-61.

[115] Ibid., cat. A4.12 (p. 161).

[116] It is not a question of more recent data proving Scranton wrong either, because when Lesbian masonry walls have been discovered since the writing of Scranton's book (in 1941), walls which have been closely dated (such as those of the temple terrace at Old Smyrna), have also been proven to be of Archaic date.

ALPHABETICAL INDEX OF SITES

Site Name	Site No.
Kaukara (Lisbori)	#87
Kladomantri (Chydira)	#182
Klimaki (Antissa)	#173
Klopedi (Agia Paraskeui)	#111
Koja Dag (Skalochori)	#193
Korakas (Kleio)	#227
Koukkaki (Agia Marina)	#40
Koukmidos (Kleio)	#231
Kouphi (Skalochori)	#162
Kourouklos (Chydira)	#178
Kourtir (Lisbori)	#91
Koutlougouni (Skalochori)	#190
Krousos (Skala Eresou)	#134
Kryo Neri (Achladeri)	#102
'Kusu-Mandrassi' (Sigri)	#149
Laka (Aphalonas)	#14
Lakerdas (Pyrgi)	#30
Lapedia (Agra)	#128
Lesbados (Sigri)	#144
Limani tou Pyrgiou (Pyrgi)	#28
Listis (Parakoila)	#129
Louta (Polichnitos)	#82
Loutra Thermis (Thermi)	#8
Loutzas (Basilika)	#94
Makara (Agra)	#131
Manosados (Kato Tritos)	#50
Megalonisi (Sigri)	#147
Megalos Lakkos (Eresos)	#175
Mesa Rongada (Ano Stauros)	#65
Mesintziki (Achladeri)	#101
Meladia (Eresos)	#142
Messa (Achladeri)	#103
Methymna (town)	#217
Mitoilia (Kato Stauros)	#64
Mitropolis (Anemotia)	#197
Monastiraki (Pyrgoi)	#57
Monastirellia (Bapheios)	#212
Monastiri tis Myrsiniotissas (Daphia)	#118
Monastiri tis Peribolis (Tzithra)	#167
Monastiri tou Kreokopou (Tzithra)	#172
Moni Leimonos (Daphia)	#119
Moni Hypsilou (Antissa)	#174
Mosyna (Napi)	#108
Myloi (Agia Marina)	#39
Mytilene (town)	#27
Nipos (Parakoila)	#125
Nisos Panagias (Mandamados)	#240
Obriokastro (Gabathas)	#161
Oikia (Sigri)	#151
Ormos Mystegnon (Mystegna)	#4
Osios Grigorios (Skopelos)	#60
Outza (Moria)	#21
Palaiokastro (Arisbi)	#116
Palaiokastro Issas (Parakoila)	#123
Paliochora (Philia)	#199
Paliochori (Komi)	#1
Paliochorion (Sigri)	#152
Paliokastro (Agra)	#188
Paliokastro (Mesagros)	#51
Paliokastro (Sigri)	#148

Site Name	Site No.
Paliokastro Korphiou (Laphionas)	#209
Paliopyrgos (Brisa)	#76
Palios (Mandamados)	#239
Pamphila (village)	#17
Panagia Kokkinou (Skalochori)	#164
Panagia tis Amalis (Agia Marina)	#43
Pastourmas (Achladeri)	#97
Patia (Aphalonas)	#13
Pedia (Skalochori)	#196
Pegia (Kleio)	#228
Pente Agioi (Pterounda)	#189
Peribola (Polichnitos)	#83
Petri (village)	#213
Pharanx (Daphia)	#117
Pharkobnar (Sigri)	#145
Pharkonias (Sigri)	#146
Phonias (Skalochori)	#195
Phousa (Ano Chalikas)	#31
Phousa (Mychou)	#48
Pigados (Sigri)	#150
Pitsilia (Agiasos)	#71
'Plain of Eresos' (Eresos)	#138
Plaka (Basilika)	#95
Plati (Nees Kydonies)	#2
Prasologos (Nees Kydonies)	#244
Prophitis Ilias (Agia Paraskeui)	#112
Prophitis Ilias (Hypsilometopo)	#221
Prophitis Ilias (Kerami)	#121
Prophitis Ilias (Kleio)	#230
Prophitis Ilias (Lisbori)	#88
Prophitis Ilias (Skalochori)	#194
Prophitis Ilias (Sykamia)	#224
Pyrgi (Chydira)	#181
Pyrgo (Gabathas)	#157
Pyrgoi Thermis (Thermi)	#11
Pyrrha (Achladeri)	#99
Rachonas (Methymna)	#216
Rousos (Hypsilometopo)	#211
Routhia (Batousa)	#168
Salbaradis (Skalochori)	#163
Saliakas (Moria)	#19
Sal-taschi (Gabathas)	#156
Seistria (Mesotopos)	#132
Selles (Skoutaros)	#205
Skala Dipiou (Kato Tritos)	#46
Skordalos (Sigri)	#143
Skoteino (Chydira)	#186
Spilios (Eresos)	#141
'Sti Manna' (Papados)	#52
Strongylos (Polichnitos)	#78
Tabari (Mesotopos)	#133
Taxiarchis (Agia Paraskeui)	#106
Taxiarchis (Kato Tritos)	#49
Taxiarchis (Mandamados)	#236
Taxiarchis tou Stenaka (Mandamados)	#242
Taxiarchis tou Troulotis (Napi)	#109
Temenos (Bapheios)	#218
Temenos (Lisbori)	#93
Thermelia (Moria)	#23
Thermokastro (Argenos)	#223

Site Name	Site No.
Tholos (Eresos)	#139
Tokatia (Achladeri)	#100
Traperia (Polichnitos)	#79
Treis Agioi (Pamphila)	#10
Trianta (Kalloni)	#120
Tsaph (Tarti)	#59
Tsephos (Gabathas)	#160
Tsesmedes (Loutra)	#44
Tsichrantas (Skoutaros)	#192
Tsiphos (Gabathas)	#155
Tsouloumountas (Sigri)	#154
Tyrrani (Chydira)	#180
Viran Köy (Hypsilometopo)	#222
Xiro (Achladeri)	#96
Xirokastrini (Kerami)	#122
Xirolimni (Skoutaros)	#191
Xylokastro (Agiasos)	#70
Ypapanti tou Christou (Plagia)	#62

CHRONOLOGICAL INDEX OF SITES

Site No.	Site Name	Neolithic	Bronze Age			Iron Age					Roman	Medieval		
		N	EBA	MBA	LBA	PG	G	A	C	HL	R	BYZ	VEN	TUR
#1	Paliochori (Komi)	-	-	-	-	-	-	-	-	-	LR-Byz		'MAge'	-
#2	Plati (Nees Kydonies)	-	EBA	-	-	-	-	-	-	-	-	Byz	'MAge', Tur	Tur
#3	Kalamos (Nees Kydonies)	-	-	-		-	-	-	-	-	-	Byz	-	Tur
#4	Ormos Mystegnon (Mystegna)	-	-	-		-	-	-	-	-	R?	EByz	'MAge'	-
#5	Agia Marina (Mystegna)	-	-	-	-	-	-	-	-	-	-	EByz	-	-
#6	Agios Thymianos (Thermi)	-	-	-	-	-	-	-	C?	-	-	-	-	-
#7	Karyes (Thermi)	-	-	-	-	-	-	-	C	HL	R	EByz, LByz/Tur		Tur
#8	Loutra Thermis (Thermi)	-	-	-	-	-	-	-	C	HL	R	-	-	-
#9	Epano Pyrgoi (Thermi)	-	-	-	-	-	-	-	-	-	-	LByz	-	-
#10	Treis Agioi (Pamphila)	-	-	-	-	-	-	-	-	-	-	EByz	-	-
#11	Pyrgoi Thermis (Thermi)	-	EBA	MBA	LBA	-	-	-	-	-	R	-	-	-
#12	Gamila (Aphalonas)	-	-	-	-	-	-	-	-	-	-	Byz	'MAge'	-
#13	Patia (Aphalonas)	-	-	-	-	-	-	-	-	-	-	Byz	'MAge', Tur	Tur
#14	Laka (Aphalonas)	-	-	-	-	-	-	-	-	HL	LR	EByz	-	Tur
#15	Katho (Panagiouda)	-	-	-	-	-	-	-	-	-	-	-	-	Tur
#16	Kalamiaris (Panagiouda)	-	-	-	-	-	-	-	-	-	-	EByz	-	-
#17	Pamphila (village)	-	-	-	-	-	-	-	C/HL		-	-	-	-
#18	Augo Atsinganas (Moria)	-	-	-	-	-	-	-	-	-	-	-	'MAge'	Tur
#19	Saliakas (Moria)	-	EBA	-	-	-	-	-	-	-	R	-	'MAge'	-
#20	Kamares (Moria)	-	-	-	-	-	-	-	-	-	R	-	-	-
#21	Outza (Moria)	-	-	-	LBA	-	-	-	-	HL	-	EByz	'MAge', Tur	Tur
#22	Katolakos (Moria)	-	-	-	-	-	-	-	-	-	R	-	-	-
#23	Thermelia (Moria)	-	-	-	-	-	-	-	-	-	-	-	-	Tur
#24	Kara-Tepe (Mytilene)	-	-	BA		-	-	-	C/HL?	C/HL?	-	-	-	-
#25	Agios Nikolaos (Pyrgi)	-	-	-	-	-	-	A	C	HL?	-	Byz	-	-
#26	Ano Latomeia Kourtzi (Aliphantas)	-	-	-	-	-	-	-	C?	-	LR	-	-	-
#27	Mytilene (town)	-	EBA	-	LBA	PG	G	A	C	HL	R	Byz	Ven	Tur
#28	Limani tou Pyrgiou (Pyrgi)	-	-	-	-	-	-	-	-	HL?	R	-	-	-
#29	Bigla (Pyrgi)	-	-	-	-	-	-	-	C/HL		LR/Byz		-	-
#30	Lakerdas (Pyrgi)	-	-	-	-	-	-	-	C/HL		R	EByz	-	-
#31	Phousa (Ano Chalikas)	-	-	-	-	-	-	-	-	-	-	-	'MAge'	-

Site No.	Site Name	Neolithic	Bronze Age			Iron Age					Roman	Medieval		
		N	EBA	MBA	LBA	PG	G	A	C	HL	R	BYZ	VEN	TUR
#32	Agios Spyridon (Ano Chalikas)	-	-	-	-	-	-	-	C	-	LR	-	-	Tur
#33	Akleidios (Mytilene)	-	-	-	-	-	-	-	-	HL	-	-	-	-
#34	Dyo Agioi (Ano Chalikas)	-	-	-	-	-	-	-	-	-	LR	EByz?, LByz/Tur	-	-
#35	Agios Bartholomaios (Taxiarchis/Ksagiani)	LN/EBA	-	-	-	-	-	-	-	-	-	-	-	-
#36	Agia Kyriaki (Agia Marina)	-	-	-	-	-	-	-	-	-	-	EByz	-	-
#37	Agia Euprepeia (Pligoni)	-	-	-	-	-	-	-	-	HL/R	-	EByz	-	-
#38	Kalamies (Agia Marina)	-	-	-	-	-	-	-	C	HL	R	EByz	-	-
#39	Myloi (Agia Marina)	-	-	-	-	-	-	-	C/HL	-	-	-	-	Tur
#40	Koukkaki (Agia Marina)	-	-	-	-	-	-	-	-	HL/R	-	-	-	-
#41	'Aja Tschiflik' (Agia Marina)	-	-	-	-	-	-	A/C	-	-	·	-	-	-
#42	Agios Georgios (Agia Marina)	-	-	-	-	-	-	A	C	-	-	-	-	-
#43	Panagia tis Amalis (Agia Marina)	-	-	-	-	-	-	-	-	-	-	Byz	-	-
#44	Tsesmedes (Loutra)	-	-	-	-	-	-	-	-	HL?	-	EByz	-	-
#45	Dibolon (Skala Loutron)	-	-	BA	-	-	-	-	C	HL	R	Byz	-	-
#46	Skala Dipiou (Kato Tritos)	-	-	-	-	-	-	-	C-EByz?		R		'MAge'?	-
#47	Agios Georgios (Kato Tritos)	-	-	-	-	-	-	-	-	HL	R	-	-	-
#48	Phousa (Mychou)	-	-	-	-	-	-	-	-	HL	-	-	-	-
#49	Taxiarchis (Kato Tritos)	-	-	-	-	-	-	-	-	-	-	-	-	-
#50	Manosados (Kato Tritos)	-	-	-	-	-	-	-	-	-	-	Byz	-	-
#51	Paliokastro (Mesagros)	-	-	-	-	-	-	-	-	-	-	EByz?	'MAge'	Tur
#52	'Sti Manna' (Papados)	-	-	-	-	-	-	-	C	HL	ER	Byz	'MAge'	Tur
#53	Agia Paraskeui (Papados)	-	-	-	-	-	-	-	-	-	-	EByz	'MAge'	-
#54	Chalatses (Perama)	-	-	MBA	LBA	-	-	-	-	-	R	-	-	-
#55	Agios Georgios tis Kourkoutas (Perama)	-	-	-	-	-	-	-	-	-	-	EByz, LByz?	-	-
#56	Brachonisi (Pyrgoi)	-	-	-	-	-	-	-	-	-	-	Byz	-	-
#57	Monastiraki (Pyrgoi)	-	-	-	-	-	-	A	-	HL	R	-	-	-
#58	Kabourolimni (Pyrgoi)	-	-	-	-	-	-	-	-	-	-	-	-	-

Site No.	Site Name	Neolithic	Bronze Age			Iron Age					Roman	Medieval		
		N	EBA	MBA	LBA	PG	G	A	C	HL	R	BYZ	VEN	TUR
#59	Tsaph (Tarti)	-	-	-	-	-	-	-	C	HL	R	EByz	-	-
#60	Osios Grigorios (Skopelos)		-	-	-	-	-	-		HL/R	R	EByz, LByz		
#61	Kastri (Plagia)	-	-			-	-	-	-	-	-	Byz	-	-
#62	Ypapanti tou Christou (Plagia)	-		BA?		-	-	-	-	LHL	R	EByz	-	-
#63	Glyphia (Drota)	-	EBA	-	-	-	-	-	-	-	-	EByz	-	-
#64	Mitoilia (Kato Stauros)	-	EBA	-	-	-	-	-	-	-	-		-	-
#65	Mesa Rongada (Ano Stauros)			-	-	-	-	-	-	-	-		-	-
#66	Agios Basilis (Kato Stauros)	-	-	-	-	-	-	-	-	-	LR	-	-	Tur
#67	Kambia (Ambeliko)	-	-	-	-	-	-	-	-	-	ER/MR LR	EByz?	-	-
#68	Agios Christophoros (Ambeliko)	-	-	-	-	-	-	-	-	-	-		-	-
#69	Dede Kambous (Ambeliko)	-	-	-	-	-	-	-	-	-	-	-	-	Tur
#70	Xylokastro (Agiasos)	-	-	-	-	-	-	-	-	-	-	-	'MAge'	
#71	Pitsilia (Agiasos)	-	-	-	-	-	-	-	-	-	-	Byz	-	Tur
#72	Kastelli (Agiasos)	-	-	-	-	-	-	-	-	-	-	Byz	-	-
#73	Karini (village)	-	-	-	-	-	-	-	-	HL	-	-	-	-
#74	Agios Phokas (Brisa)	-	EBA	-	-	-	LG	A	C	HL	ER	EByz, MByz	-	-
#75	Achilopigado (Brisa)	-	-	-	-	-	-	-	-	-	LR/EByz?		-	-
#76	Paliopyrgos (Brisa)	-	-	BA?	-	-	-	-	-	-	-	-	Ven	-
#77	Brysi tou Deligianni (Brisa)	-	EBA	-	-	-	-	-	C/HL	-	-	-	-	-
#78	Strongylos (Polichnitos)	-	-	-	-	-	-	-	C/HL	-	-	Byz	-	Tur
#79	Traperia (Polichnitos)	-	-	-	-	-	-	-	-	-	R	Byz	-	-
#80	Garbias (Polichnitos)	-	-	-	-	-	-	-		C-EByz?			'MAge'	-
#81	Bougazi (Polichnitos)	-	-	-	-	-	-	-	C/HL	-	-	-	-	-
#82	Louta (Polichnitos)	-	-	-	-	-	-	-	C/HL	-	R, LR-Byz	-	-	-
#83	Peribola (Polichnitos)	-	-	-	-	-	-	A/C	-	-	R	EByz	'MAge'	-
#84	Chalakies (Polichnitos)	LN	EBA	-	-	-	-	-	C	-	R	-	-	-
#85	Ara (Polichnitos)	-	-	-	-	-	-	-	C?	HL	R	EByz	-	-

Site No.	Site Name	Neolithic	Bronze Age			Iron Age					Roman	Medieval		
		N	EBA	MBA	LBA	PG	G	A	C	HL	R	BYZ	VEN	TUR
#86	Agios Ioannis (Lisbori)	-	-	-	-	-	-	-	-	HL	R?	EByz, MByz	Ven	Tur
#87	Kaukara (Lisbori)	-	-	-	-	-	-	A	-	-	-	EByz	-	-
#88	Prophitis Ilias (Lisbori)	-	EBA	-	-	-	-	-	-	-	-	MByz	'MAge'	-
#89	Damandri (Polichnitos)	-	-	-	-	-	-	-	-	HL/R?		Byz?	'MAge'	Tur
#90	Astratgos (Lisbori)	-	-	-	-	-	-	-	-	-	-	EByz, LByz?	-	-
#91	Kourtir (Lisbori)	LN	EBA	MBA	LBA	-	G	-	C	-	R	E-LByz	Ven	Tur
#92	Aspres Petres (Lisbori)	-	-	-	-	-	-	-	-	-	LR?	Byz	-	-
#93	Temenos (Lisbori)	-	-	-	-	-	-	-	-	HL	R	Byz	Ven	-
#94	Loutzas (Basilika)	-	-	-	-	-	-	-	-	-	R, LR?	Byz	'MAge'	Tur
#95	Plaka (Basilika)	-	-	-	-	-	-	-	C/HL		LR-EByz?		-	-
#96	Xiro (Achladeri)	-	-	-	-	-	-	A	-	-	R	-	-	-
#97	Pastourmas (Achladeri)	-	-	-	-	-	-	-	-	-	-	-	-	Tur
#98	Agios Dimitrios (Achladeri)	-	-	-	-	-	-	-	-	-	-	EByz	-	-
#99	Pyrrha (Achladeri)	-	EBA?	MBA?	LBA	PG	G	A	C	HL	R	LByz/Tur	-	-
#100	Tokaria (Achladeri)	-	-	-	-	-	-	-	-	-	R	EByz	-	-
#101	Mesinziki (Achladeri)	-	-	-	-	-	-	-	-	-	-	-	'MAge'	-
#102	Kryo Neri (Achladeri)	-	-	-	-	-	-	-	C	HL	R, LR-Byz	-	'MAge'	-
#103	Messa (Achladeri)	-	-	-	-	-	-	A	LC-EHL		-	EByz, LByz	-	-
#104	Chiftlik (Achladeri)	-	-	-	-	-	-	-	-	-	-	-	-	-
#105	Agios Georgios Chalinadou (Agia Paraskeui)	-	-	-	-	-	-	-	-	-	-	EByz	'MAge'	Tur
#106	Taxiarchis (Agia Paraskeui)	-	-	-	-	-	-	-	-	-	-	EByz	-	-
#107	Agios Dimitrios (Agia Paraskeui)	-	-	-	-	-	-	-	-	-	-	-	-	Tur
#108	Mosyna (Napi)	-		BA?		-	-	-	-	-	-	-	-	-
#109	Taxiarchis tou Troulotis (Napi)	-		BA?	-	-	-	-	-	-	-	EByz	-	-
#110	Agios Therapon (Napi)	-	-	-	-	-	-	-	-	-	-	EByz	-	-
#111	Klopedi (Agia Paraskeui)	-	EBA	-	-	-	LG	A	C?	HL?	R	-	-	-
#112	Prophitis Ilias (Agia Paraskeui)	-	EBA	MBA	LBA	-	-	A	C/HL		LR		'MAge'	-

Site No.	Site Name	Neolithic	Bronze Age			Iron Age					Roman	Medieval		
		N	EBA	MBA	LBA	PG	G	A	C	HL	R	BYZ	VEN	TUR
#113	*Agia Photia (Agia Paraskeui)*	N	-	-	-	-	-	-	-	C/HL?	-	-	-	-
#114	*Gerna (Agia Paraskeui)*	N	EBA	-	-	-	-	-	-	-	-	EByz	-	Tur
#115	*Agios Giannis (Arisbi)*	-	EBA	-	-	-	-	-	-	HL	-	EByz	'MAge'	-
#116	*Palaiokastro (Arisbi)*	-	EBA	MBA	-	-	-	A	C	HL	R	Byz/Ven?	'MAge'	-
#117	*Pharanx (Daphia)*	-	-	-	-	-	-	-	-	-	-	-	-	Tur
#118	*Monastiri tis Myrsiniotissas (Daphia)*	-	-	-	-	-	-	-	-	-	-	Byz	-	Tur
#119	*Moni Leimonos (Daphia)*	-	-	-	-	-	-	-	-	-	-	Byz	-	Tur
#120	*Triania (Kalloni)*	-	-	-	-	-	-	-	C	HL	-	LR-Byz	-	Tur
#121	*Prophitis Ilias (Kerami)*	-	-	-	-	-	-	A?	-	HL	-	Byz	-	-
#122	*Xirokastrini (Kerami)*	-	-	-	-	-	-	A	-	HL	-	Byz	Ven?, 'MAge', Tur?	-
#123	*Palaiokastro Issas (Parakoila)*	-	-	-	-	-	-	A/C?	-	-	-	Byz/Tur		
#124	*Kastrelli (Parakoila)*	-	-	-	-	-	-	-	-	-	-	-	'MAge'	Tur
#125	*Nipos (Parakoila)*	-	-	-	-	-	-	-	C/HL	-	-	-	-	-
#126	*Aetos (Parakoila)*	-	-	-	-	-	-	-	C/HL	-	-	-	-	-
#127	*Chontro Bigli (Agra)*	-	-	-	-	-	-	-	C/HL	-	-	-	-	-
#128	*Lapedia (Agra)*	-	-	-	-	-	-	-	-	HL	-	-	-	-
#129	*Listis (Parakoila)*	-	-	-	-	-	-	-	C?	-	-	-	-	-
#130	*Apothiki (Agra)*	-	-	-	-	-	-	A	C	HL	R	-	'MAge'	-
#131	*Makara (Agra)*	-	EBA	-	LBA	-	-	A	C?	HL	-	Byz	-	Tur
#132	*Seistria (Mesotopos)*	-	EBA	MBA?	-	-	-	-	-	-	-	EByz	'MAge'	-
#133	*Tabari (Mesotopos)*	-	BA	-	-	-	-	-	-	HL	ER	-	-	-
#134	*Krousos (Skala Eresou)*	-	EBA/MBA	-	-	-	-	-	C	HL	LR	Byz	-	-
#135	*Bigla (Skala Eresou)*	-	-	-	-	-	-	A	C	HL	R	EByz	Ven	-
#136	*Agios Andreas (Skala Eresou)*	-	-	-	-	-	-	-	-	-	-	EByz, LByz	-	Tur
#137	*Aphentellis (Skala Eresou)*	-	-	-	-	-	-	-	-	-	-	EByz	-	-
#138	*'Plain of Eresos' (Eresos)*	-	EBA	-	-	-	-	A	-	HL	-	-	-	-
#139	*Tholos (Eresos)*	-	-	-	-	-	-	-	-	-	R	-	-	-
#140	*Blitsi (Eresos)*	-	-	-	-	-	-	-	-	HL	-	-	-	-
#141	*Spilios (Eresos)*	-	-	-	-	-	-	A	-	-	-	-	-	-
#142	*Meladia (Eresos)*	-	-	-	-	-	-	-	-	HL	-	-	-	-

Site No.	Site Name	Neolithic	Bronze Age			Iron Age					Roman	Medieval		
		N	EBA	MBA	LBA	PG	G	A	C	HL	R	BYZ	VEN	TUR
#143	Skordalos (Sigri)	-	-	-	-	-	-	-	-	-	-	-	-	-
#144	Lesbados (Sigri)	-	-	-	-	-	-	-	-	-	-	-	-	-
#145	Pharkobnar (Sigri)	-	-	-	-	-	-	A	-	HL	HL/R?	-	-	-
#146	Pharkonias (Sigri)	-	-	-	-	-	-	A?	-	-	-	-	-	Tur
#147	Megalonisi (Sigri)	-	-	BA?	-	-	-	-	-	-	-	EByz	-	-
#148	Paliokastro (Sigri)	-	-	-	-	-	-	-	-	-	R?, LR-Byz	EByz	Ven, 'MAge'	Tur
#149	'Kusu-Mandrassi" (Sigri)	-	-	-	-	-	-	-	-	-	-	-	-	-
#150	Pigados (Sigri)	-	-	-	-	-	-	-	-	HL	-	-	-	-
#151	Oikia (Sigri)	-	-	-	-	-	-	-	-	HL	-	-	-	-
#152	Paliochorion (Sigri)	-	-	-	-	-	-	-	-	-	-	-	'MAge'	-
#153	Agios Nikolaos (Sigri)	-	-	-	-	-	-	-	-	-	R	LR-Byz, LByz-Tur	-	-
#154	Tsouloumounias (Sigri)	-	-	-	-	-	-	-	-	-	-	-	-	-
#155	Tsiphos (Gabathas)	-	-	-	-	-	-	-	-	-	R	-	-	-
#156	Sal-taschi (Gabathas)	-	-	-	-	-	-	-	-	HL	R, LR-Byz	-	'MAge'	-
#157	Pyrgo (Gabathas)	-	EBA	-	-	-	-	-	-	-	R, LR-Byz	-	-	'MAge', Tur
#158	Agioi Archangeloi (Gabathas)	-	EBA	-	-	-	-	-	-	-	R	EByz, Byz/Tur	-	-
#159	Agios Georgios (Gabathas)	-	-	-	-	-	-	-	-	-	-	LR-Byz, LByz/Tur	-	-
#160	Tsephos (Gabathas)	-	EBA?	-	-	-	-	-	-	-	-	-	-	-
#161	Obriokastro (Gabathas)	-	EBA?	MBA	LBA	-	EG-LG	-	-	HL	R	Byz	Ven	Tur
#162	Kouphi (Skalochori)	-	-	-	-	-	-	-	C/HL	-	-	-	-	-
#163	Salbaradis (Skalochori)	-	-	-	-	-	-	-	-	-	-	EByz, LByz/Tur?	-	-
#164	Panagia Kokkinou (Skalochori)	-	-	-	-	-	-	-	-	-	R	EByz	-	Tur
#165	Kastri (Skalochori)	-	-	-	-	-	-	A	-	-	-	-	-	-
#166	Apastra (Gabathas)	-	-	-	-	-	-	A/C?	-	-	-	EByz	-	-
#167	Monastiri tis Peribolis (Tzithra)	-	-	-	-	-	-	-	-	-	-	Byz?	-	Tur
#168	Routhia (Batousa)	-	-	-	-	-	-	A	-	-	-	-	-	-
#169	Kabouros (Skalochori)	-	-	-	-	-	-	-	-	-	-	-	Byz/Tur	-
#170	Agia Kyriaki (Batousa)	-	-	-	-	-	-	-	-	-	LR-Byz	-	-	-
#171	Agia Paraskeui (Tzithra)	-	-	-	-	-	-	-	-	-	-	Byz?	'MAge', Tur	-

Site No.	Site Name	Neolithic	Bronze Age			Iron Age					Roman	Medieval		
		N	EBA	MBA	LBA	PG	G	A	C	HL	R	BYZ	VEN	TUR
#172	Monastiri tou Kreokopou (Tzithra)	-	-	-	-	-	-	-	-	-	-	LByz	-	Tur
#173	Klimaki (Antissa)	-	-	-	-	-	-	-	-	-	-	Byz	-	-
#174	Moni Hypsilou (Antissa)	-	-	-	-	-	-	-	-	-	-	Byz	-	Tur
#175	Megalos Lakkos (Eresos)	-	-	-	-	-	-	A	-	-	-	-	-	-
#176	Agios Alexandros (Eresos)	-	-	-	-	-	-	-	-	-	R	LByz	-	-
#177	Aetos (Eresos)	-	-	-	-	-	-	-	-	C/HL	-	-	-	-
#178	Kourouklos (Chydira)	-	-	-	-	-	-	A/C?	-	-	-	-	-	-
#179	Agios Ilias (Chydira)	-	-	-	-	-	-	-	-	-	LR-Byz		-	-
#180	Tyrrani (Chydira)	N/EBA		-	-	-	-	-	-	-	-	-	-	-
#181	Pyrgi (Chydira)	-	-	-	-	-	-	A/C?	-	-	-	-	-	-
#182	Kladomantri (Chydira)	-	-	-	-	-	-	A/C?	-	-	-	-	-	-
#183	Gigi (Chydira)	-	-	-	-	-	-	A	-	C/HL?	-	-	-	-
#184	Batoudia (Chydira)	-	-	-	-	-	-	A/C	-	-	-	-	-	-
#185	Balana (Chydira)	-	-	-	-	-	-	A	-	-	-	-	-	-
#186	Skoteino (Chydira)	-	-	-	-	-	-	-	-	-	LR-Byz		-	-
#187	Bigla (Agra)	-	-	-	-	-	-	A	-	-	-	-	-	-
#188	Paliokastro (Agra)	-	-	-	-	-	-	-	-	-	-	-	'MAge'	-
#189	Pente Agioi (Pterounda)	-	-	-	-	-	-	A	-	-	-	Byz	-	Tur
#190	Koutlougouni (Skalochori)	-	-	-	-	-	-	A	-	-	-	-	-	-
#191	Xirolimni (Skoutaros)	-	-	-	-	-	-	-	-	-	R	EByz?	'MAge'	-
#192	Tsichranias (Skoutaros)	-	-	-	-	-	-	-	C	-	R	EByz	-	-
#193	Koja Dag (Skalochori)	-	-	-	-	-	-	A	-	-	-	-	-	-
#194	Prophitis Ilias (Skalochori)	-	-	-	-	-	-	A	-	HL	-	-	-	-
#195	Phonias (Skalochori)	-	-	-	-	-	-	A	-	-	-	-	-	-
#196	Pedia (Skalochori)	-	-	-	-	-	-	-	-	-	R	EByz	'MAge'	-
#197	Mitropolis (Anemotia)	-	-	-	-	-	-	-	-	HL/R?		EByz	-	Tur
#198	Erimopyli (Philia)	-	-	-	-	-	-	-	-	C/HL?		-	-	Tur
#199	Paliochora (Philia)	-	-	-	-	-	-	-	-	HL/R?		-	'MAge', Tur	
#200	Katopetro (Laphionas)	-	-	-	-	-	-	-	-	-	-	-	-	-
#201	Ambelia Skoteinou (Philia)	-	-	-	-	-	-	A	-	-	-	-	-	-
#202	Ametelli Skoteinou (Laphionas)	-	-	-	-	-	-	A	-	-	-	-	-	Tur

Site No.	Site Name	Neolithic	Bronze Age			Iron Age					Roman	Medieval		
		N	EBA	MBA	LBA	PG	G	A	C	HL	R	BYZ	VEN	TUR
#203	Agios Alexandros (Laphionas)	-	-	-	-	-	-	-	-	-	-	EByz	-	Tur
#204	Chlios (Skoutaros)	-	-	-	-	-	-	-	-	-	-	-	-	Tur
#205	Selles (Skoutaros)	-	-	-	-	-	-	A	-	-	-	-	-	-
#206	Kalejik (Skoutaros)	-	-	-	-	-	-	-	-	-	LR-Byz	-	'MAge'	-
#207	Agios Georgios (Petra)	-	-	-	-	-	-	-	-	-	LR-Byz	-	'MAge'	-
#208	Agios Dimitrios (Petra)	-	-	-	-	-	-	-	-	-	R	EByz	-	-
#209	Paliokastro Korphiou (Laphionas)	-	-	-	-	-	-	-	-	-	LR-Byz	-	-	-
#210	Agios Dimitrios (Hypsilometopo)	-	-	-	-	-	-	-	-	-	-	EByz	-	-
#211	Rousos (Hypsilometopo)	-	-	-	-	-	-	-	-	HL	-	-	-	-
#212	Monastirellia (Bapheios)	-	-	-	-	-	-	A	C/HL		R	-	'MAge'	Tur
#213	Petri (village)	-	-	-	-	-	-	-	-	-	-	-	-	-
#214	Achilopigada (Petri)	-	-	-	-	-	-	-	C/HL		-	-	-	Tur
#215	Agia Kyriaki (Petra)	-	-	-	-	-	-	-	-	-	-	Byz?	-	-
#216	Rachonas (Methymna)	-	-	-	-	-	-	-	-	-	-	-	-	Tur
#217	Methymna (town)	-	EBA	-	LBA	PG	G	A	C	HL	R	EByz, LByz	Ven	Tur
#218	Temenos (Bapheios)	-	-	-	-	-	-	-	C	-	-	-	-	-
#219	Ekklise Bagir (Bapheios)	-	-	-	-	-	-	-	C/HL		LR-Byz	-	-	-
#220	Agios Thomas (Argenos)	-	-	-	-	-	-	-	-	-	-	-	-	-
#221	Prophitis Ilias (Hypsilometopo)	-	-	-	-	-	-	A	-	-	-	-	-	-
#222	Viran Köy (Hypsilometopo)	-	-	-	-	-	-	-	-	-	-	-	'MAge'	-
#223	Thermokastro (Argenos)	-	-	-	-	-	-	-	-	-	-	-	'MAge'	-
#224	Prophitis Ilias (Sykamia)	-	-	-	-	-	-	-	-	-	-	EByz	-	-
#225	Agia Anastasia (Kleio)	-	-	-	-	-	-	-	-	-	-	EByz	-	-
#226	Agia Sotira (Kleio)	-	-	-	-	-	-	-	-	-	-	Byz?	-	-
#227	Korakas (Kleio)	-	-	-	-	-	-	-	-	-	-	-	Ven	Tur
#228	Pegia (Kleio)	-	-	-	-	-	-	-	-	-	LR-Byz	-	'MAge'	-
#229	Agios Blasis (Kleio)	-	-	-	-	-	-	-	-	-	-	-	'MAge'	-
#230	Prophitis Ilias (Kleio)	-	-	-	-	-	-	-	C?	-	-	-	-	-
#231	Koukmidos (Kleio)	-	-	-	-	-	-	-	-	-	-	-	-	Tur

Site No.	Site Name	Neolithic	Bronze Age			Iron Age					Roman	Medieval		
		N	EBA	MBA	LBA	PG	G	A	C	HL	R	BYZ	VEN	TUR
#232	*Kastri (Kapi)*	-	-	-	-	-	-	A/C?		-	-	-	-	-
#233	*Karanik Çay (Kapi)*	-	-	-	-	-	-	-	-	-	-	-	-	Tur
#234	*Agia Photia (Napi)*	-	-	-	-	-	-	-	-	-	-	-	'MAge'	
#235	*Drakou Pidima (Napi)*	-	-	-	-	-	-	A	-	C/HL	-	-	-	-
#236	*Taxiarchis (Mandamados)*	-	-	-	-	-	-	-	-	-	-	-	-	Tur
#237	*Agia Sotira (Kleio)*	-	EBA	-	-	-	-	A	-	C/HL	-	Byz/Tur		
#238	*Angourelia Sarakinas (Mandamados)*	-	-	-	-	-	-	-	-	-	-	-	-	-
#239	*Palios (Mandamados)*	-	-	-	-	-	-	-	-	HL	R	EByz	-	Tur
#240	*Nisos Panagias (Mandamados)*	-	-	BA	-	-	-	-	-	-	-	-	-	-
#241	*Agios Stephanos (Mandamados)*	-	-	-	-	-	-	-	-	-	-	LByz	-	-
#242	*Taxiarchis tou Stenaka (Mandamados)*	-	-	-	-	-	-	-	-	-	LR	-	'MAge'	Tur?
#243	*Kabakli (Mandamados)*	-	-	BA	-	-	-	-	-	-	-	-	-	Tur
#244	*Prasologos (Nees Kydonies)*	-	-	BA	-	-	-	-	-	-	-	-	-	-

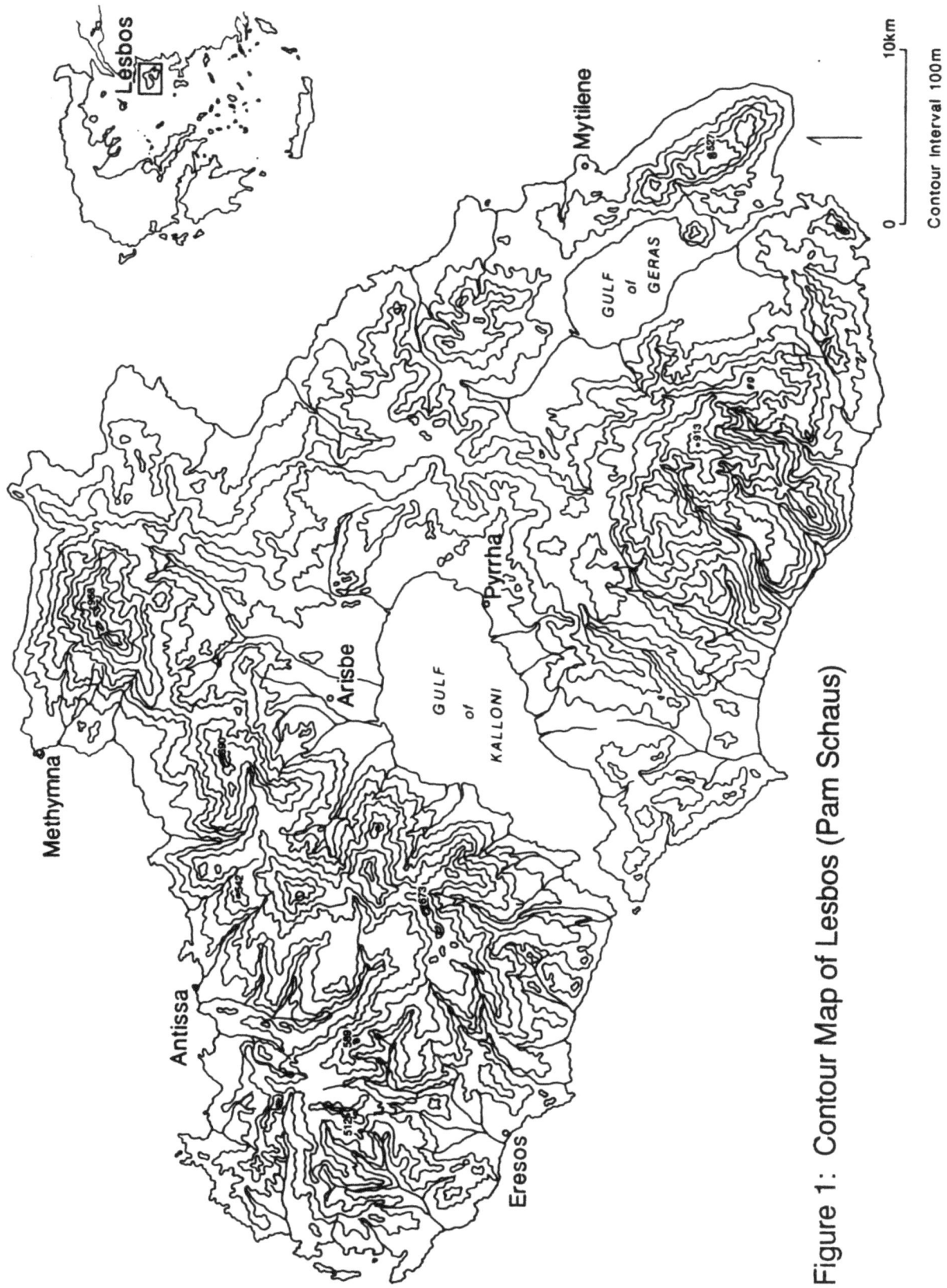

Figure 1: Contour Map of Lesbos (Pam Schaus)

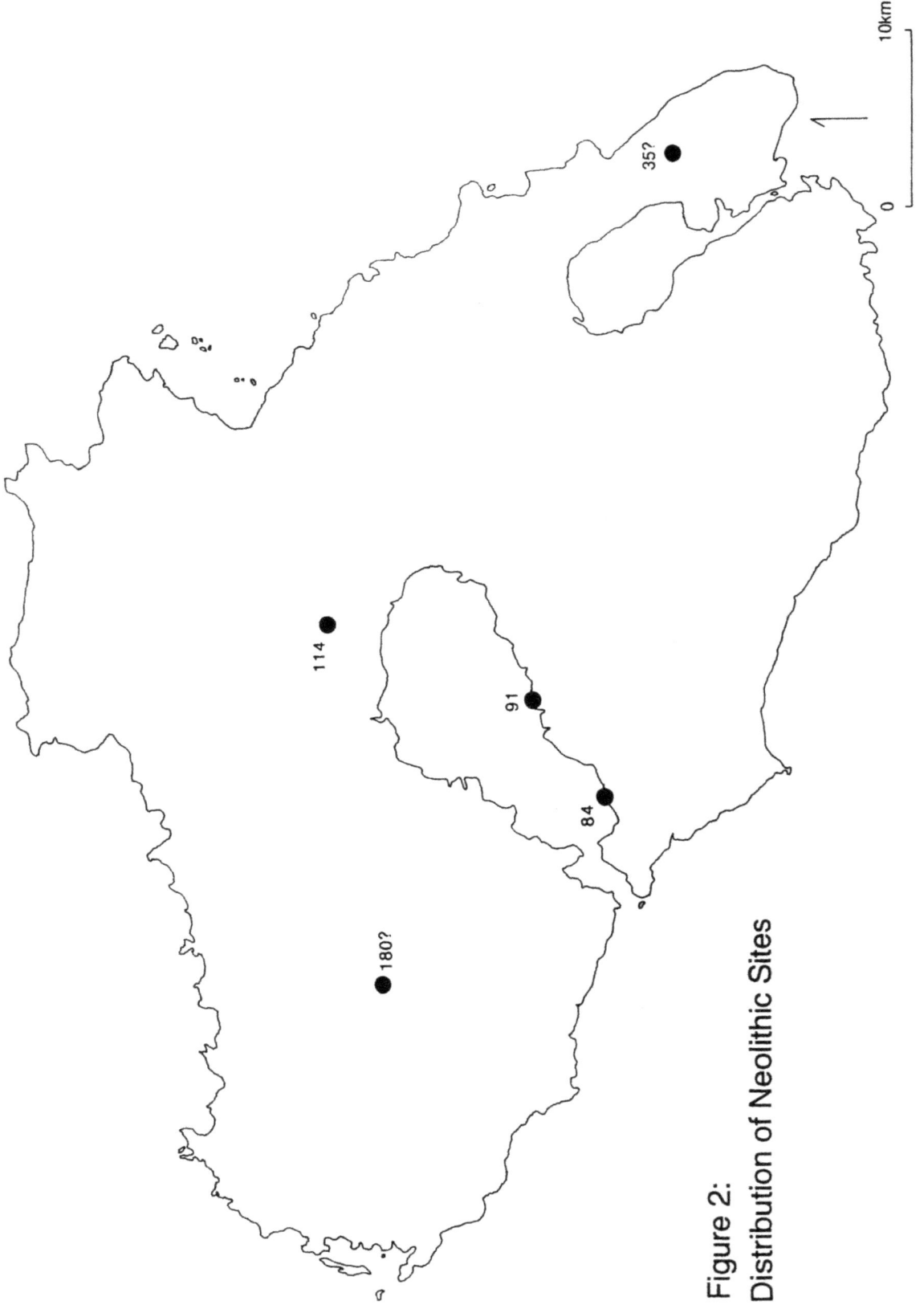

Figure 2:
Distribution of Neolithic Sites

35?

114

91

84

180?

10km

0

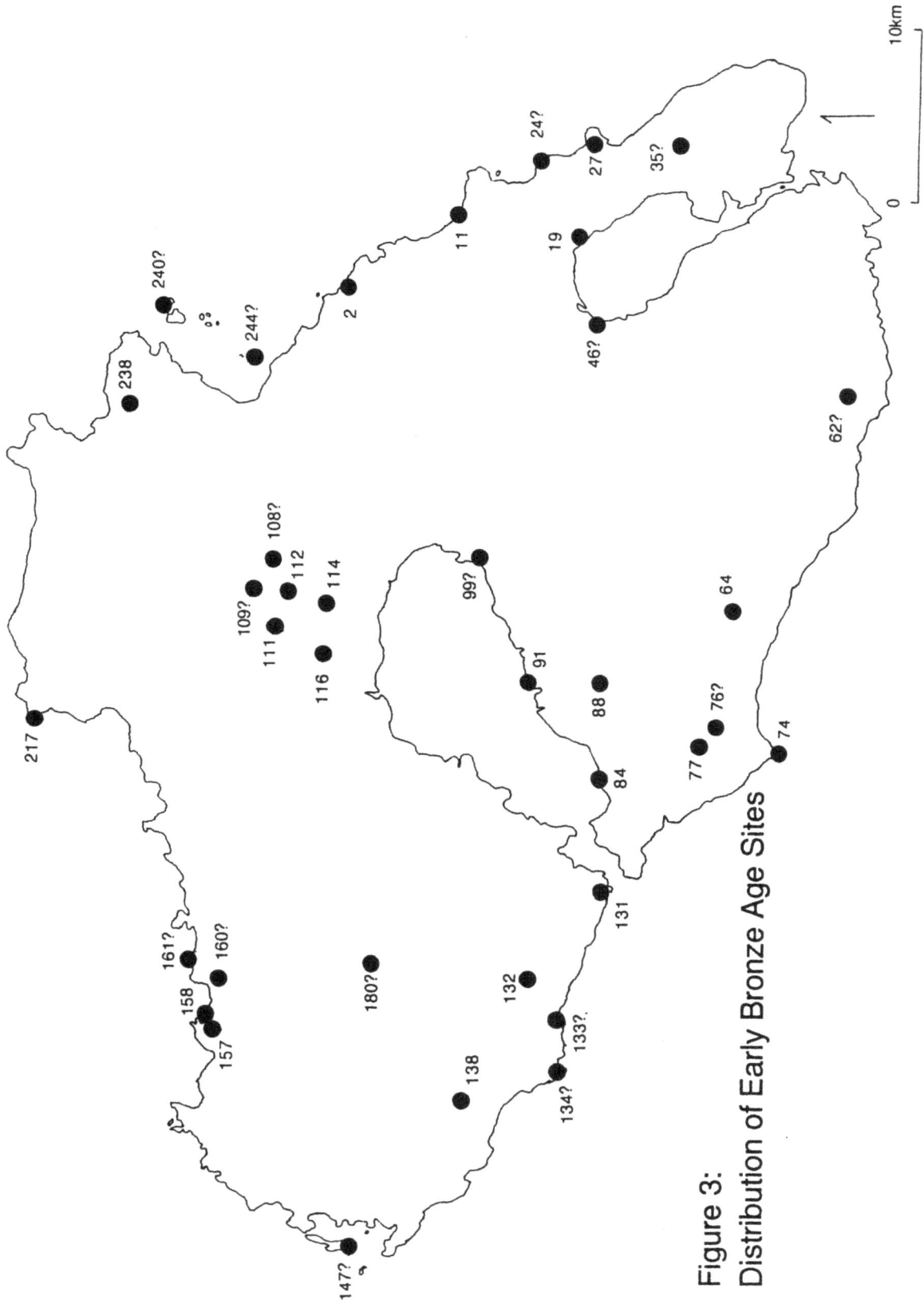

Figure 3:
Distribution of Early Bronze Age Sites

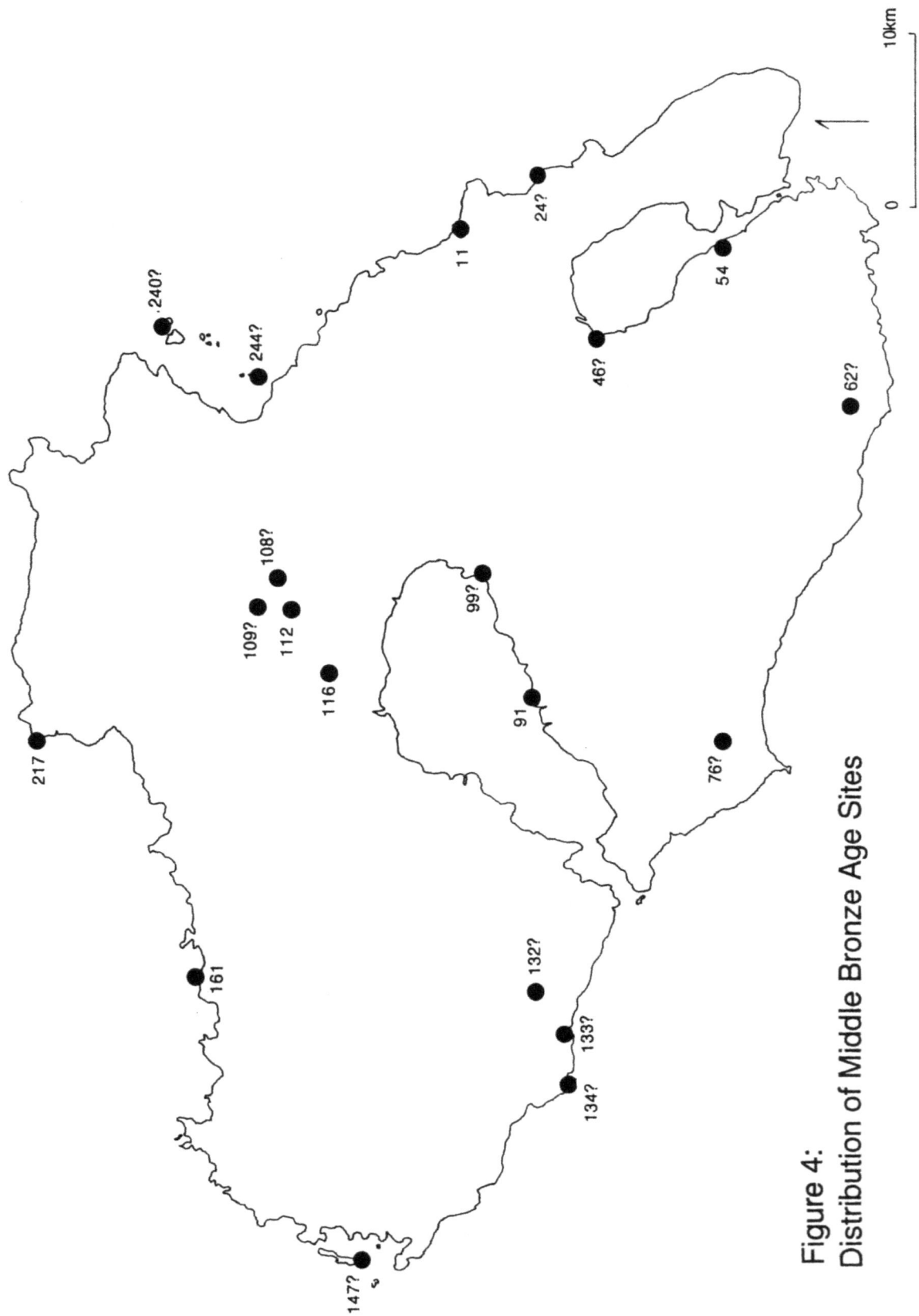

Figure 4:
Distribution of Middle Bronze Age Sites

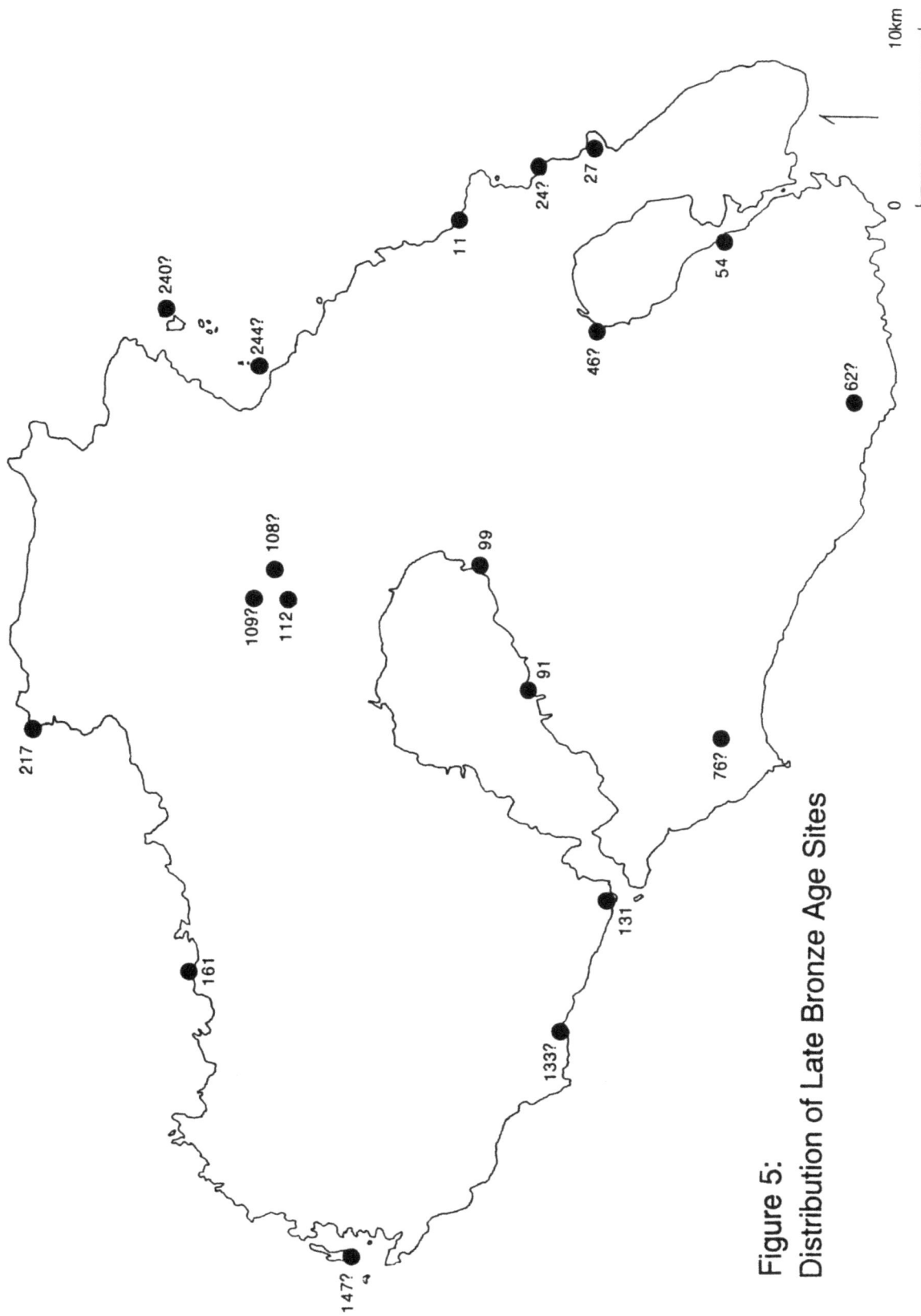

Figure 5:
Distribution of Late Bronze Age Sites

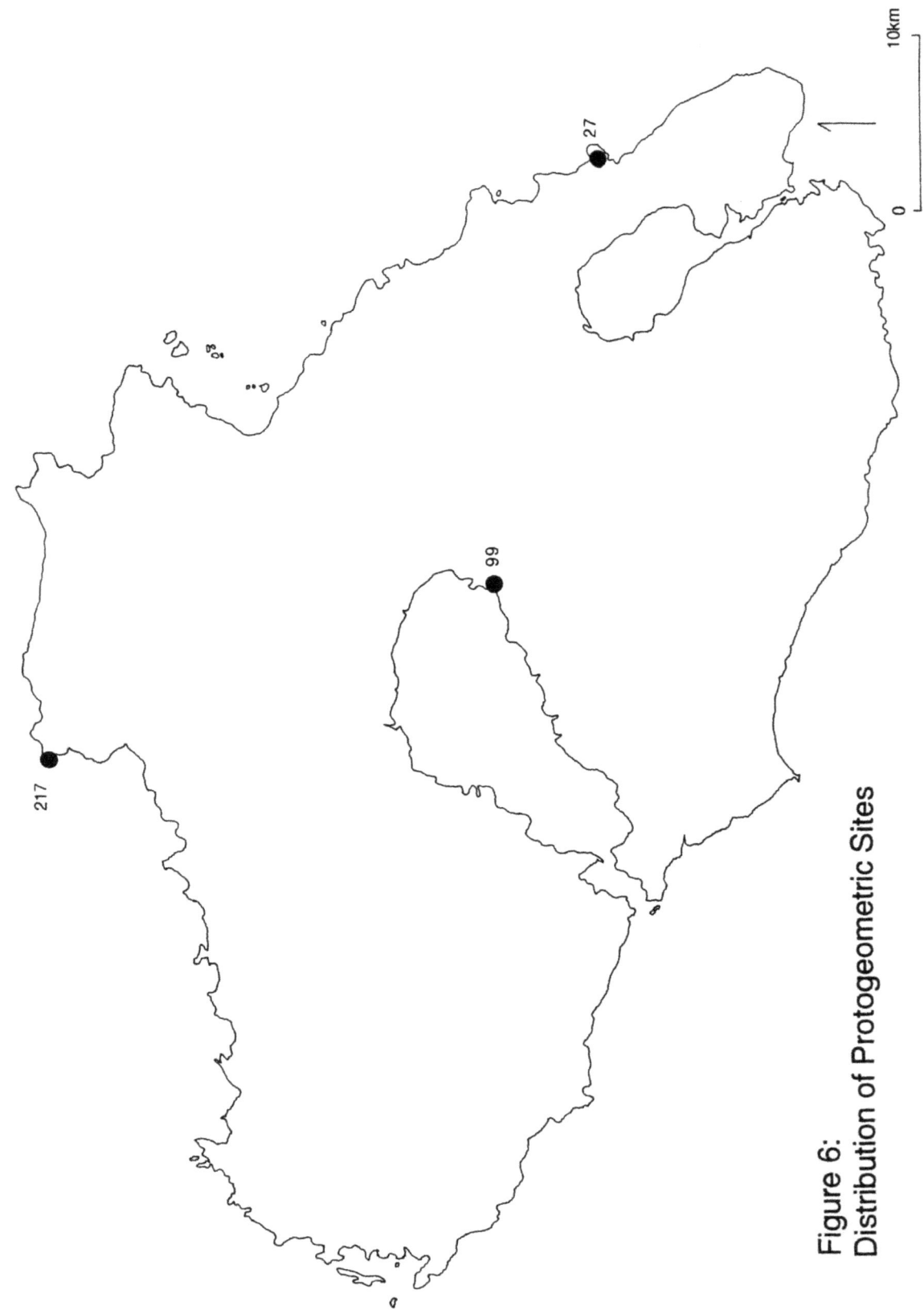

Figure 6:
Distribution of Protogeometric Sites

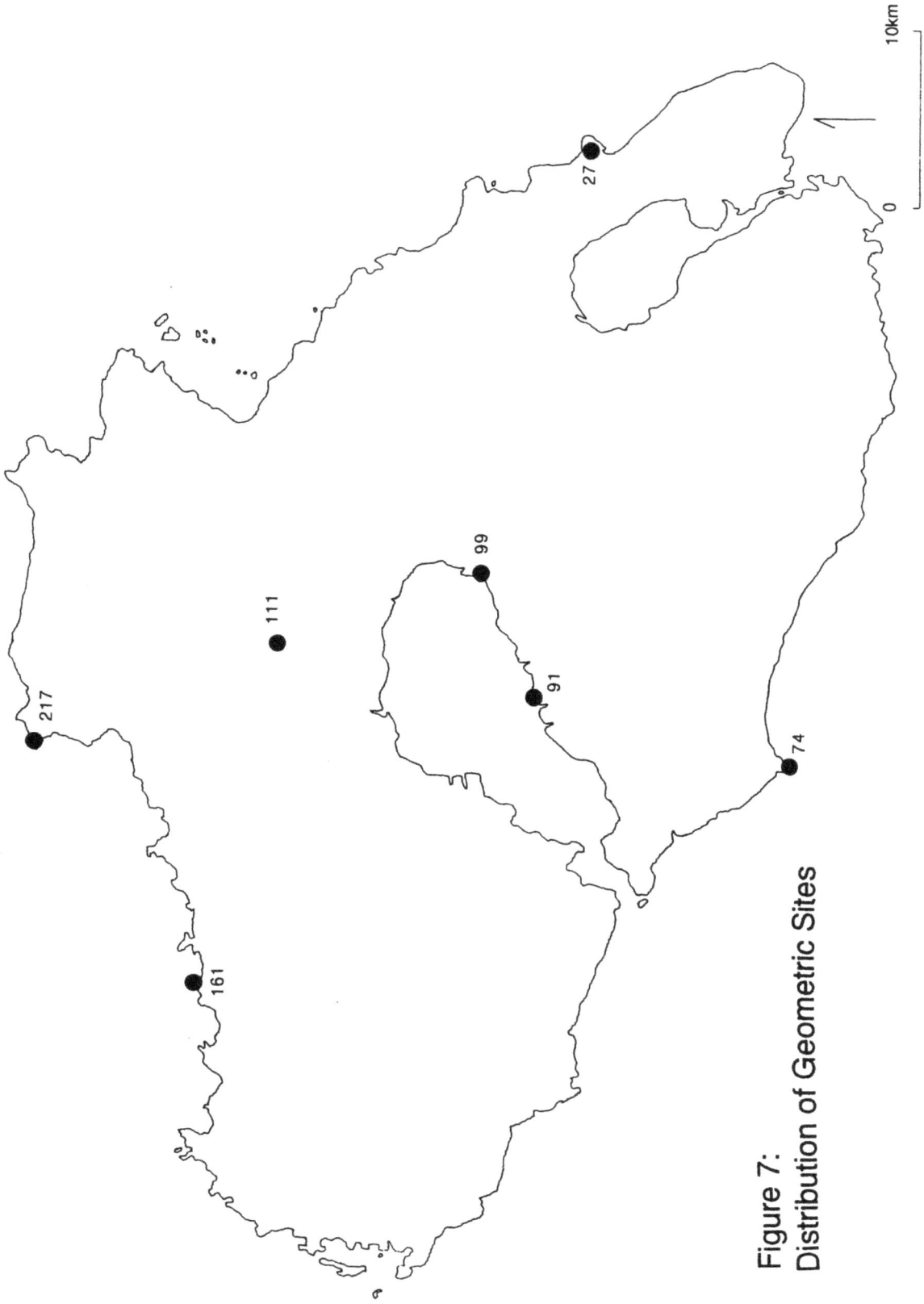

Figure 7:
Distribution of Geometric Sites

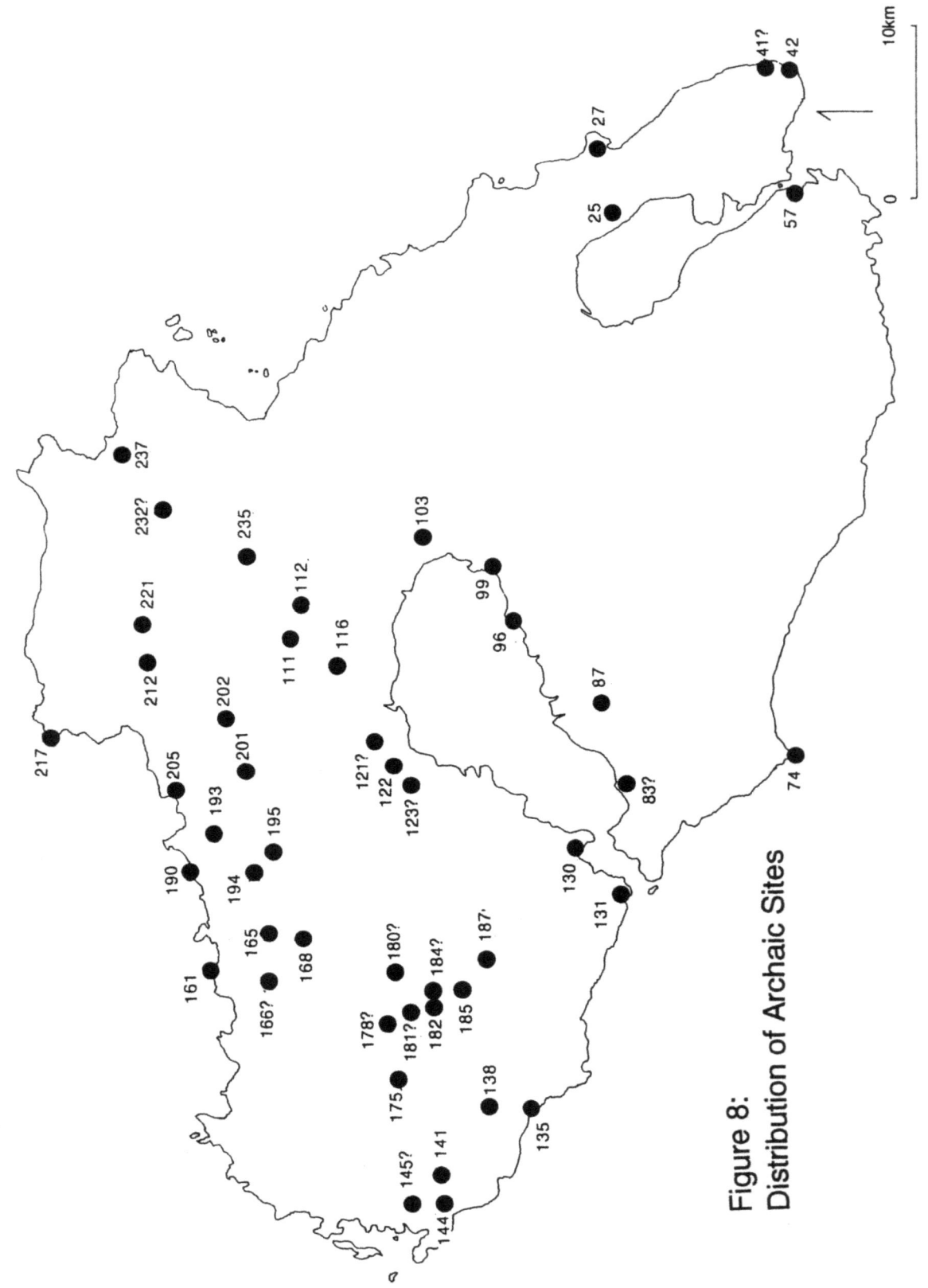

Figure 8:
Distribution of Archaic Sites

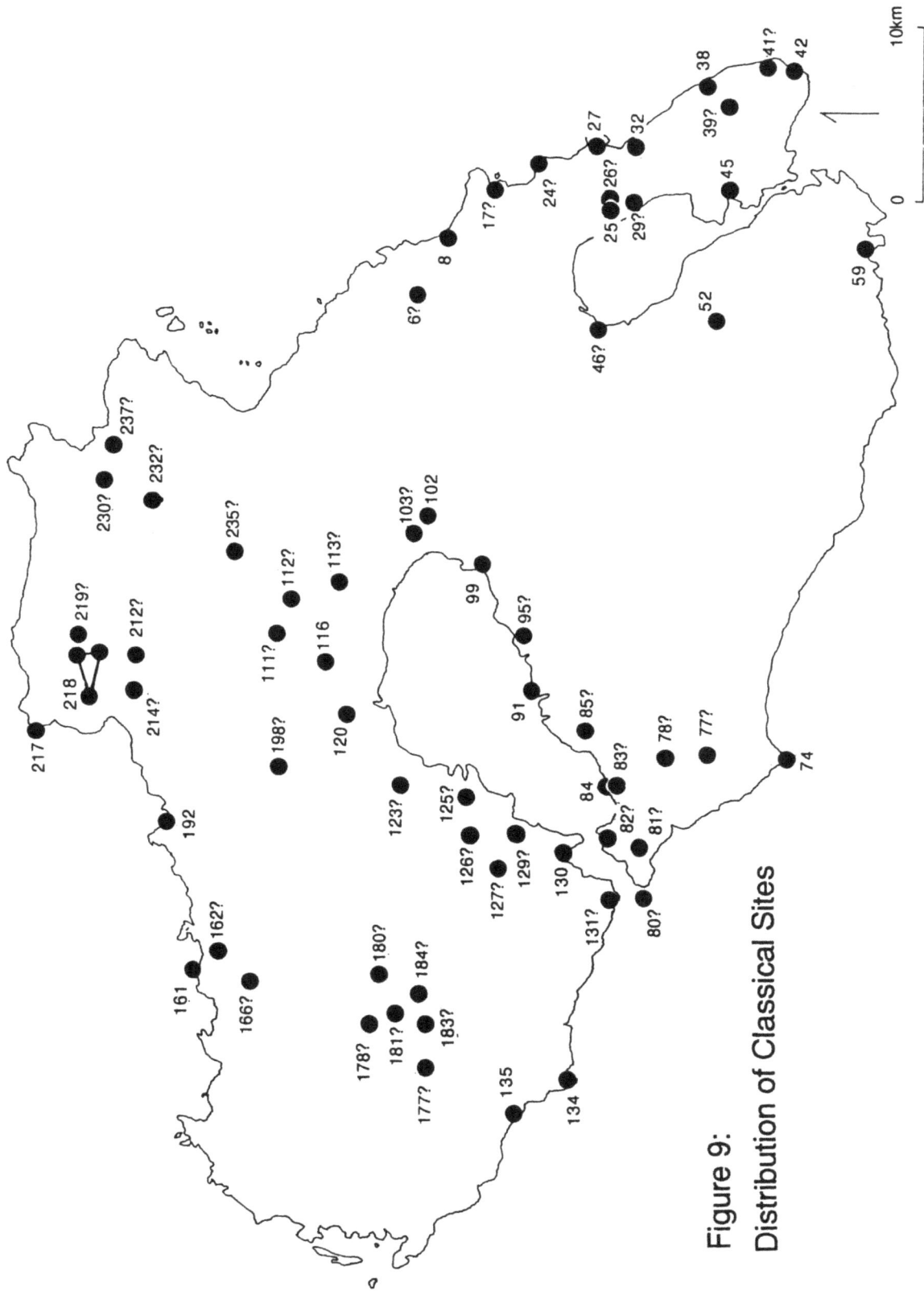

Figure 9:
Distribution of Classical Sites

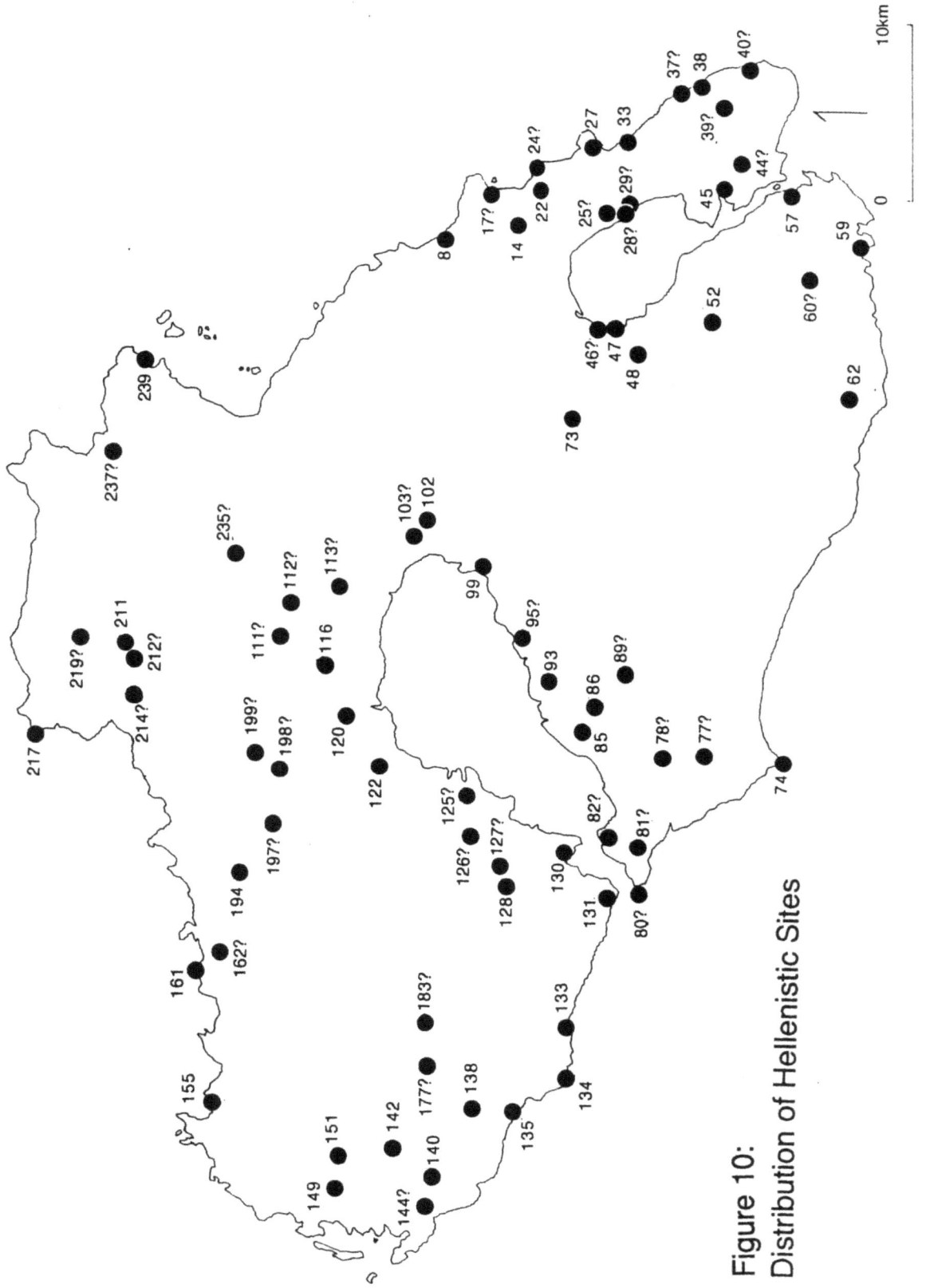

Figure 10:
Distribution of Hellenistic Sites

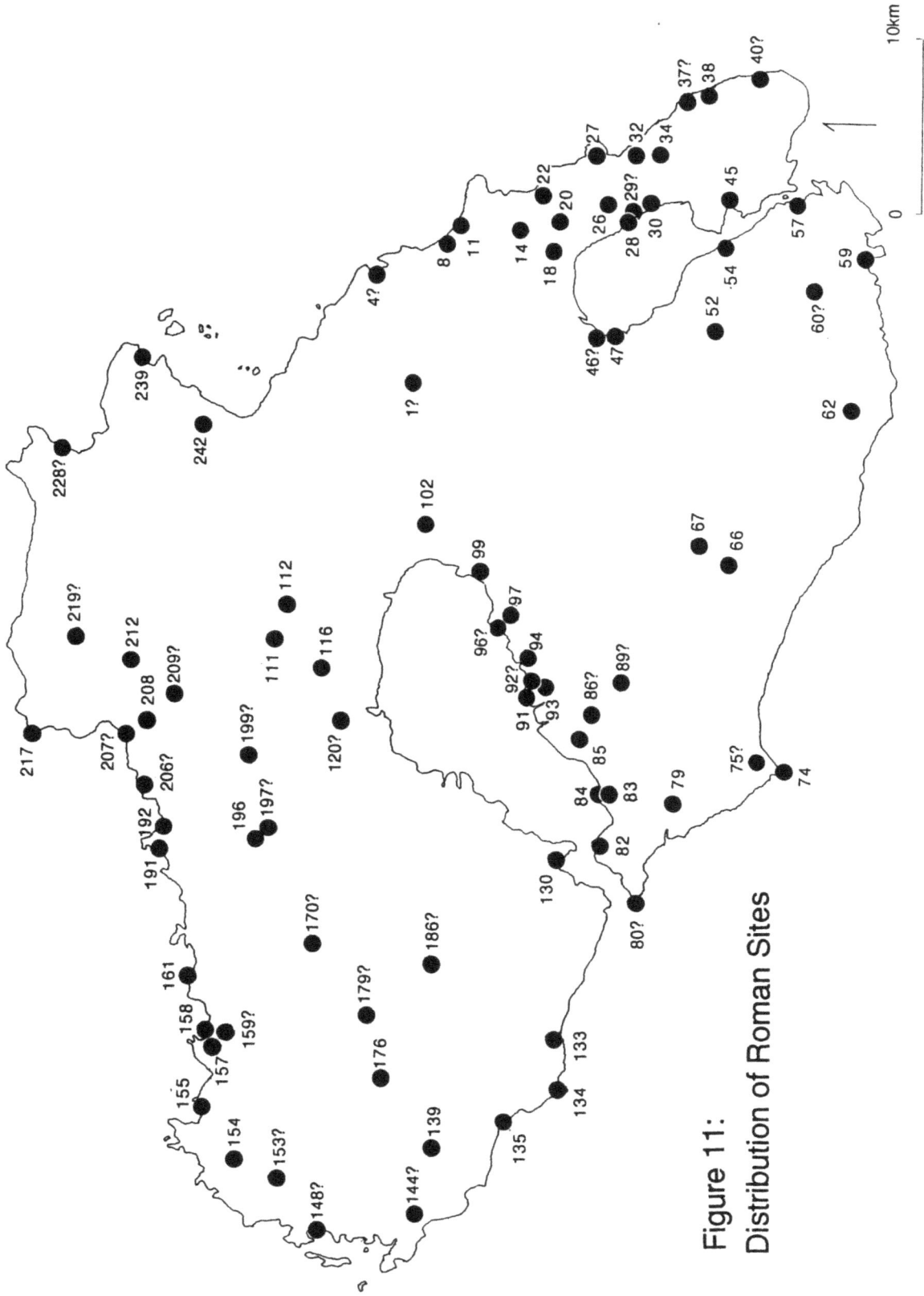

Figure 11:
Distribution of Roman Sites

10km

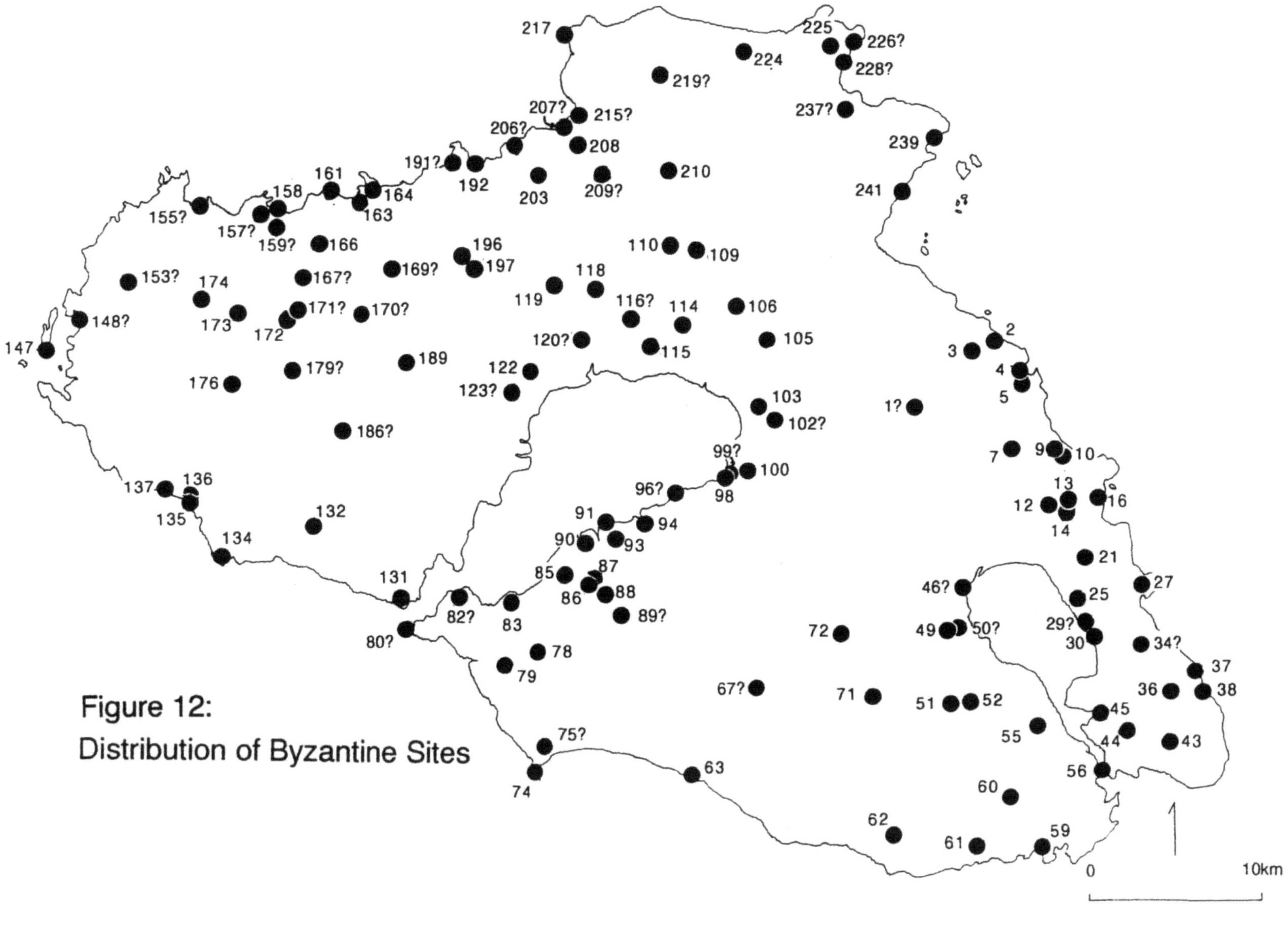

Figure 12:
Distribution of Byzantine Sites

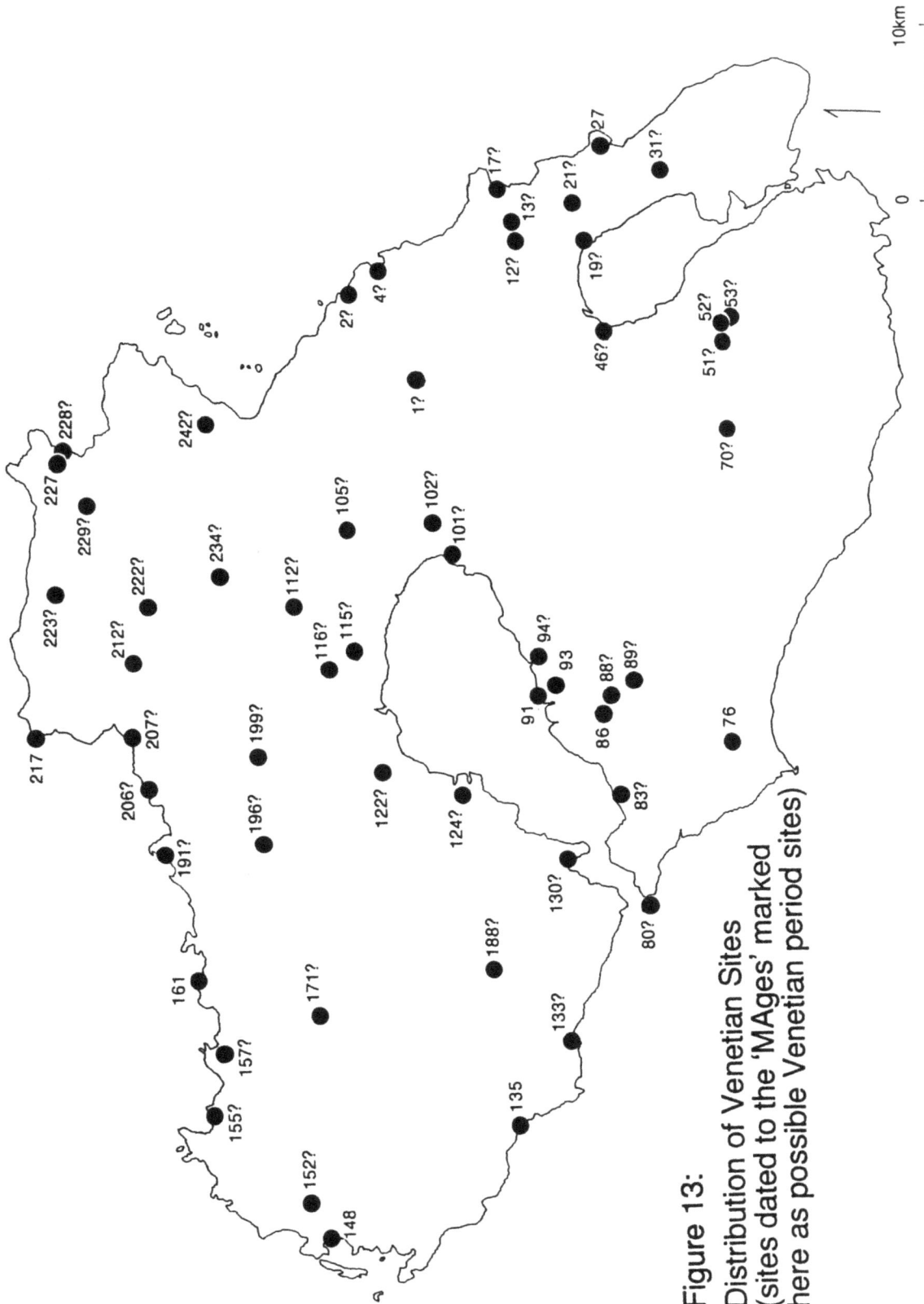

Figure 13:
Distribution of Venetian Sites
(sites dated to the 'MAges' marked
here as possible Venetian period sites)

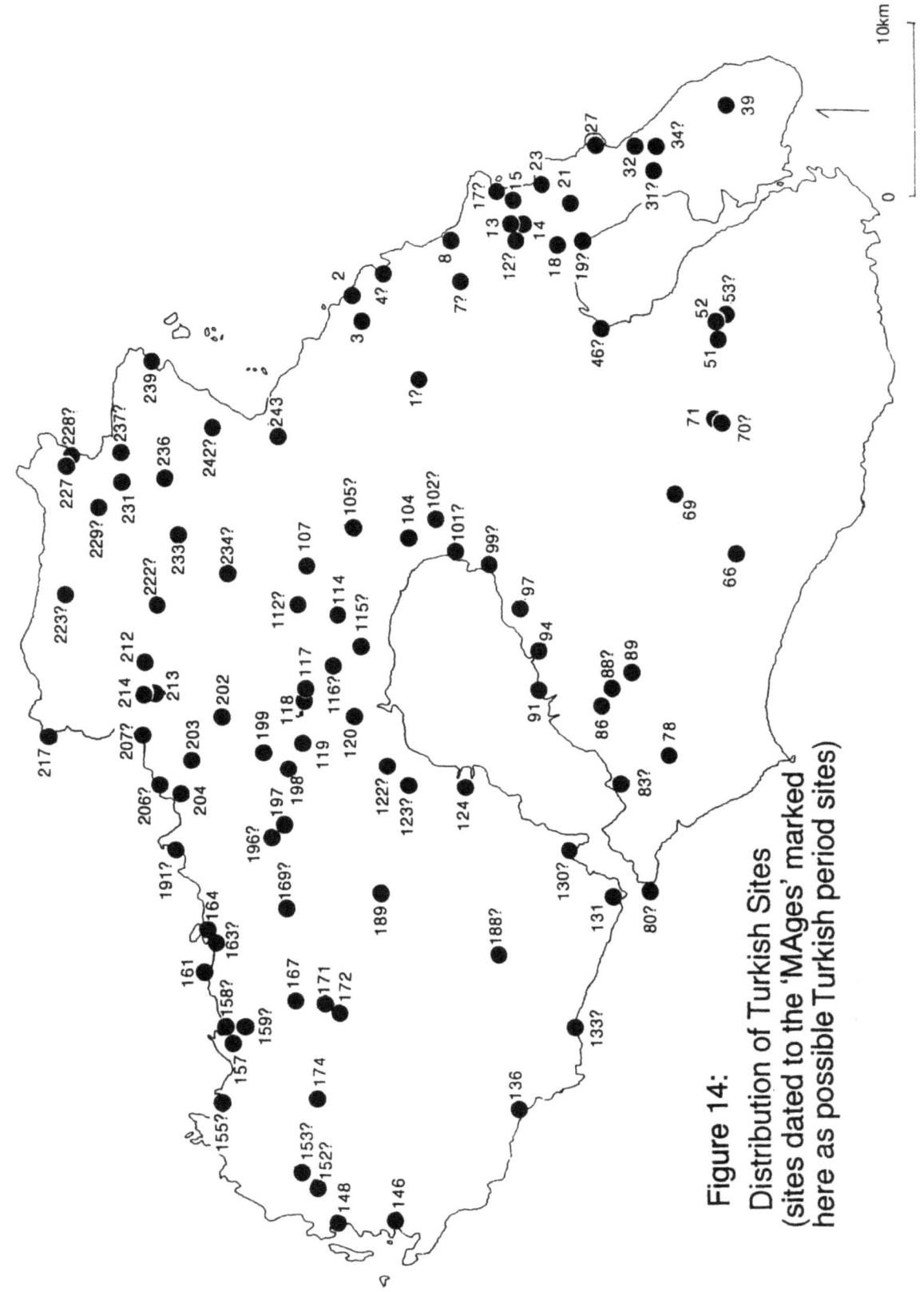

Figure 14:

Distribution of Turkish Sites
(sites dated to the 'MAges' marked
here as possible Turkish period sites)

Χω.[ρίον] Πέτρ(α)

Χω.[ρίον] Νάπ[α

Χω.[ρίον] Πυρρίου

Χω.[ρίον] Λευκὴ ἀκ[τὴ
σὺν τεμένει

Χω.[ρίον] Τύδαι
Ελπι[δήφορος

Γερασαι[

Χω.[ρίον] Κώμης

Χω.[ρίον] Μακριανῶν

Χω.[ρίον] Σικοῦντος

Χω.[ρίον]
Ἡρακλῆς

Χω.[ρίον]
Κέντρον

Χω.[ρίον] Μέσου ἀγροῦ

Χω.[ρίον] Πατρικοῦ

Χω.[ρίον] Σκόπελος

ἐν τῷ χωρίω
ἐπάνω τᾶς Κιλλάω[

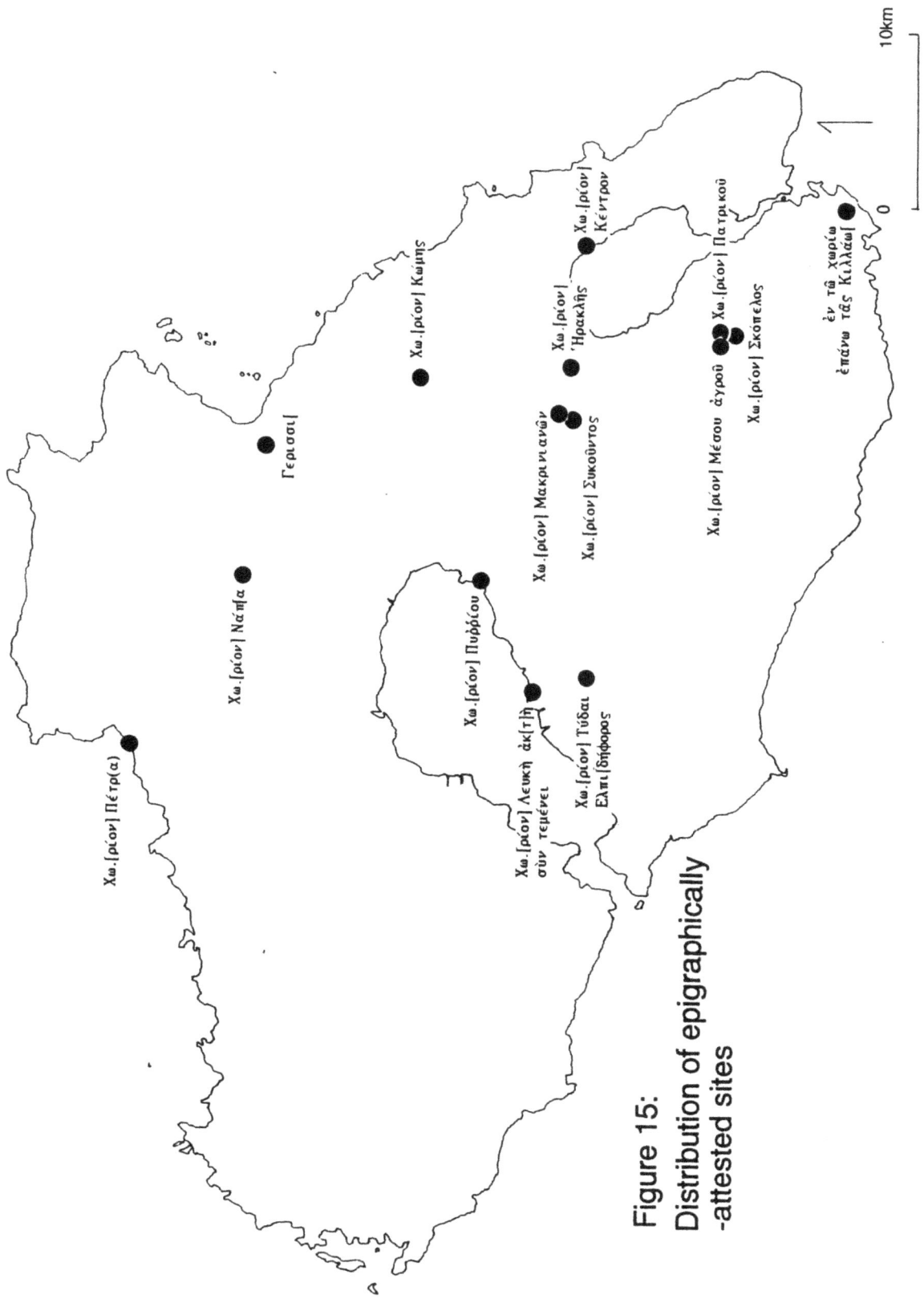

Figure 15:
Distribution of epigraphically
-attested sites

Figure 16: Lesbian masonry wall at Selles. (Axiotis, 1992 I, 277.) Reproduced by kind permission of Dr. M. Axiotis. (Exact scale of wall not given in the publication)

Figure 17: Large-scale Lesbian masonry wall at Methymna. (Buchholz, pl. 5 c.) Reproduced by kind permission of Prof. Dr. H.-G. Buchholz. (Exact scale of wall not given in the publication)

Figure 18: Detail of Lesbian masonry wall on the acropolis at Antissa. (BSA W. Lamb archive.)

Figure 19: Detail of Lesbian masonry wall at Apothiki. (Koldewey, pl. 15. 4.)

Figure 20:   Detail of Lesbian masonry wall at the Drakou Pidima. (Kontis, 1973, fig. 32 [p. 58].)
(Exact scale of wall not given in the publication)

Figure 21:   Detail of Lesbian masonry wall at Arisbe (Palaiokastro). (Koldewey, pl. 14. 5.)

Figure 22:   Block from Lesbian masonry wall on the acropolis at Eresos. (Scranton, fig. 5 [p. 29].)
             (Exact scale of blocks not given in the publication)

Figure 23:   Naturally curved block having fallen from the acropolis at Eresos.

Figure 24: The Lesbian masonry structure at Apothiki from a distance. (Koldewey, pl. 15. 3.)
(For scale of wall see fig. 19)

Figure 25: The Lesbian masonry wall at Xirokastrini. (Scranton, fig. 4 [p. 26].)
(Exact scale of wall not given in the publication)

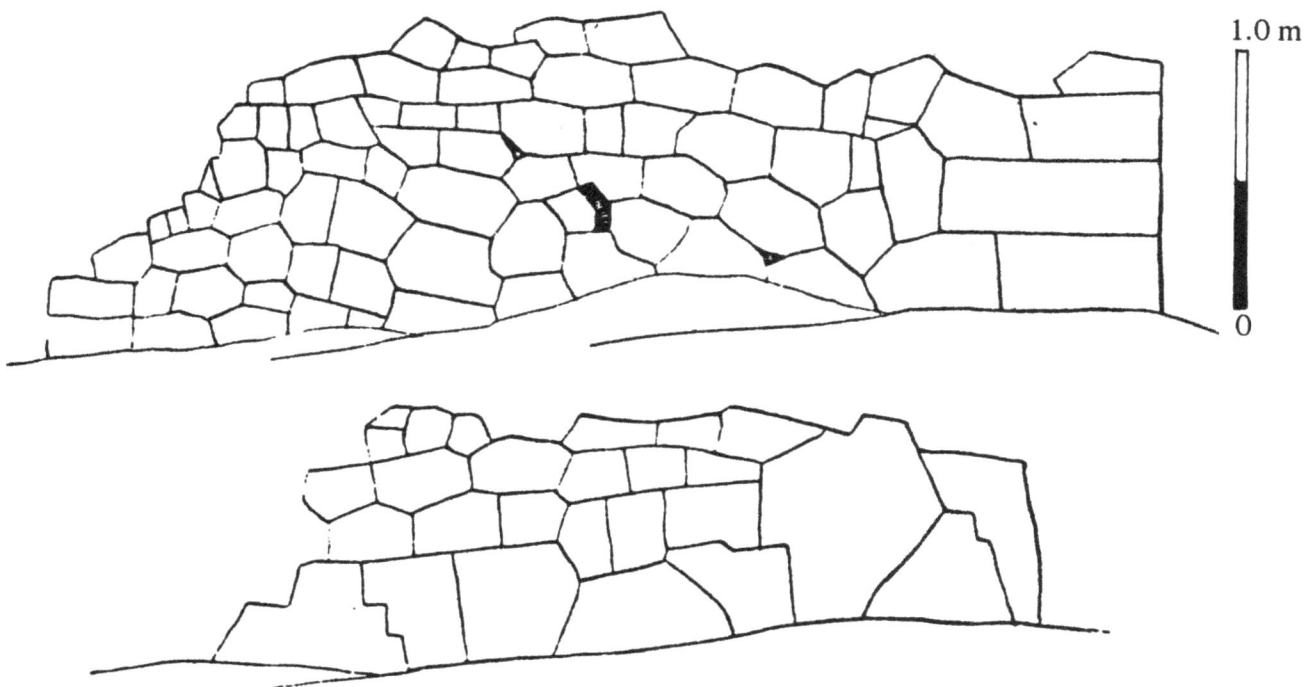

Figure 26: Lesbian masonry wall at Makara exhibiting squared corner blocks. (Koldewey, p. 87.)
(Rectangular blocks at right corner of top wall stated by Koldewey (ibid.) to be 1 m high)

Figure 27: Lesbian masonry wall at Xirokastrini exhibiting squared corner blocks. (Koldewey, pl. 14. 6-7.)

Figure 28: Detail of the terrace wall at Apothiki. (Axiotis, 1992 II, 524.) Reproduced by kind permission of Dr. M. Axiotis. (For scale of wall see fig. 19)

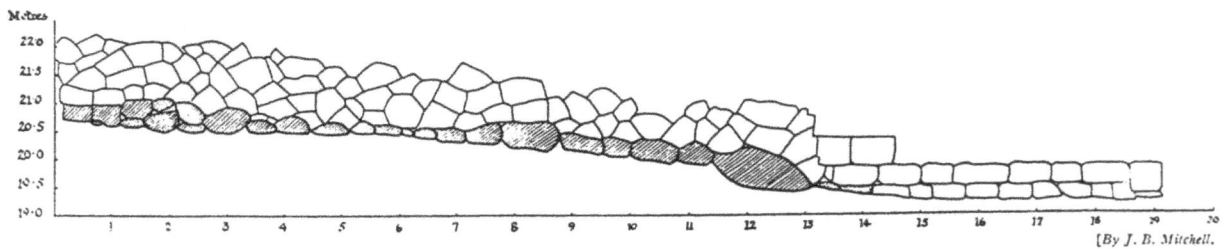

FIG. 4.—WALL, NORTH OF THE ACROPOLIS.

[By J. B. Mitchell.

Figure 29: Elevation of Lesbian masonry wall on the south side of the acropolis at Antissa. (Lamb, 1930-31 fig. 4 [p. 173].)

Figure 30:   Small-scale Lesbian masonry wall near the harbour at Methymna. (Buchholz, pl. 5 b.)
              Reproduced by kind permission of Verlag Philipp von Zabern (Mainz).
              (Exact scale of wall not given in the publication)

Figure 31:   Antissa, Lesbian masonry wall of the second apsidal building. (BSA W. Lamb archive.)

Figure 32: Lesbian masonry wall at Mytilene. (Kontis, 1973, fig. 41 [p. 76].)
(Exact scale of wall not given in the publication)

www.ingramcontent.com/pod-product-compliance
Lightning Source LLC
Chambersburg PA
CBHW051302270326
41926CB00030B/4701